Baha'u'llah

Baha'u'llah

A Short Biography

MOOJAN MOMEN

ONEWORLD
OXFORD

Baha'u'llah
A Oneworld Book

Published by Oneworld Publications 2007

Copyright © Moojan Momen 2007

ISBN-13: 978–1–85168–469–4

Typeset by Jayvee, Trivandrum, India
Cover design by Design Deluxe
Printed and bound by Thomson-Shore Inc., USA

Oneworld Publications
185 Banbury Road
Oxford OX2 7AR
England
www.oneworld-publications.com

Contents

Introduction

The religion founded by Baha'u'llah has in the 160 years since its inception spread to every country in the world[1] and its administrative institutions have been set up in every country where there is not a legal barrier to their establishment.[2] Its membership comprises of large numbers of converts from all of the other major religious traditions of the world and from every major culture and ethnic group. Its attraction for some people possibly rests in its combination of spirituality with modernity – the application of spiritual principles to the problems of the modern world; others are attracted by its community structure that encourages and facilitates the participation of all; still others are attracted by the deep spirituality of the prayers and scriptures and the example of the life of the founder, Baha'u'llah, and of his son and successor, 'Abdu'l-Baha.

This book gives a brief account of the life, works, claims and teachings of the founder of the Baha'i Faith, Baha'u'llah. His life story involves many trajectories. One trajectory is a geographical one that takes us from Iran to Iraq to what was then the capital of the Ottoman Empire, Istanbul (in present-day Turkey), to Edirne (also in present-day European Turkey), and finally to 'Akka, in what was then the Ottoman province of Syria and what is today the state of Israel. Another trajectory is a social one in which Baha'u'llah went from a position at the apex of society in the royal court to that of an outcast, exile and prisoner. The most important trajectory, however, is the religious and spiritual one which saw Baha'u'llah born into a traditional Muslim family, become a member of the Babi movement, which was considered a heretical innovation, and finally advance his own claim: that he had inaugurated a religious dispensation which not only abrogated the Islamic one but was the fulfilment of the prophecies of all religions.

Baha'u'llah's vision, which forms the basis of his teachings, is that of an essential unity and interconnectedness among all humanity. This unity is in turn the product of a vision of religion itself being essentially one phenomenon that has evolved through stages with the advent of the founders of the various religions of the world. At the apex of this vision is the concept that there is only one ultimate reality, God, and that the differing ideas about ultimate reality that exist in the various religious systems of the world are in fact merely conceptions of this one reality coming from different viewpoints.

Baha'u'llah's aim was not just to present to humanity a new global vision of a united and peaceful world. He also outlined and inaugurated a way of organising society so as to bring this vision into reality. Baha'u'llah recognised that it was the hierarchical nature of our present social structure that prevented many groups, such as women and minorities, from playing a full social role. He thus laid down the principles and outlined the framework of the structures and processes that would enable the creation of a more egalitarian and participative society. It would take many years for these plans to come to fruition and the Baha'i community even today is working out the details of how to apply the principles that Baha'u'llah gave and how to give form to the framework of social structures and processes that he outlined.

At the centre of the Baha'i Faith stands the person of Baha'u'llah. By laying claim to the high station of being the Manifestation of the Names and Attributes of God for this age, the voice of God on earth, he challenged those around him and those in the present day to investigate and respond to this claim. Some have dismissed his claims and labelled him a heretic, blasphemer or charlatan. Much of the world has simply not noticed these claims and has passed him by. His followers maintain however that it is his teachings that hold the key to solving the problems of the world and that however much the world might ignore or oppose him and his teachings now, eventually the worsening condition of humanity will force the world to examine these for clues as to how to tackle these problems.

This book is an attempt to tell the life story of this individual who made such claims and expounded such teachings. In telling this story, the aim has been to tell his story as far as possible in his own words or in the words of his family and close companions. In addition, this book surveys the writings of Baha'u'llah and attempts to give an outline of his teachings. It is of course impossible to condense the whole of the life-story of Baha'u'llah and adequately to outline his writings and teachings in the space of such a small book. It is therefore unfortunately inevitable that distortions and omissions have crept into the work by the process of summarizing and compressing. The reader is invited, after reading this book, to explore aspects of these subjects in other more detailed works which are listed in the bibliography.

In order to avoid having too many footnotes, the general sources for each chapter are summarised in the Sources and References section at the back of the book. Although in general the Baha'i system of transliteration has been used for names and Persian and Arabic words, insofar as possible diacritical marks have been removed. They are only inserted where there may be doubt as to how a word is pronounced and then only on the first occurrence of a word, except in quotations where transliteration is kept as in the source. Full transliterations of names and words can be found in the index.

ONE

Early Life

Iran at the beginning of the nineteenth century was asleep. The world around it was beginning to change rapidly but it was largely unaware of this. In Europe, the Industrial Revolution was starting to transform life in all its aspects: food, clothes, housing, work, transport, the city landscape, the environment – nothing was spared its effects. Politically the age of the colonialist expansion into India and Africa was just beginning and even China and Japan were eventually unable to resist foreign penetration. Intellectually, the effects of the Age of Enlightenment were removing religion from the central position that it had always occupied and replacing it with science as the guarantor of truth. But just as the world was being roused into a flurry of activity, Iran was settling into a comfortable repose after a turbulent eighteenth century which had seen the two-hundred year Safavid dynasty overthrown and a seventy-year period of turmoil. At the end of the eighteenth century, the Qajar tribe had imposed its authority over the whole of Iran and settled into a system of government where every governorship of the provinces and every high government position was sold off to the highest bidder who would then act as a tax farmer, milking his position for whatever returns it offered until he was replaced. There was no law or system of government beyond the will of the king or of the local governor. They had the power of life and death over their subjects, who could be killed for even the most trivial reason. Even the state treasury was very rudimentary with officials being allocated in lieu of salary the taxes of certain villages, of which they in effect became lords and from which they were responsible for collecting their salaries as taxes. The nomadic tribes which were at least a third of the population were virtually independent.

Baha'u'llah's family came from Nur, a district in the Iranian province of Mazandaran, the province in north Iran at the south end of the Caspian Sea. This province has high mountain peaks in the south descending to the northern coastal plain bordering the sea. Because of the dense sub-tropical jungles of the lower parts of the province (a stark contrast to the dry desert conditions in much of the rest of Iran), it was always a difficult area for invaders to penetrate. The Zoroastrian royalty and nobility fled to these parts after the Arab Islamic invasion of Iran in the seventh century and Baha'u'llah's family are said to have been descended from the last Zoroastrian monarch of Iran. Even when the people of this area finally converted to Islam centuries after that invasion, they mainly converted to the Zaydi form of Shi'i Islam as distinct from the Sunni Islam of most of the rest of Iran. It was only when the Safavid monarchs imposed Twelver Shi'i Islam on the whole country that Mazandaran fell into line with the rest of Iran.

The noble families of the Nur district, including Baha'u'llah's family, had for generations provided the kings of Iran with well-educated government officials: civil servants who would collect taxes, keep accounts, pay the army and generally administer the government. Baha'u'llah's father, Mirza Buzurg Nuri, rose in the ranks of these civil servants to become the minister to a royal prince who was the commander of the royal guards. He was later a vizier (minister), an official responsible for the collection of taxes, in a province. He was given the village of Takur in the Nur region in lieu of salary and he built a fine mansion there by the side of the Nur river as a family home. Nuri was close friends with Mirza Abu'l-Qasim Farahani Qa'im-Maqam, who was the first minister at the court of the Crown Prince. When the Crown Prince acceded to the throne as Muhammad Shah, Qa'im-Maqam became Prime Minister. He was one of the few Iranians who had woken up to the fact that the world was passing Iran by and that the country needed to modernize if it was not to be swallowed up by the colonialist forces that threatened it: Russia from the north and Britain from the south. Baha'u'llah's father was a close associate of Qa'im-Maqam and so when, in 1835, Muhammad Shah turned against Qa'im-Maqam and had him executed, a not uncommon fate for Qajar Prime Ministers, Baha'u'llah's father fell into disfavour also, particularly as he was at odds with the new Prime Minister, Haji Mirza Aqasi. He lost his position and much of his wealth, and even his mansion in Takur was all but destroyed in a flood. He fell ill and eventually died in the spring of 1839.

Baha'u'llah's father was also renowned as a calligrapher. Indeed, his real name was 'Abbas and he had been given the designation Buzurg (meaning "great") by the king because of his calligraphic prowess. As was customary among Iran's nobility, Mirza Buzurg had an extensive family. He took three wives and also had three concubines. The mother of Baha'u'llah was his second wife, Khadijih Khanum. She was from the Namadsáb family of the village of Fiyúl, a short distance south of Takur. This family had pre-existing ties to the family of Mirza Buzurg since an older sister of Mirza Buzurg was already married into the family. Khadijih Khanum had been married before to a certain Aqa Sultan and had three children from her previous marriage. With Aqa Buzurg she had five further children (two daughters and three sons; one son died while young). It was the custom of the family to spend the winter months in Tehran, where Mirza Buzurg would attend to his government duties, and the summer in the family home in Takur. Baha'u'llah, the fourth child, was born on 12 November 1817 in the family home in the 'Údlaján quarter of Tehran. His given name was Husayn 'Ali but he is generally now known by the title he took in later life, Bahá'u'lláh (the glory of God).

Mirza Buzurg Nuri, the father of Baha'u'llah

BAHA'U'LLAH'S EARLY LIFE

In keeping with the high social position of the family, Baha'u'llah was taught by private tutors. He would have been taught reading, writing and arithmetic; he would have memorized parts of the Qur'an and also Persian poetry.[3] Most of the poetry that he was taught would have been the mystical poetry of the Sufi poets of Iran (Sufism is Islamic mysticism) and, in later years, Baha'u'llah often quoted Sufi poets such as Rumi and 'Attar and used Sufi imagery in his writings.

We do not have a great deal of information about Baha'u'llah's early years. It is said that he showed great sharpness of mind and profundity of understanding from an early age and was the pride of his father. He was disinterested in material things and loved nature. There are a few episodes that Baha'u'llah himself recalls in his later writings and which therefore can be said to have made an impression on him. He describes for example a puppet show that he saw during his older half-brother's marriage feast:

> When I was still a child and had not yet attained the age of maturity, my father made arrangements in Tihrán for the marriage of one of my older brothers, and as is customary in that city, the festivities lasted for seven days and seven nights. On the last day it was announced that the play 'Sháh Sultán Salím' would be presented. A large number of princes, dignitaries, and notables of the capital gathered for the occasion. I was sitting in one of the upper rooms of the building and observing the scene. Presently a tent was pitched in the courtyard, and before long some small human-like figures, each appearing to be no more than about a hand's span in height, were seen to emerge from it and raise the call: 'His Majesty is coming! Arrange the seats at once!' . . . there appeared, arrayed in regal majesty and crowned with a royal diadem, a kingly figure, bearing himself with the utmost haughtiness and grandeur, at turns advancing and pausing in his progress, who proceeded with great solemnity, poise and dignity to seat himself upon his throne.
>
> At that moment a volley of shots was fired, a fanfare of trumpets was sounded, and king and tent were enveloped in a pall of smoke. When it had cleared, the king, ensconced upon his throne, was seen surrounded by a suite of ministers, princes, and dignitaries of state who, having taken their places, were standing at attention in his presence. A captured thief was then brought before the king, who gave the order that the offender should be beheaded. Without a moment's delay the chief executioner cut off the thief's head, whence a blood-like liquid came forth . . .

This Youth regarded the scene with great amazement. When the royal audience was ended, the curtain was drawn, and, after some twenty minutes, a man emerged from behind the tent carrying a box under his arm.

'What is this box,' I asked him, 'and what was the nature of this display?'

'All this lavish display and these elaborate devices,' he replied, 'the king, the princes, and the ministers, their pomp and glory, their might and power, everything you saw, are now contained within this box.'

I swear by My Lord Who, through a single word of His Mouth, hath brought into being all created things! Ever since that day, all the trappings of the world have seemed in the eyes of this Youth akin to that same spectacle. They have never been, nor will they ever be, of any weight and consequence . . .[4]

In another place, Baha'u'llah writes of how sad he was when as a child he read the story of the Banu Qurayzah, a Jewish tribe of Medina in the time of the prophet Muhammad whose menfolk had all been executed on the orders of the head of their alliance after they had betrayed their allies. He says that although he realised that what had happened was necessary and was by the decree of God, nevertheless he was greatly saddened by the story and earnestly entreated God for love and unity among all the peoples of the earth.

Baha'u'llah was also evidently keenly affected by and opposed to all manifestations of injustice. On one occasion when a government tax inspector had three times unjustly demanded payments from Baha'u'llah's father, Baha'u'llah, although still young, had ridden for two days to Tehran and there presented his father's case before the government, thus leading to the tax collector's dismissal.

As he grew into a young man, Baha'u'llah exhibited great sagacity and insight. The following story is told by 'Abdu'l-Baha, Baha'u'llah's son. One day while still a youth, Baha'u'llah went to visit Shaykh Muhammad Taqi Mujtahid Nuri, one of the great clerics of Iran at this time who was known as 'Allámih (the very learned) Nuri, at his home in the village of Yalrúd, near Takur. 'Allámih had around him a group of his senior students whom he was teaching. He asked four of them, who had almost completed their studies and were about to receive their certificates, about an Islamic Tradition that says that Fatimih, the daughter of Muhammad, was the best of the women in the world except for the one to whom Mary gave birth. 'Allámih asked these four what this Tradition meant, since Mary had no daughter. Each gave an explanation that did not satisfy their teacher. Then Baha'u'llah suggested that this Tradition was merely emphasizing the high station of Fatimih by saying that only an imaginary person could be likened to her. The teacher was silent, but when Baha'u'llah had left he upbraided his pupils saying that he had expected more from them than this: that a mere youth would explain what they who wore a turban and the garb of the learned and had almost completed their studies had failed to discern.

Baha'u'llah also records that on one occasion, when visiting his future mother-in-law, he listened to a cleric with a large turban expounding on whether the arch-angel Gabriel was the greater or Qanbar, the servant of the Imam 'Ali. He writes that although he was still but a boy, he was astonished at the ignorance of these elders and when an opportunity came, he expressed his thoughts saying that since Gabriel is stated in Qur'an to be the one through whom the Word of God is revealed to the prophet Muhammad, then even Qanbar's master the Imam 'Ali would not reach that station. Baha'u'llah states that some time later, he visited Qum and was dismayed to find the same cleric expounding the same sort of pointless and fruitless discourse.

MARRIAGE AND CHILDREN

In about 1832, Baha'u'llah's older sister Sárih married Mirza Mahmud, a son of Mirza Isma'il Vazir (minister) of Yalrud.

Three years later in about October 1835, Baha'u'llah himself, at the age of eighteen, married the sister of Mirza Mahmud, Ásiyih Khanum. She was reported to have been beautiful, kind and caring. After the fall from power and death of Baha'u'llah's father in 1839, the family lost their home and Baha'u'llah rented a house in the 'Udlaján Quarter of Tehran for his wife, mother and most of his step-mothers and their children. It was here that the couple's surviving children were born (they had seven children in all but only three survived to adulthood). Their eldest surviving son was born in 1844 and was named 'Abbas after his grandfather but is better known by the title he took 'Abdu'l-Baha (the servant of Baha'u'llah). Next in 1846 came a daughter, Fatimih Sultan Khanum, who in later years was known by the titles Bahiyyih Khanum and the Greatest Holy Leaf, and then in 1850 a son, Mirza Mahdi, who was given the title the Purest Branch. Bahiyyih Khanum was very close to her mother and remembered her thus:

> I wish you could have seen her as I first remember her, tall, slender, graceful, eyes of a dark blue – a pearl, a flower amongst women . . .
>
> I have been told that even when very young, her wisdom and intelligence were remarkable. I always think of her in those earliest days of my memory as queenly in her dignity and loveliness, full of consideration for everybody, gentle, of a marvellous unselfishness, no action of hers ever failed to show the loving-kindness of her pure heart; her very presence seemed to make an atmosphere of love and happiness whenever she came, enfolding all comers in the fragrance of gentle courtesy.[5]

As was customary and expected of his social position, Baha'u'llah took a second wife, his cousin Fatimih in about 1848. Fatimih was a daughter of the older sister of Mirza Buzurg who had also married into the Namadsab family of Fiyul. Thus the two were related on both their father's and mother's side. Fatimih had been married to the above-mentioned Shaykh Muhammad Taqi 'Allámih Nuri when he was very old and she was very young.[6] When he died, there may have been family pressure for the young widow who was in a socially difficult position to be given the security of a marriage within the family. From this marriage of Fatimih to Baha'u'llah there were six children with three male and one female child surviving to adulthood. In later years in Baghdad in about 1862, Baha'u'llah took a third wife, Gawhar Khanum of Kashan but she remained in Baghdad when Baha'u'llah left for Istanbul and only joined Baha'u'llah later in 'Akka in about 1885. There was a single daughter from this marriage.

Baha'u'llah had been expected to enter into the state civil service like his father. Although the Prime Minister Haji Mirza Aqasi had enmity towards Baha'u'llah's father, he appears to have taken a liking to Baha'u'llah and offered him a good position in the government. Baha'u'llah, however, declined, probably because he did not want to be enmeshed in the bribery and corruption that surrounded the royal court.

In later years Haji Mirza Aqasi turned against Baha'u'llah over a village called Quch-Hissar that had belonged to Baha'u'llah's father. Haji Mirza Aqasi had ridden through this village that lay to the south of Tehran and had taken a liking to it; he pressured Baha'u'llah to give it to him. Baha'u'llah replied that the property was not solely his but belonged also to a number of his siblings who were not of age. When he saw that the Prime Minister was determined to obtain the property by fair means or foul, however, he transferred ownership of the property to the Shah's sister. When the Prime Minister tried again to take the village by force, the Shah's sister complained to her brother and the Prime Minister was ordered to desist. Needless to say the Prime Minister was furious at Baha'u'llah and began to scheme against him.

Baha'u'llah was not interested in social advancement and lucrative government positions. He contented himself with managing the property that he had inherited from his father and earning a much more modest income in that way. He had property in Takur in the upper part of the Nur district where he would spend the summer months and in Dárkalá in lower Nur where he would spend the winter months. He also had a house in Tehran. Baha'u'llah's daughter Bahiyyih Khanum describes thus what she remembered in later years of the life of Baha'u'llah and Asiyih Khanum in Tehran:

> Even in the early years of their married life, they, my father and mother, took part as little as possible in State functions, social ceremonies, and the luxurious habits of ordinary highly placed and wealthy families in the land of Persia; she, and her noble-hearted husband, counted these worldly pleasures meaningless, and preferred rather to occupy themselves in caring for the poor, and for all who were unhappy, or in trouble. From our doors nobody was ever turned away; the hospitable board was spread for all comers.[7]

Panorama of Tehran. In the background are the Alburz mountains which separate Tehran from Mazandaran

The Cause of the Bab
(1844–1853)

In the late summer of 1844, Baha'u'llah had almost reached the age of 27. It was at this time that news reached him of a young man in Shiraz, Sayyid 'Ali Muhammad the Báb. This man, who at 24 was a mere youth and a merchant, had dared to put forward religious claims. He had taken the titles of Dhikru'lláh (meaning 'the Remembrance of God') and Bab (meaning 'Gate'), which people took to mean that he was the Gate to the Hidden Imam, the Messianic figure that all of Iran's Shi'i Muslims were expecting. In his first book, issued in 1844 and widely distributed, he had challenged not just the people but even the most learned of the clerical class and the king himself to acknowledge his religious authority and precedence over all people:

> All praise be to God Who hath, through the power of Truth, sent down this Book unto His servant, that it may serve as a shining light for all mankind . . . Verily this is none other than the sovereign Truth; it is the Path which God hath laid out for all that are in heaven and on earth . . . Verily this is the true Faith of God, and sufficient witness are God and such as are endowed with the knowledge of the Book. This is indeed the eternal Truth

which God, the Ancient of Days, hath revealed unto His omnipotent Word – He Who hath been raised up from the midst of the Burning Bush . . .

O King of Islám! Aid thou, with the truth, after having aided the Book, Him Who is Our Most Great Remembrance, for God hath, in very truth, destined for thee, and for such as circle round thee, on the Day of Judgement, a responsible position in His Path. I swear by God, O Sháh! If thou showest enmity unto Him Who is His Remembrance, God will, on the Day of Resurrection, condemn thee . . .

O concourse of divines! Fear God from this day onwards in the views ye advance, for He Who is Our Remembrance in your midst, and Who cometh from Us, is, in very truth, the Judge and Witness. Turn away from that which ye lay hold of, and which the Book of God, the True One, hath not sanctioned, for on the Day of Resurrection ye shall, upon the Bridge, be, in very truth, held answerable for the position ye occupied . . . And unto you We have sent down this Book which truly none can mistake . . .

O People of the Qur'an! Ye are as nothing unless ye submit unto the Remembrance of God and unto this Book . . .

O Peoples of the East and the West! Be ye fearful of God concerning the Cause of the true Joseph and barter Him not for a paltry price established by yourselves, or for a trifle of your earthly possessions . . .[8]

These challenging words were stirring the people of Iran, causing some to adhere to them and their author and others to oppose him vigorously and eventually violently. The Bab had first declared his mission to Mulla Husayn Bushru'i in Shiraz in the south of Iran during the evening of 22 May 1844. Bushru'i and the other seventeen first disciples of the Bab were called by him the Letters of the Living. These were all young people who had been students of Sayyid Kazim Rashti, the second leader of what had come to be known as the Shaykhi school (after its founder Shaykh Ahmad al-Ahsa'i). Rashti's teaching had included admonitions to his students that the day of the promised return of the Hidden Imam was close and that they should watch carefully for signs of it. Rashti had refused to appoint a new leader of the

Shaykhi school and thus at his death many of his students spread out to look for a new leader. It was this quest that had taken them to Shiraz and to the Bab. Over a period of several months the Bab gathered around him the Letters of the Living and then he dispersed them to all parts of Iran and neighbouring countries to spread the news of his claim. One of the Letters of the Living was a woman who was known as Qurratu'l-'Ayn and was eventually given the title of Tahirih. She did not meet the Bab but was included among the Letters of the Living by virtue of a letter she wrote to the Bab.

Baha'u'llah first heard of the call of the Bab in the late summer of 1844. Mulla Husayn Bushru'i was directed by the Bab to go north to Isfahan, Tehran and then Khurasan. When he arrived in Tehran, he took up residence in one of the religious colleges in the city, the Pay-Minar College (also known as the Mirza Salih College), which was the headquarters of the Shaykhi movement in the city. The leading Shaykhi of Tehran rejected Bushru'i's message but another Shaykhi scholar resident in the school, Mulla Muhammad Mu'allim Nuri, was much attracted to the message. In the course of conversation, Bushru'i asked about the family of the late minister Mirza Buzurg, and Mulla Muhammad, who was tutor to Baha'u'llah's son, 'Abdu'l-Baha, and the other children in Baha'u'llah's household, replied praising Baha'u'llah greatly.[9] Thereupon, Bushru'i gave him a scroll written by the Bab to deliver to Baha'u'llah.

We do not know precisely what this scroll that Bushru'i had brought from the Bab said but it evoked an immediate response from Baha'u'llah. Upon reading it, he realised that the writer of these words was not just claiming to be the representative of the Hidden Imam but was claiming divine revelation. He immediately declared: 'Whoso believes in the Qur'an and recognises its Divine origin, and yet hesitates, though it be for a moment, to admit that these soul-stirring words are endowed with the same regenerating power, has most assuredly erred in his judgment and has strayed far from the path of justice.'[10]

BAHA'U'LLAH IN NUR

Although Baha'u'llah never met the Bab, he became one of his most active and effective followers. Baha'u'llah first converted his family in Tehran to the new religion and then proceeded to Nur, where he acquainted his friends and other family with the Babi Faith, most of whom became Babis. His half-brother Azal, who was to play a significant role in later years, was only twelve years old at this time and became a follower of the Bab in 1846. Only his uncle Shaykh 'Azizu'llah opposed him and tried to stir up other clerics against him. Eventually word of Baha'u'llah's success spread around Nur and later in 1848 Mulla Muhammad Tunukabuni, who had taken the place of his deceased father-in-law, the above mentioned 'Allamih Nuri, as the senior cleric in Nur, was compelled to send two of his prominent students (who were also sons-in-law of 'Allamih Nuri) to investigate the matter. At this time Baha'u'llah was in the northern part of Nur near the coast propagating the new religion in the village of Darkala, which was part of his inheritance from his father. The two sons-in-law of Mulla Muhammad found him there and after listening to his discourse were won over. Baha'u'llah went to the nearby village of Sa'adatabad, where Mulla Muhammad had his winter quarters, to visit him. He refused however to discuss the message that Baha'u'llah had brought, saying that he had consulted a random verse in the Qur'an and the omens were not favourable for such a discussion.[11]

BAHA'U'LLAH IN TEHRAN

Baha'u'llah returned to Tehran and made his home there one of the main centres for Babi activities in the city. At this time all sorts of people from the high and low strata of society were becoming Babis and Baha'u'llah's house was large enough to accommodate meetings. Prominent Babis travelling through Tehran would visit and often stayed at his home. Mulla Husayn Bushru'i was among those who visited Baha'u'llah both on his way to and from Maku in the far north-west of Iran where the Bab had been imprisoned by the Shah at the instigation of the Prime Minister (who feared for his position if the Shah should come under the influence of the Bab). Baha'u'llah also spent time at a delightful orchard and garden that he partly owned in Murgh Mahallih, to the north of Tehran. Here on one occasion he held a meeting of 150 of the Babis of Tehran.

These activities would have continued but for an event that occurred on 25 October 1847 in Qazvin, a town 150 kilometres north-west of Tehran. There the uncle of the female Letter of the Living Tahirih, mentioned above, was murdered by a Shaykhi who had been angered by his continual cursing of the Shaykhi movement and its leaders. This uncle of Tahirih, who was also her father-in-law, had been one of the most prominent clerics in Iran and had been loud in his condemnations of both the Shaykhis and the Babis. Tahirih and the Babis were blamed for the murder and Tahirih was confined to the house of her father, while several Babis were arrested, beaten and sent in chains to Tehran. This episode was to be just the first in an increasingly violent campaign against the Babis, led by the Islamic religious leaders who feared for their positions and livelihood with the advances being made by the new religion.

The situation for Tahirih was very dangerous since the uncle's son, who was also Tahirih's divorced husband, was furious and was likely to have Tahirih killed. Baha'u'llah arranged to have a Babi woman from Qazvin who had access to the house of Tahirih's father help Tahirih to escape. Tahirih was secretly brought to Baha'u'llah's house in Tehran and he transferred her to the house of Mirza Aqa Khan Nuri (who was later to be Prime Minister and who at that time was in exile in Kashan) and asked the latter's sister to look after her.

Baha'u'llah also gave every assistance that he could to the Babi prisoners that had been sent to Tehran from Qazvin, paying for their food and intervening with the authorities on their behalf. When one of the prisoners escaped, Baha'u'llah was accused of being complicit in this and was himself imprisoned in the home of one of the city officials. When it was demonstrated that he was innocent, he was released. During this time, Tahirih was frequently in the house of Baha'u'llah in Tehran and on one occasion, Vahid (Sayyid Yahya Darabi), who was later to be the leader of the Babis in the Nayriz upheaval of 1850, had come from visiting the Bab in Maku. 'Abdu'l-Baha recalls:

> One day the great Siyyid Yahyá, surnamed Vahíd, was present there. As he sat without, Táhirih listened to him from behind the veil. I was then a child, and was sitting on her lap. With eloquence and fervour, Vahíd was discoursing on the signs and verses that bore witness to the advent of the new Manifestation. She suddenly interrupted him and, raising her voice, vehemently declared: 'O Yahyá! Let deeds, not words, testify to thy faith, if thou art a man of true learning. Cease idly repeating the traditions of the past, for the day of service, of steadfast action, is come. Now is the time to show forth the true signs of God, to rend asunder the veils of idle fancy, to promote the Word of God, and to sacrifice ourselves in His path. Let deeds, not words, be our adorning!'[12]

THE CONFERENCE OF BADASHT, 1848

In June and July 1848, a significant meeting of the Babis occurred at the village of Badasht. The site of the meeting appears to have been accidental in that Tahirih had, shortly after her arrival in Tehran, set off in response to the Bab's call for his followers to gather in Khurasan, the north-east province of Iran. Baha'u'llah followed a few days later as did many other Babis. These Babis travelling towards Khurasan met another group of Babis led by Quddus, the foremost Letter of the Living, who were travelling in the opposite direction, at the village of Badasht. Here Baha'u'llah rented two gardens, one for Quddus and one for Tahirih, and he pitched his tent together with the other Babis in an area between the two gardens, where a stream flowed. Baha'u'llah also saw to the provision of food for all eighty-one of those who attended. This was the first opportunity that the Babi movement had had to debate and consult about a number of issues: what it was that they stood for; how to achieve their goals in the face of a rising tide of opposition; and how to achieve the release of the Bab from his captivity in Maku. It is a measure of the prestige of Baha'u'llah among the Babis that, despite the presence at this gathering of many learned and prominent Babis, Baha'u'llah led the prayers during at least some of the conference.[13] Baha'u'llah also gave new names to all those present, names which the Bab later confirmed. It was at this time that Tahirih was given her title and Baha'u'llah himself took the title Baha.

Up to this time, the Bab had refrained from provoking unnecessary opposition by phrasing his writings very carefully so that those who were not aware of their implication would not find in them any radical break with Islam. However, the Babi religion was now moving into a phase where its break with Islam was to be made more clear. One of the functions of the conference of Badasht was to make the Babis aware that their religion was not just a reform of Islam but was a new religion, abrogating the Islamic dispensation. Since it was clear that this would shock many of the Babis, a plan was made by Baha'u'llah, Quddus and Tahirih that the latter two would debate issues, Tahirih taking a radical position advocating a complete break with Islam and Quddus taking a conservative position. In this way, the Babis could gradually be educated about the implications of the Bab's claims.

The most memorable and dramatic incident that highlighted this new direction that the Babi movement was taking occurred in Baha'u'llah's tent one day. Baha'u'llah, Quddus and most of the other Babis were sitting together conversing when a message came from Tahirih that she wished to see Quddus. Quddus declined to go. Then suddenly Tahirih herself entered the tent without the customary veil. She was made up and adorned but had no face veil on. Shock and consternation spread throughout the assembly. Tahirih, whom the Babis regarded as the return of Fatimih, the daughter of the prophet Muhammad, whose very name was associated in Muslim minds with chastity and virtue, had appeared before them shattering all customary Islamic notions of what was appropriate behaviour for a woman. 'The Trumpet is sounding! The great Trump is blown! The universal Advent is now proclaimed!' she announced. Some of the Babis were unable to accept this, left the gathering and repudiated the new religion. One man even cut his own throat, so upset was he at this turn of events. Even Quddus thought Tahirih had gone too far and unsheathed his sword as if to strike her. Baha'u'llah described the situation thus:

> How great was the consternation that seized the companions on that day! Fear and bewilderment filled their hearts. A few, unable to tolerate that which was to them so revolting a departure from the established customs of Islám, fled in horror from before her face. Dismayed, they sought refuge in a deserted castle in that neighbourhood.[14]

After recovering from their shock, the Babis understood the point that was being made so dramatically. Baha'u'llah helped to effect a complete reconciliation between Tahirih and Quddus. From that time on, the participants at Badasht looked to the implementation of the laws of the Bab and abandoned their former Islamic practices. A new order had begun.

The conference of Badasht lasted 22 days and at the end, to indicate that the disagreements between Qudddus and Tahirih had only been superficial, they left together. Baha'u'llah also left with them. A short distance away at Niyala, however, the party were attacked and dispersed.

Baha'u'llah proceeded to Bandar Jaz (Gaz), a port at the south-eastern corner of the Caspian Sea. When there, one of those accompanying Baha'u'llah fell ill. Baha'u'llah sent Tahirih on to Nur with a companion while he remained in Bandar Jaz. It was while he was here that orders came from Muhammad Shah for his arrest. The notables of the town who were his hosts urged him to catch a boat that was sailing to Russia and thus escape; the Russian agent in the town was willing to help but

Baha'u'llah refused to do this. The next day a courier arrived with news of the death of Muhammad Shah and everyone forgot about the royal edict.

The accession of Nasiru'd-Din Shah did not bring any relief to the Babis in general however. The new Prime Minister Mirza Taqi Khan, who had the title Amir Nizam but who is better known by the later title Amir Kabir, was determined to impose order on the country and looked upon the Babis as a dangerous challenge to his authority.

SHAYKH TABARSI, 1848

Baha'u'llah travelled on from Bandar Jaz to 'Aliyabad (now called Qa'imshahr) in Mazandaran, and from there he went to the village of Afra where the owner of the village was his host. Nearby, some three hundred or more Babis under the leadership of Mulla Husayn Bushru'i had been attacked and taken up a defensive position at the shrine of Shaykh Tabarsi. Baha'u'llah went together with his host to Shaykh Tabarsi and inspected the defences that the Babis were erecting there. He ordered a group of six men to go to nearby Sari and demand the release of Quddus who was being detained there. This mission was successful and Quddus joined the Babis at Shaykh Tabarsi. Baha'u'llah, who had expended all the money that he had with him in the provisions for the conference at Badasht, decided to return home where he could raise some more money and buy provisions for the Babis at Shaykh Tabarsi.

Baha'u'llah travelled to Nur, where Tahirih was now in hiding, and to Tehran. Having raised money and gathered provisions, he set out for Shaykh Tabarsi in late November 1848 with a group of Babis, including his half-brother Azal, Mulla Baqir Tabrizi, one of the Letters of the Living, and Haji Mirza Jani of Kashan. By this time, however, the new Shah and his Prime Minister had ordered royal troops to the area and had set up a siege around Shaykh Tabarsi. Baha'u'llah and his companions reached within fifteen kilometres of Shaykh Tabarsi and then

The Mosque in Amul where Baha'u'llah was interrogated and
subjected to the bastinado

they rested for the night. But the people of the area had been
warned to look out for Babis trying to reach Shaykh Tabarsi and
some people informed the soldiers in the neighbourhood of the
presence of Baha'u'llah's party. They surrounded the party,
arrested them and led them off to the nearby town of Amul.

The governor of Amul was away leading some of the troops
that were besieging Shaykh Tabarsi and had left the deputy governor in charge. When the prisoners arrived, this deputy governor summoned the leading clerics and dignitaries of the town to
join him in the main mosque of the town. He had not expected
someone of Baha'u'llah's rank and social standing to be among
the prisoners and was dismayed at his precipitous actions in
summoning the clerics to this gathering. Hoping to appease the
tumult that had arisen in the town on the news of the arrival of
the Babi captives, he addressed the Babis sharply and reprimanded them for their actions. Baha'u'llah answered the accusations calmly and deliberately.

Then a piece of writing was found on one of the Babi captives.
It was given to the senior cleric present who, assuming it to be a

writing of the Bab, proceeded to mock its poor grammar and style. Baha'u'llah replied that the words that he was criticising were not those of the Bab but of the Shi'i holy figure the Imam 'Ali. The cleric fell silent but others present clamoured for the prisoners to be put to death. The deputy governor tried to assuage the passions of the mob by ordering that Mulla Baqir be subject to the bastinado (beating on the soles of the feet with sticks), but Baha'u'llah intervened, saying Mulla Baqir was his guest and that he himself was responsible for anything that Mulla Baqir had done. The deputy governor successively tried to have Haji Mirza Jani and Azal bastinadoed and Baha'u'llah intervened similarly for each of them. In the end the deputy governor had no choice but to order Baha'u'llah, despite his high social rank, to be bastinadoed. Following this the Babis were imprisoned by the clerics present in a room adjoining the mosque. Fearing that harm would come to the captives, however, the deputy governor ordered his men to go quietly by night and make a hole in the wall at the rear of the room. Through this Baha'u'llah and the other captives were led away to the deputy governor's house where they were treated with great consideration by their host. When the governor returned, he had been so affected by the bravery shown by the Babis at Shaykh Tabarsi that he apologized to the prisoners and set them free, allowing them to return to Tehran.

The Babis at Shaykh Tabarsi, who were ordinary civilians unused to warfare, were besieged and attacked by local militias and royal troops and even with canons. They held out for a total of seven months until, driven by hunger, they acceded to the offer of a truce and safe passage sent to them from the royal prince who commanded the government troops and who had pledged his word upon the holy Qur'an. When the Babis emerged, the royal prince immediately broke his word and ordered a general massacre of the Babis. Eight of the Letters of the Living, including Quddus and Mulla Husayn Bushru'i perished in this conflict.

Baha'u'llah returned to Tehran and resumed his role at the heart of the Babi community there. With the rising tide of persecutions of the Babis, there was an ever-increasing role for him in organising and encouraging the Babis of Tehran, intervening with the authorities for Babis who were in prison or under attack, supporting those Babis who lost everything as a result of the persecutions, explaining to influential persons in the government circles to which he had access the true nature of the Babi movement and trying to defuse the growing antagonism towards the Babis. His home remained a meeting-place for local Babis. Baha'u'llah was in communication with the Bab, who was now imprisoned in the fortress of Chihriq in north-west Iran. Haji Sayyah, the courier of the Bab, came to Baha'u'llah's house on several occasions with letters from the Bab and carried back replies.

Once the persecution of the Babis had begun in earnest, Baha'u'llah's social position made it very dangerous for him if the government realised what a key role he was playing in the Babi community. Therefore some of the Babis came together and consulted on how to protect him. They considered that the best plan would be to divert attention away to someone who was less in the public eye and would therefore be in less danger:

> Because Baha'u'llah had become well-known and much talked about in connection with this [Babi] Cause among the people, the ulama [Muslim clerics] and the ministers of the government in the capital city, Tehran, and the hearts and minds of all were turned towards him, Mulla 'Abdu'l-Karim Qazvini,[15] who was one of the most earliest and most respected of the Babis [he had been a secretary of the Bab] and Mirza Musa Kalim, Baha'u'llah's full brother, came and jointly suggested to Baha'u'llah: 'Considering the enmity and spitefulness of the ulama and the might of the state and the power of the Prime Minister Mirza Taqi Khan [Amir Kabir], you are in great danger. Therefore it would be a wise precaution to turn people's attention towards someone else so that you would be protected from persecution and harm for the time being.' Nor did they consider it prudent for certain considerations to involve an outsider [in these arrangements], therefore the lot fell upon Mirza Yahya [Azal], who was Baha'u'llah's [half-]brother.

And so, Baha'u'llah wrote on his [Azal's] behalf to the Bab and replies were received. He [Azal] thus became the recipient of great favour and was appointed a leader and source of guidance to the Babis, and was given the titles Vahíd and Azal. In most of the tablets he received, however, he was warned explicitly that if at any time, He Whom God shall make manifest, the one promised in the Bayan [the main book of the Bab], should appear, he would be the bearer of a new revelation and the authoritative centre of the Faith and Azal was bidden to direct himself and all others to that great revelation.[16]

The year 1850 brought matters to a head. In two towns in Iran, Zanjan in the north (on the road between Tehran and Tabriz) and Nayriz in the south, where there were large numbers of Babis, they were put under pressure by the Islamic clerics acting in concert with the government. They took up defensive positions and were soon outnumbered by government troops together with artillery, sent to besiege them. In Nayriz, the Babis under Sayyid Yahya Vahid were tricked after one month into emerging from behind their defences and massacred; in Zanjan, they were gradually worn down by repeated attacks over seven months. On 19 February that year, the execution of seven prominent Babis occurred in Tehran. In the middle of the year, on 9 July, the Bab himself was brought from his place of confinement in Chihriq and executed in Tabriz in north-west Iran.

About six weeks before his execution, the Bab had packed all of the documents, seals and rings into a chest and entrusted them to Mulla Baqir, one of the Letters of the Living, to take them to Mulla 'Abdu'l-Karim Qazvini, his secretary, who was in Qum. Qazvini opened the chest and found it contained a sheet of blue paper on which the Bab had inscribed in a delicate, skilful penmanship about five hundred verses in the form of a pentacle all consisting of derivatives of the word 'Baha'. Qazvini was instructed in a letter from the Bab to deliver the chest to Baha'u'llah in Tehran.

'PILGRIMAGE' TO KARBALA, 1851–1852

About a year after the execution of the Bab, the Prime Minister, the Amir Kabir, summoned Baha'u'llah into his presence and said to him quite bluntly that he was sure that Baha'u'llah was a main factor in the resilience of the Babis. Baha'u'llah records what occurred at that meeting in early June 1851, thus:

> The Amír-Nizám [Amir Kabir] . . . asked Us one day to see him. He received Us cordially, and revealed the purpose for which he had summoned Us to his presence. 'I am well aware,' he gently insinuated, 'of the nature and influence of your activities, and am firmly convinced that were it not for the support and assistance which you have been extending to Mullá Husayn and his companions, neither he nor his band of inexperienced students would have been capable of resisting for seven months the forces of the imperial government. The ability and skill with which you have managed to direct and encourage those efforts could not fail to excite my admiration. I have been unable to obtain any evidence whereby I could establish your complicity in this affair. I feel it a pity that so resourceful a person should be left idle and not be given an opportunity to serve his country and sovereign. The thought has come to me to suggest to you that you visit Karbilá in these days when the Sháh is contemplating a journey to Isfahán. It is my intention to be enabled, on his return, to confer upon you the position of Amír-Díván [head of the royal court], a function you could admirably discharge.' We vehemently protested against such accusations, and refused to accept the position he hoped to offer Us. A few days after that interview, We left Tihrán for Karbilá.[17]

The Prime Minister's suggestion that Baha'u'llah go to Karbala was the customary way in Iran of exiling prominent persons who could not be kept in prison. Baha'u'llah consented to leave for Iraq although he was unwilling to go because the situation of the Babis in Tehran had become critical. Following the execution of the Bab, there had been a struggle for power. While Baha'u'llah's half-brother Azal had been given by the Bab some degree of leadership, he was too young to be able to exert any influence. Instead there had been a struggle between Shaykh 'Ali 'Azim, a turbulent cleric from Khurasan, and Sayyid Basir, a blind Indian mystic. The former had won towards the end of 1850 and was now talking of taking revenge for the execution of the Bab. Baha'u'llah was very much opposed to such talk and had tried to lead the Babis in the opposite direction towards continuing to spread the religion of the Bab by persuasive argument and by their personal example. Even while he was in Kirmanshah en route for Karbala, he sent one of the Babis, Nabil Zarandi, as a messenger back to Tehran to try to persuade Azal who had come under the influence of 'Azim to leave Tehran, but he refused.

In Iraq, Baha'u'llah first visited Baghdad where he found the situation among the Babi community there equally critical in the wake of the execution of the Bab. The Babis there, even the most learned and senior of them, had fallen under the spell of a certain Sayyid 'Uluvv and were following his leadership and superstitious ideas. Baha'u'llah managed to persuade them of the falseness of their new views and even managed to persuade Sayyid 'Uluvv to abandon his claim. In Karbala also Baha'u'llah met with the Babi community and encouraged them.

The Amir Kabir who had exiled Baha'u'llah fell from power in November 1851 and was murdered on the orders of the Shah in February 1852. The new Prime Minister was Mirza Aqa Khan Nuri, from the same Nuri clan as Baha'u'llah. After he had been in office a few months, he sent a message to Baha'u'llah inviting him to return to Tehran. Upon Baha'u'llah's arrival in Tehran in April or May 1852, the Prime Minister asked his own brother to act as host to Baha'u'llah. While this was a great honour, it restricted Baha'u'llah's freedom of action. Indeed it is likely that part of the new Prime Minister's plan was to be able to tell the Shah that he had the Babi situation under firm control and had one of their prominent leaders under close supervision.

THE ATTEMPT ON THE LIFE OF THE SHAH

The situation among the Babis in Tehran had deteriorated greatly during Baha'u'llah's absence. The group of Babis led by 'Azim had been meeting regularly at the home of Sulayman Khan, whose family had held high positions in the royal court. The group had however come increasingly under the domination of Husayn Jan, a new convert from Milan near Tabriz, who had great charisma and held his audiences spellbound. He was advocating an increasingly violent strategy.

During the summer months, the court moved, as usual, to the cooler villages north of Tehran. The Prime Minister's estates were in the village of Afchih and it was here that he took Baha'u'llah in June. Just as Baha'u'llah was transferring to Afchih, he did manage to meet with 'Azim and urgently tried to dissuade 'Azim from the course he was taking. According to Nabil:

> I have heard it stated by Áqáy-i-Kalím [Baha'u'llah's brother] that in the course of that journey [to Afchih] Bahá'u'lláh was able to meet 'Azím, who had been endeavouring for a long time to see Him, and who in that interview was advised, in the most emphatic terms, to abandon the plan he had conceived. Bahá'u'lláh condemned his designs, dissociated Himself entirely from the act it was his intention to commit, and warned him that such an attempt would precipitate fresh disasters of unprecedented magnitude.[18]

But even 'Azim was no longer fully in charge. He found himself increasingly pushed aside at the meetings at Sulayman Khan's house by Husayn Jan and was unable to bring the Babis to their senses. On 14 August 1852, they even refused to allow him in to the meeting. The following day, three Babis made an inept and unsuccessful attempt on the life of the Shah (they had only loaded their pistols with bird-shot). The Shah was only slightly wounded but was beside himself with rage at this event. The authorities captured two of the Babi assailants and tortured them until they revealed that they were Babis and that they had been gathering at the house of Sulayman Khan. A raid was launched on the house and some twelve Babis arrested there. Further torture and further arrests followed. The servant of Sulayman Khan was taken around the city and whomever he identified as having come to the house of Sulayman Khan was arrested.

Baha'u'llah had been at Afchih when news of the attempt on the life of the Shah reached him. The Prime Minister's brother wrote to him that the Shah's mother in particular was denouncing Baha'u'llah as the leader of the conspiracy against her son and was trying to drag the Prime Minister into this as an accomplice. Baha'u'llah knew it would not be long before he was arrested and so he set out from Afchih towards the royal camp at Shimiran. Arriving at the village of Zargandih, he went to his sister Nisa's house. She was married to the Persian secretary of the Russian Legation in Tehran and her house was in the compound of the Russian Legation. Baha'u'llah was however recognized as he went in and the Persian government demanded that he be handed over to them. The Russian Minister complied after extracting certain assurances from the Persian government that Baha'u'llah would receive a fair trial. Baha'u'llah was led away towards Tehran in chains.

> All along the route, He was pelted and vilified by the crowds whom His enemies had succeeded in convincing that He was the sworn enemy of their sovereign and the wrecker of his realm. Words fail me to portray the horror of the treatment which was meted out to Him as He was being taken to the Siyáh-Chál of Tihran. As He was approaching the dungeon, and old and decrepit woman was seen to emerge from the midst of the crowd, with a stone in her hand, eager to cast it at the face of Baha'u'llah. Her eyes glowed with a determination and fanaticism of which few women of her age were capable. Her whole frame shook with rage as she stepped forward and raised her hand to hurl her missile at Him. 'By the Siyyidu'sh-Shuhadá [grandson of the prophet Muhammad], I adjure you,' she pleaded, as she ran to overtake those into whose hands Bahá'u'lláh had been

delivered, 'give me a chance to fling my stone in his face!' 'Suffer not this woman to be disappointed,' were Bahá'u'lláh's words to His guards, as He saw her hastening behind Him. 'Deny her not what she regards as a meritorious act in the sight of God.'[19]

THE BLACK PIT (SIYAH CHAL)

The arrested Babis were chained together and crowded into an underground, disused water cistern that was being used as a dungeon. It was called the Siyáh Chál (the Black Pit) and was dark and dank. To keep up their spirits, Baha'u'llah divided them into two groups and they would chant through the night with one group saying the fist half of the refrain: 'God is sufficient unto me; He verily is the All-Sufficing' and the other group responding: 'In Him let the trusting trust.' Baha'u'llah's own description of that Black Pit includes the following:

> We were consigned for four months to a place foul beyond comparison. As to the dungeon in which this Wronged One and others similarly wronged were confined, a dark and narrow pit were preferable. Upon Our arrival We were first conducted along a pitch-black corridor, from whence We descended three steep flights of stairs to the place of confinement assigned to Us. The dungeon was wrapped in thick darkness, and Our fellow-prisoners numbered nearly a hundred and fifty souls: thieves, assassins and highwaymen. Though crowded, it had no other outlet than the passage by which We entered. No pen can depict that place, nor any tongue describe its loathsome smell. Most of these men had neither clothes nor bedding to lie on. God alone knoweth what befell Us in that most foul-smelling and gloomy place! . . .
>
> Shouldst thou at some time happen to visit the dungeon of His Majesty the Shah, ask the director and chief jailer to show thee those two chains, one of which is known as Qará-Guhar, and the other as Salásil. I swear by the Daystar of Justice that for four months this Wronged One was tormented and chained by one or the other of them.[20]

On one occasion, Baha'u'llah spoke about his captivity thus:

> The weight of the chain placed about Our neck was difficult to bear [the heaviest chain used weighed over fifty kilograms], but having the thumbs of both hands bound together behind the back was even more aggravating. The royal guards were unyielding, but the executioners would show us kindness. One even offered Me tea and some grapes, but as I was freighted with chains and My hands were bound, I was unable to accept them.[21]

Baha'u'llah's son 'Abdu'l-Baha was eight years old at this time. He describes a visit that he made to his father in this dungeon:

> They sent me with a black servant to His blessed presence in the prison. The warders indicated the cell, and the servant carried me in on his shoulders. I saw a dark, steep place. We entered a small, narrow doorway, and went down two steps, but beyond those one could see nothing. In the middle of the stairway, all of a sudden we heard His blessed voice: 'Do not bring him in here', and so they took me back. We sat outside, waiting for the prisoners to be led out. Suddenly they brought the Blessed Perfection [Baha'u'llah] out of the dungeon. He was chained to several others. What a chain! It was very heavy. The prisoners could only move it along with great difficulty. Sad and heart-rending it was.[22]

The Shah had given orders that whoever could be identified as a Babi should be put to death. They brought the servant of Sulayman Khan to Baha'u'llah and tried to induce him to identify Baha'u'llah but he declined (because of course Baha'u'llah had not been one of those who had attended the gatherings at Sulayman Khan's house). Moreover, 'Azim, whom they also questioned about Baha'u'llah's involvement in the plot, refused to implicate him. Most of the other Babis were however led out one by one and put to death. At this time, the two most senior of the remaining Letters of the Living, Tahirih and the Bab's secretary, perished. The Shah had decided that all the members of the government and court should be given the opportunity to show their loyalty. And so each of the Babis was given to a different group and the various government ministries and departments of the court competed with each other to find the most gruesome ways in which to put the Babi that they had been assigned to death. An Austrian army officer who was training the shah's troops wrote a lengthy account of these events, a part of which follows:

His [the shah's] last edict still further enjoins on the Royal servants the annihilation of the sect [the Babis]. If these simply followed the Royal command and rendered harmless such of the fanatics as are arrested by inflicting on them a swift and lawful death, one must needs, from the Oriental standpoint, approve of this; but the manner of inflicting the sentence, the circumstances which precede the end, the agonies which consume the bodies of the victims until their life is extinguished in the last convulsion are so horrible that the blood curdles in my veins if I now endeavour to depict the scene for you, even in outline. Innumerable blows with sticks which fall heavily on the back and soles of the feet, brandings of different parts of the body with red-hot irons, are such usual inflictions that the victim who undergoes only such caresses is to be accounted fortunate. But follow me my friend, you who lay claim to a heart and European ethics, follow me to the unhappy ones who, with gouged-out eyes, must eat, on the scene of the deed, without any sauce, their own amputated ears; or whose teeth are torn out with inhuman violence by the hand of the executioner; or whose bare skulls are simply crushed by blows from a hammer; or where the bazar is illuminated with unhappy victims, because on right and left the people dig deep holes in their breasts and shoulders and insert burning wicks in the wounds. I saw some dragged in chains through the bazar, preceded by a military band, in whom these wicks had burned so deep that now the fat flickered convulsively in the wound like a newly extinguished lamp ... The more fortunate suffered strangulation, stoning or suffocation: they were bound before the muzzle of a mortar, cut down with swords, or killed with dagger thrusts, or blows from hammers and sticks. Not only the executioner and the common people took part in the massacre: sometimes Justice would present some of the unhappy Babis to various dignitaries and the Persian [recipient] would be well content, deeming it an honour to imbrue his own hands in the blood of the pinioned and defenceless victim. Infantry, cavalry, artillery, the ghulams or guards of the King, and the guilds of butchers, bakers, etc., all took their fair share in these bloody deeds.[23]

Part of the plan conceived at the house of Sulayman Khan had been that Azal, Baha'u'llah's half-brother, would go to his home district of Nur and create an uprising of the Babis there at the same time as the attempt on the life of the Shah. Only a handful of people rallied to Azal and nothing came of the planned uprising but it gave the enemies of the Babis in the Nur area, such as Baha'u'llah's uncle Shaykh 'Azizu'llah, the opportunity to send alarming and exaggerated reports to the Shah. The Shah, still recovering from his wounds, was in no mood to assess these reports properly and merely ordered the Prime Minister to send a force to Nur to suppress the Babis. Mirza Aqa Khan Nuri, the Prime Minister, was in a difficult situation. Being from Nur himself, he had reliable reports that there was no insurrection going on there, but he knew that, if he were to insist on this before the Shah, he could be confirming suspicions that he himself was in league with the Babis. He therefore felt he had no choice but to send a force to Nur. He thought he would mitigate the effects of this by sending as the adviser to this force his nephew Abu Talib Khan whose sister was married to Mirza Muhammad Hasan, a half-brother of Baha'u'llah, and was resident in Takur. Unfortunately the Prime Minister had misjudged his nephew and when the troops arrived in Takur it was Abu Talib Khan who led them in attacking the houses of the Babis, looting and killing. Baha'u'llah's house in Takur was among those pillaged. About twenty of the Babis were led back to Tehran where a number of them died in prison.

During this period that Baha'u'llah spent in the Black Pit, he had an experience which he himself designates as the birth of his mission. He has described this in different ways and so it may well have been a series of experiences rather than a single experience. In one place he has described it thus:

> Day and night, while confined in that dungeon, We meditated upon the deeds, the condition, and the conduct of the Bábís, wondering what could have led a people so high-minded, so noble, and of such intelligence, to perpetrate such an audacious and outrageous act against the person of His Majesty. This Wronged One, thereupon, decided to arise, after His release from prison, and undertake, with the utmost vigour, the task of regenerating this people.
>
> One night, in a dream, these exalted words were heard on every side: 'Verily, We shall render Thee victorious by Thyself and by Thy Pen. Grieve Thou not for that which hath befallen Thee, neither be Thou afraid, for Thou art in safety. Erelong will God raise up the treasures of the earth – men who will aid Thee through Thyself and through Thy Name, wherewith God hath revived the hearts of such as have recognized Him' . . .
>
> During the days I lay in the prison of Tihrán, though the galling weight of the chains and the stench-filled air allowed Me but little sleep, still in those infrequent moments of slumber I felt as if something flowed from the crown of My head over My breast, even as a mighty torrent that precipitateth itself upon the earth from the summit of a lofty mountain. Every limb of My body would, as a result, be set afire. At such moments My tongue recited what no man could bear to hear.[24]

In another place he describes the experience in terms of a vision:

> While engulfed in tribulations I heard a most wondrous, a most sweet voice, calling above My head. Turning My face, I beheld a Maiden – the embodiment of the remembrance of the name of My Lord – suspended in the air before Me. So rejoiced was she in her very soul that her countenance shone with the ornament of the good pleasure of God, and her cheeks glowed with the brightness of the All-Merciful. Betwixt earth and heaven she was raising a call which captivated the hearts and minds of men. She was imparting to both My inward and outer being tidings which rejoiced My soul, and the souls of God's honoured servants.

Pointing with her finger unto My head, she addressed all who are in heaven and all who are on earth, saying: By God! This is the Best-Beloved of the worlds, and yet ye comprehend not. This is the Beauty of God amongst you, and the power of His sovereignty within you, could ye but understand. This is the Mystery of God and His Treasure, the Cause of God and His glory unto all who are in the kingdoms of Revelation and of creation, if ye be of them that perceive. This is He Whose Presence is the ardent desire of the denizens of the Realm of eternity, and of them that dwell within the Tabernacle of glory, and yet from His Beauty do ye turn aside.[25]

RELEASE AND EXILE

Despite the fury of the Shah's mother against him, Baha'u'llah himself could not be condemned to death because of the undertaking that the Persian government had given the Russian Minister and because no evidence had been found against him. Therefore after four months in the Black Pit, the government ordered the release of Baha'u'llah with the condition that he go into exile. His own home had been looted and wrecked and so he went to stay with his half-brother to recover his health. The Russian Minister immediately offered Baha'u'llah asylum in Russian territory. Baha'u'llah, however, refused this. Probably his main consideration was that, whatever may have been the Russian Minister's intention, if he had gone to Russian territory, he and the Babi movement would have become instruments of Russian policy, in the struggle that Russia and Britain were engaged upon to gain supremacy in Iran. Baha'u'llah was given a month in which to leave the country. He chose to make his place of exile Baghdad which at that time was the capital of the province of the Ottoman Empire that forms a large part of the present country of Iraq.

On 12 January 1853, a month after his release from prison, during a bitterly cold winter, Baha'u'llah and his family set off over the mountains to Baghdad. Accompanying Baha'u'llah and his immediate family were his brother Mirza Musa, known as Kalim, and his half-brother Mirza Muhammad Quli, as well as representatives of the Iranian and Russian governments. They were ill-prepared for the cold they encountered and Baha'u'llah's wife, Asiyih Khanum, was far advanced in pregnancy and not in a fit condition for the jolting of riding on a mule (she must have lost this child as a result of the rigours of the journey as there is no child of hers recorded as being born at this time). The family had lost all of their wealth and possessions. Priceless works of art and manuscripts that had been owned by Baha'u'llah's father were looted and their other possessions destroyed. Asiyih Khanum sold most of what remained of her marriage treasures, jewels, embroidered garments and other belongings to raise funds to prepare for the journey. With all their assets gone, they were reduced to selling the gold buttons on Asiyih Khanum's wedding clothes for food on the journey itself. Some of the family suffered from frostbite on the way. Bahiyyih Khanum, the daughter of Baha'u'llah, remembered in particular:

> When we came to a city, my dear mother would take the clothes and wash them at the public baths; we also were able to have baths at those places. She would carry the cold, wet clothes away in her arms – drying them was an almost impossible task; her lovely hands, being unused to such coarse work, became very painful.
>
> We sometimes stayed at a caravanserai – a sort of rough inn. Only one room was allowed for one family, and for one night – no longer. No light was permitted at night, and there were no beds. Sometimes we were able to have tea, or again a few eggs, a little cheese, and some coarse bread.
>
> My father was so ill that he could not eat the rough food – my mother was very distressed and tried to think of some way of getting different food, as he grew more weak through eating nothing.
>
> One day she had been able to get a little flour, and at night, when we arrived at the caravanserai, she made a sweet cake for him. Alas! – the misfortune – being dark, she used salt instead of sugar. So the cake was uneatable![26]

Baha'u'llah refers to the hardship of his imprisonment and of this journey in a prayer he wrote addressing God:

> My God, My Master, My Desire! . . . Thou hast created this atom of dust through the consummate power of Thy might, and nurtured Him with Thine hands which none can chain up . . . Thou hast destined for Him trials and tribulations which no tongue can describe, nor any of Thy Tablets adequately recount. The throat Thou didst accustom to the touch of silk Thou hast, in the end, clasped with strong chains, and the body Thou didst ease with brocades and velvets Thou hast at last subjected to the abasement of a dungeon. Thy decree hath shackled Me with unnumbered fetters, and cast about My neck chains that none can sunder. A number of years have passed during which afflictions have, like showers of mercy, rained upon Me . . . How many the nights during which the weight of chains and fetters allowed Me no rest, and how numerous the days during which peace and tranquillity were denied Me, by reason of that wherewith the hands and tongues of men have afflicted Me! Both bread and water which Thou hast, through Thy all-embracing mercy, allowed unto the beasts of the field, they have, for a time, forbidden unto this servant, and the things they refused to inflict upon such as have seceded from Thy Cause, the same have they suffered to be inflicted upon Me, until, finally, Thy decree was irrevocably fixed, and Thy behest summoned this servant to depart out of Persia, accompanied by a number of frail-bodied men and children of tender age, at this time when the cold is so intense that one cannot even speak, and ice and snow so abundant that it is impossible to move.[27]

THREE

Baghdad (1853–1863)

Baha'u'llah arrived in Baghdad on 8 April 1853. The journey from Tehran had been very difficult and had lasted three months. After a few days in Baghdad, Baha'u'llah moved to Kazimayn, a Shi'i shrine city which at that time was some five kilometres north-west of Baghdad (it has since become incorporated into the city). The Iranian consul suggested to him that since Kazimayn tended to be full of rather fanatical elements, it would be safer for Baha'u'llah if he lived in Baghdad itself in the mainly Persian-speaking quarters on the west bank of the Tigris river. Baha'u'llah consented to this and rented a house there. His younger half-brother, Azal, who with the death of other leading Babis was now increasingly being regarded as the leader of the Babi community, had escaped from Nur after the failed uprising there and arrived in Baghdad in disguise and under an assumed name about two months after Baha'u'llah. Since he was not under any royal edict of exile, Baha'u'llah tried to persuade him to return to Iran and rally the Babi community there, but he declined to go.

Although Baha'u'llah had had the experience in the Black Pit of Tehran, described in the previous chapter, and felt a flood of spiritual power within him, he refrained at this time, and indeed for the whole of his ten-year stay in Baghdad, from openly announcing any claim. He decided instead to put his energies into reviving the fortunes of the Babi community both in Baghdad and in Iran. He describes the situation of the Babis at the time of his arrival thus: 'Upon Our arrival in Iraq We found the Cause of God sunk in deep apathy and the breeze of divine revelation stilled. Most of the believers were faint and dispirited, nay utterly lost and dead.'[28] Baha'u'llah began both to urge them to put away thoughts of revenge against the Shah and the clerics who had brought them so much suffering and to guide them towards manifesting in their lives the high ethical teachings to be found in the writings of the Bab.

A number of the most influential Iranian and Arab Babis in Kazimayn and Baghdad found the leadership that they sorely needed in Baha'u'llah and gathered around him. Increasing numbers of Babis also began to visit Baghdad from Iranian cities such as Kashan, Isfahan and Yazd. These met with Baha'u'llah and returned to their homes singing his praises to the Babi communities there. One of those who joined the circle that was gathering around Baha'u'llah in Baghdad was a youth, Mirza Aqa Jan, who arrived in Baghdad from Kashan in September 1853. He was in later years to become the principal secretary of Baha'u'llah. Azal observed these developments from a distance. On the one hand, he had gone into hiding out of fear and had forbidden any Babis from trying to seek him out. On the other hand, he was jealous of the fact that Baha'u'llah was the centre of a growing band of admirers. He therefore began to spread rumours about Baha'u'llah, causing dissension and disunity among the Babis. He was aided in his scheming by a certain Sayyid Muhammad Isfahani, who had attached himself to Azal and was goading him into these actions.

Matters came to a head with the visit of Mirza Kamalu'd-Din Naraqi who belonged to one of the foremost clerical families in Iran and had himself studied the Islamic sciences. He had become a Babi and had come to Baghdad to meet Azal. When Azal refused to meet him, he asked for a commentary on a verse of the Qur'an. He was greatly disappointed at what Azal produced and turned instead to Baha'u'llah, who produced the Tablet of All Food (the shorter writings of Baha'u'llah which were usually written for individuals are called 'tablets' and this Qur'anic verse, 3:93, begins with the words 'all food', see p. 157). The production of this tablet and Kamalu'd-Din's enthusiastic reception of it caused great resentment in Azal and he and Isfahani redoubled their efforts to spread false accusations about Baha'u'llah. This resulted in heated exchanges with those who had become fervent admirers of Baha'u'llah.

Baha'u'llah was distraught at this turn of events. In a letter to his cousin Maryam, he wrote: 'O Maryam! From the land of Tá [Tehran], after countless afflictions, We reached 'Iraq, at the bidding of the Tyrant of Persia, where, after the fetters of our foes, We were afflicted by the perfidy of Our friends.'[29] Mirza Aqa Jan reported that one night, just after dawn, he had seen Baha'u'llah emerge from his house, his night-cap still on his head, showing signs of great perturbation and saying:

'These creatures are the same creatures who for three thousand years have worshipped idols, and bowed down before the Golden Calf. Now, too, they are fit for nothing better. What relation can there be between this people and Him Who is the Countenance of Glory? What ties can bind them to the One Who is the supreme embodiment of all that is lovable?' 'I stood,' declared Mírzá Áqá Ján, 'rooted to the spot, lifeless, dried up as a dead tree, ready to fall under the impact of the stunning power of His words. Finally, He said: 'Bid them recite: "Is there any Remover of difficulties save God? Say: Praised be God! He is God! All are His servants, and all abide by His bidding!" Tell them to repeat it five hundred times, nay, a thousand times, by day and by night, sleeping and waking, that haply the Countenance of Glory may be unveiled to their eyes, and tiers of light descend upon them.' He Himself, I was subsequently informed, recited this same verse, His face betraying the utmost sadness.[30]

SOJOURN IN THE MOUNTAINS OF KURDISTAN, 1854–6

Seeing that his presence in Baghdad was in danger of splitting the community, Baha'u'llah decided to leave the scene of the conflict

for the mountains 300 kilometres to the north of Baghdad which
are the domains of the Kurdish people. He took with him one
attendant, Aqa Abu'l-Qasim Hamadani, who was not well-
known among the Babis, and left suddenly, informing no-one of
where he was going. Dressed in the garb of a dervish, those Sufis
who wander from town to town, he took the name Darvish
Muhammad and assumed the life of a hermit, living in a cave in
the mountains of Kurdistan. Hamadani lived in the town of
Sulaymaniyyih as a merchant and obtained provisions for
Baha'u'llah, who would occasionally visit the town to go to the
public baths. Baha'u'llah's daughter remembered what he had
described of his life in these mountains: 'The food was easy to
describe – coarse bread, a little cheese was the usual diet; sometimes, but very rarely, a cup of milk; into this would be put some
rice, and a tiny bit of sugar. When boiled together, these scanty
rations provided the great treat of a sort of rice pudding.'[31]

Baha'u'llah has himself described his motivation in leaving
Baghdad and his life in these mountains thus:

> In the early days of Our arrival in this land [Iraq], when We dis-
> cerned the signs of impending events, We decided, ere they hap-
> pened, to retire. We betook Ourselves to the wilderness, and
> there, separated and alone, led for two years a life of complete
> solitude. From Our eyes there rained tears of anguish, and in
> Our bleeding heart there surged an ocean of agonizing pain.
> Many a night We had no food for sustenance, and many a day
> Our body found no rest. By Him Who hath My being between
> His hands! notwithstanding these showers of afflictions and
> unceasing calamities, Our soul was wrapt in blissful joy, and
> Our whole being evinced an ineffable gladness. For in Our
> solitude We were unaware of the harm or benefit, the health or
> ailment, of any soul. Alone, We communed with Our spirit,
> oblivious of the world and all that is therein.[32]

Baha'u'llah had inherited a fine calligraphic hand from his
father. During one of Baha'u'llah's trips into the town of
Sulaymaniyyih, a paper with Baha'u'llah's penmanship fell into
the hands of one of the Sufi shaykhs (leader, teacher, holy man)

of Sulaymaniyyih. Realising that this 'Darvish Muhammad' was something more than he appeared to be, this Sufi shaykh went to him and was soon learning from him. Baha'u'llah was invited to teach the famous *Meccan Revelations* of Shaykh Muhyi'd-Din Ibn al-Arabi (one of the best known but most abstruse works of Islamic mystical philosophy) at the retreat of the Nakhshbandi-Khalidi Sufi order in the town. Then he was invited to compose a poem in the style of one of the most famous of Sufi poems, the *Ta'iyyih* by the Egyptian Sufi Ibn al-Fárid. Baha'u'llah wrote some 2000 verses of which he chose 127 and presented them as the Ode of the Dove.

In the absence of Baha'u'llah, the Babi community in Baghdad had sunk to low levels of degradation. Azal was directing a campaign that was increasing the divisions among the Babis. He ordered the death of rival claimants to the leadership such as Dayyan in the Adharbayjan province of Iran, while surrounding himself with ruffians who stole from the pilgrims who came to the shrines at Kazimayn. The Babi community became

The Sufi Retreat (Takiyyih) in Sulaymaniyyih where
Baha'u'llah lived and taught for a time

the object of vilification and contempt among the people of Iraq. Seeing the deteriorating state of the Babi community, a number of people advanced claims to leadership of it, some claiming to be 'He whom God shall make manifest', the messianic figure that is frequently mentioned in the later writings of the Bab.

At one stage in the latter part of 1855, Abu'l-Qasim Hamadani went to Hamadan in order to sell some goods and was returning with cash when he was set upon by robbers and left for dead. He survived long enough to tell those who found him the identity of the robbers and that the money they had stolen belonged to Darvish Muhammad who could be found by enquiring in Sulaymaniyyih. News of this murder and of the murdered man's final words was published in the Iranian government newspaper of the time, which eventually reached the Persian consulate in Baghdad. Baha'u'llah's brother, Kalim, and son, 'Abdu'l-Baha, were visiting the Iranian consulate one day when someone read out the account of Hamadani's murder. Instinctively Kalim and 'Abdu'l-Baha knew that 'Darvish Muhammad' was Baha'u'llah. They discussed this among the Babis in Baghdad and plans were made for two of the Babis to go to Sulaymaniyyih with petitions and try to persuade Baha'u'llah to return and save the Babi community from the low state into which it had fallen.

These two Babis went to Sulaymaniyyih and waited until they saw Baha'u'llah. However, witnessing the great love and affection which the people of the town had for Baha'u'llah, they dared not openly talk of his return to Baghdad. They merely presented the petitions that they had brought and retired to the caravanserai where they were quartered. Baha'u'llah visited them there and was at first unwilling to accede to their request that he return. He pointed to the treachery and back-biting to which he had been subjected in Baghdad and contrasted this with the sincere devotion and high regard with which he was held among the Kurds. The Babis said that they would then remain in Sulaymaniyyih and many other Babis would undoubtedly migrate there also. Baha'u'llah eventually relented and agreed to return to Baghdad, explaining his reasons for doing so thus to one of the two Babis who had come:

> But for My recognition of the fact that the blessed Cause of the Primal Point [the Bab] was on the verge of being completely obliterated, and all the sacred blood poured out in the path of God would have been shed in vain, I would in no wise have consented to return to the people of the Bayán [the Babis], and would have abandoned them to the worship of the idols their imaginations had fashioned.[33]

In one of his writings, Baha'u'llah states that, although when he had left Baghdad he had no thought of returning, it was the summons of God, the 'Mystic Source', which caused him to return:

> Our withdrawal contemplated no return, and Our separation hoped for no reunion. The one object of Our retirement was to avoid becoming a subject of discord among the faithful, a source of disturbance unto Our companions, the means of injury to any soul, or the cause of sorrow to any heart. Beyond these, We cherished no other intention, and apart from them, We had no end in view. And yet, each person schemed after his own desire, and pursued his own idle fancy, until the hour when, from the Mystic Source, there came the summons bidding Us return whence We came. Surrendering Our will to His, We submitted to His injunction.[34]

Baha'u'llah told his admirers in Sulaymaniyyih of his decision to go to Baghdad and consoled them with the promise that they could visit him there, provided they came in small numbers so as not to excite the suspicions of the authorities. He then set off with the two Babis to return to Baghdad. They arrived there on 19 March 1856, almost exactly two years after Baha'u'llah had departed.

RETURN TO BAGHDAD, 1856–1858

Upon Baha'u'llah's return to Baghdad, he discovered the low morale and degraded state of the Babi community. 'We found no more than a handful of souls, faint and dispirited, nay utterly lost and dead,' was Baha'u'llah description of what he found, 'The Cause of God had ceased to be on any one's lips, nor was any heart receptive to its message.'[35] Gradually, Baha'u'llah began to rebuild the Babi community and restore its self-respect and prestige.

The domestic arrangements in Baghdad are remembered thus by Bahiyyih Khanum, the daughter of Baha'u'llah:

> Mírzá Músá [Baha'u'llah's brother] and his wife were always devoted to Bahá'u'lláh. This uncle, Mírzá Músá, who came into exile with us, was a very kind helper in everything. At one time he did almost all the cooking, for which he had a talent, he would also help with the washing.
>
> Ásíyih Khánum, my dear mother, was in delicate health, her strength was diminished by the hardships she had undergone, but she always worked beyond her force.
>
> Sometimes my father himself helped in the cooking, as that hard work was too much for the dainty, refined, gentle lady. The hardships she had endured saddened the heart of her divine husband, who was also her beloved Lord. He gave this help both before his sojourn in the wilderness of Sulaymániyyih, and after his return.[36]

Gradually the house of Baha'u'llah became a focal point for not only the Babis but even of Iranian princes and notables who were living in exile in Baghdad. There was a stream of Kurdish visitors from Sulaymaniyyih and the Kurdish leader 'Abdullah Pasha Baban became devoted to Baha'u'llah. Learned Arab Sunni scholars of Baghdad such as Shaykh 'Abdu'l-Qadir Gilani, Shaykh 'Abdu's-Salam Shawwaf and Ibn al-Alusi from the eastern half of Baghdad now began to cross the river to visit Baha'u'llah. Visitors to Baghdad, such as Manekji Sahib, the Zoroastrian agent who had been sent by his co-religionists in India to improve the lot of the Zoroastrians in Iran, when he was in Baghdad in 1861 to 1862, also called on Baha'u'llah for advice and assistance.

Baha'u'llah's reputation and standing among the ordinary people of Baghdad also grew. At first, after his return from the mountains of Kurdistan, Baha'u'llah remained in his house. But from about 1858, it became his custom to go daily to one of two well-known coffee shops in Baghdad, one at either end of the bridge across the Tigris that linked east Baghdad with west Baghdad. He would sit there and talk to the people about the teachings of the Bab. These two coffee houses became very crowded as people began to flock to hear him. He thus became very well known in Baghdad and was the acknowledged leader of the Babi community. People who felt they had been unjustly treated began coming to his door asking him to intervene in their case and assist them. Ustad Muhammad 'Ali Salmani who was with him in Baghdad, describes Baha'u'llah's typical daily routine at this time:

> It was the custom of the Blessed Beauty [Baha'u'llah] when He lived in Baghdad to partake of His morning tea in the *andarún* [inner apartment of his house]. He would then go out to the *bírúní* [reception room]. This *bírúní* which He had was a single clean and tidy room . . .
>
> And so, Bahá'u'lláh would come to this room. He would walk about and pace up and down and the friends would visit Him. Here in the *bírúní* He would remain about half an hour or an hour. After that, He would proceed to a coffeehouse. There was in Baghdad a Siyyid Habíb the Arab, who was the *kadkhudá* [headman of a city quarter] of Old Baghdad. This man had a coffeehouse which Bahá'u'lláh would frequent, and as a general thing this is where the people would come to be with Him. Áqá Najaf-'Alí and Áqá Muhammad-Ibráhím, who were permanent servitors of Bahá'u'lláh, would also be present. Sometimes, I too would go along.
>
> Here Bahá'u'lláh would partake of coffee every day, and the water pipe would be prepared for Him . . . He would smoke a very little, and would converse with the people. His purpose in going to this coffeehouse was to spread the Faith. It was an excellent establishment. Siyyid Habíb was not a believer, but he was a fine man – and very unassuming. After an hour or an hour and a half, Bahá'u'lláh would leave here and return to His living quarters until afternoon. Then He would again set out for

another visit to the coffeehouse and stay until sundown. After that, He would go back to His *andarún*, or sometimes to the *bírúní*. There the friends would usually remain together until two hours after sunset, and then go their separate ways. And, sometimes Bahá'u'lláh would be present.

All the great of Baghdad, and the ulama [the Muslim clerics, mainly Sunni], and the magistrates, would present themselves here at this coffeehouse with extreme deference. Bahá'u'lláh, however, would never go to their homes. The inhabitants of Baghdad (that is, the Sunnis) would speak, one and all, of the utter perfection of Bahá'u'lláh. Many a time they would refer difficult questions to Him and request Him to solve them.[37]

There was also an ever increasing stream of Babis who came to Baghdad from all parts of Iran: Yazd, Shiraz, Isfahan, Mashhad, Kashan, Qazvin and Tehran. Some of those who arrived in Baghdad after having been forced to leave their homes as a result of persecution stayed; most, however, returned to their towns, enthused by their visit to Baha'u'llah and carrying with them the stream of writings that were now flowing from Baha'u'llah's pen. As a result, Baha'u'llah's reputation among the Babis of Iran was growing. They had found someone around whom they could rally, who would revive their faith and restore their prestige. Most of those who had advanced claims to leadership of the Babi community recognized at this time Baha'u'llah's superiority and grouped around him, even though he had as yet still not advanced any claim of his own.

Most of the Babis lived in houses around the house of Baha'u'llah and they were so poor that several of them occupied each room. They each scratched out a living and whatever they earned they would pool together, purchase food and have their meals together. 'Many a night, no less than ten persons subsisted on no more than a pennyworth of dates. No one knew to whom actually belonged the shoes, the cloaks, or the robes that were to be found in their houses. Whoever went to the bazaar could claim that the shoes upon his feet were his own, and each one who entered the presence of Baha'u'llah could affirm that the cloak and robe he then wore belonged to him.'[38] Baha'u'llah himself asserts in one of his writings that: 'There was a time in Iraq, when the Ancient Beauty [Baha'u'llah] . . . had no change of linen. The one shirt He possessed would be washed, dried and worn again.'[39]

Although Baha'u'llah was trying to improve the morals of the Babi community, there were still elements in that community who were less affected by Baha'u'llah efforts and these caused Baha'u'llah many problems. On one occasion in about 1858, for example, one of them, a young Arab Babi, took it into his head to kill two Iranians who were at the centre of attacks on the Babis. He killed one and severely wounded the other. The wounded man managed to reach the house of the governor 'Umar Pasha. When the latter heard that the culprit was a Babi, he wanted to summon Baha'u'llah to the Governorate. An indication of the high regard with which Baha'u'llah was held by the people of Baghdad is the fact that the governor was told by his advisers that it was inappropriate to treat someone of Baha'u'llah's standing in such a manner. The governor therefore sent one of his men to Baha'u'llah to enquire about the matter. This man returned fully satisfied with Baha'u'llah's answers and the governor eventually sent the wounded man himself to Baha'u'llah to obtain justice. On another occasion, an official of the Iranian consulate came to Baha'u'llah and said that they had arrested a number of the criminal element among the Iranians of Baghdad and one of them had claimed a relationship to Baha'u'llah. Baha'u'llah responded thus:

> 'Tell him, no one in this world can claim any relationship to Me except those who, in all their deeds and in their conduct, follow My example, in such wise that all the peoples of the earth would be powerless to prevent them from doing and saying that which is meet and seemly.' 'This brother of Mine,' He further declared to that official, 'this Mírzá Músá, who is from the same mother and father as Myself, and who from his earliest childhood has kept Me company, should he perpetrate an act contrary to the interests of either the state or religion, and his guilt be

established in your sight, I would be pleased and appreciate your action were you to bind his hands and cast him into the river to drown, and refuse to consider the intercession of any one on his behalf.'[40]

Baha'u'llah's half-brother, Azal, continued to try to undermine him. He remained in hiding, sometimes disguised as a shoe seller or chalk merchant and sometimes removing himself to Basra or Najaf, but would issue instructions through Sayyid Muhammad Isfahani and a small number of others who gathered around him. This band of people who gathered around Azal caused Baha'u'llah many problems since they also called themselves Babis but their standards of behaviour were lamentable. One day, one of the Iranian princes resident in Baghdad complained to Baha'u'llah that Azal and Sayyid Muhammad Isfahani had been heard to boast that they would pull down the Shi'i holy shrine at Kazimayn and build a coffee shop in its place. Baha'u'llah replied that these sorts of people had no connection with him. He then wrote to Azal and his followers asking why, if they were calling themselves Babis, they were deliberately instigating the hatred of the people towards the cause of the Bab.

There were some others also who were not pleased with the presence of Baha'u'llah in Baghdad. An Iranian Kurd who was the leading figure in the bazaar was continually cursing and abusing the Babis. He was reprimanded by the Iranian consul in Baghdad but this only aroused the anger of the Kurdish community in Baghdad and they determined to attack the Babis and kill them all – there was a community of about 2000 Shi'i Iranian Kurds in Baghdad and only about thirty Babi men at this time. All of the latter, Arabs and Iranians, gathered around Baha'u'llah's house to defend it. Baha'u'llah, however, refused to cower in his house and went as usual to a coffee shop. Returning in the evening he loudly proclaimed that he was not afraid of death in such a way that the Kurds who were standing by to attack him were thrown into confusion and dispersed. One night, an armed group of these Kurds came to the house of

Baha'u'llah, demanding to see him. Although the Babis were fearful that these men had come to assassinate Baha'u'llah, the latter told them to allow the men in and let them keep their arms. Baha'u'llah welcomed the men warmly and, ignoring their refusal to sit down, their surliness and their constant handling of their weapons, launched into a discourse on the sufferings of the Imam Husayn, a holy figure from Shi'i history who was martyred. These Kurds who were Shi'is were much affected by this discourse and at the end of it bowed low before Baha'u'llah and left.

It may be noted in passing that Baha'u'llah was particularly affected by the story of the sufferings and martyrdom of the Imam Husayn, the grandson of the prophet Muhammad who had been martyred at Karbala in 680 CE. During his time in Baghdad, he always kept the ten days of mourning for the Imam at the beginning of the Muslim month of Muharram and would make a pilgrimage to the shrine at Kazimayn on the tenth day. Moreover he would host recitals of poetry lamenting the martyrdom of Imam Husayn at his home during these ten days and it was reported that when a particularly moving poem about this episode by the sixteenth-century Iranian poet Muhtasham was being recited, tears would flow from his eyes.[41]

At this time, the foremost cleric of the Shi'i world was Shaykh Murtada Ansari, who taught his students at Najaf (160 kilometres south of Baghdad). He had a great reputation for his knowledge, piety and fairness. One of his associates, Sayyid Muhammad Mujtahid came to Baghdad on one occasion and through an intermediary asked for a secret meeting at night with Baha'u'llah. They conversed for some three hours and at the end of this time Sayyid Muhammad pronounced himself satisfied with what he had heard. He then returned to Najaf. One day, after Ansari had completed his classes, there was general discussion about the Babis and the usual accusations were voiced. Ansari halted the discussion saying that everything that was being said was merely hearsay and could not be relied upon but that if anyone had investigated the matter for themselves, they should speak. At this juncture, Sayyid Muhammad announced that he had in fact recently conversed with Baha'u'llah and offered to give an account of what had passed between them. Ansari asked him to proceed but, as soon as he began to speak, some of the clerics present started to voice objections in a loud and rude manner. Ansari got up, angry at this, and left the room. One of those present however, Mirza 'Ali Naqi Mujtahid was sufficiently interested to go to Baghdad and seek out Baha'u'llah, and he eventually converted. He returned to Ansari and informed him of his findings. From that time onwards, whenever anyone asked Ansari about the Babis, he would reply that Baghdad was only a short distance away and that the enquirer should investigate the matter there since in matters of belief one should not follow a religious leader but should investigate for oneself.

Another of the students of Ansari was Aqa Muhammad Qa'ini, who was later given the title Nabil Akbar by Baha'u'llah. He was one of very few people to whom Ansari gave a certificate of ijtihad – the certificate that enabled a person to call themselves a mujtahid and to give judgements on Islamic law independently. He was already a Babi when he came from Najaf to Baghdad and visited Baha'u'llah. He himself has described how, considering himself the most learned person present at the gatherings at the house of Baha'u'llah, he used to sit at the head of the room and take it upon himself to address those present on a religious topic and to answer the questions that were asked while Baha'u'llah sat in the middle of the room and poured tea for the visitors. Qa'ini describes how Baha'u'llah began by just making occasional comments on what was being discussed but after a time he spoke more and eventually, as Qa'ini realised that his own contributions were worth little in the face of Baha'u'llah's words, Qa'ini fell silent and allowed Baha'u'llah to speak uninterrupted. In this way, Qa'ini became one of a small but growing number of Babis who became certain that Baha'u'llah was 'He whom God shall make manifest', the messianic figure whom the Bab had promised and whom the Babis ardently expected.

Another who came to this conclusion was Shams-i Jihan Khanum, a Qajar princess, an aunt of Nasiru'd-Din Shah, known by her pen-name of Fitnih, who had become a Babi through Tahirih in Tehran. She came to Baghdad and, in a poem she wrote, she describes her unsatisfactory experience with Mirza Yahya and his followers, how her faith was restored by meeting Baha'u'llah and of how she realised his true station.

Mirza Malkam Khan, who was forming secret societies in Iran and stirring up a demand for reform, wrote to Baha'u'llah suggesting that he join him in this work. Baha'u'llah replied to him that the very people whom he thought were supporting him would soon be out for his blood. Soon after this in late 1861, Malkam Khan fell from favour, was expelled from Iran and arrived in Baghdad. He came to Baha'u'llah for help, but Baha'u'llah did not think it wise to allow him to stay in his house and arranged for him to live elsewhere. Then word reached Malkam Khan that Qazvini, the Iranian consul, had orders to arrest him and send him back to Iran. Malkam Khan asked Baha'u'llah for help and the latter sent him to the governorate and asked the governor to ensure his safety. The governor arranged for Malkam Khan to proceed to Istanbul. A few other Iranian political exiles, such 'Abbas Mirza (later given the title of Mulk-Árá), the king's exiled half-brother, and Mirza Fadlu'lláh Nuri, the brother of the former Prime Minister, tried to gain favours from Baha'u'llah but he refused to involve himself in their schemings.

During the last few years in Baghdad, the British consul-general there, Arnold Burrowes-Campbell, came to recognize the prestige of Baha'u'llah and offered him British protection and transfer either to England or India. Baha'u'llah declined this offer much as he had previously declined the offer of Russian protection.

Another episode indicative of the great respect with which Baha'u'llah was held in Baghdad towards the end of his stay there was that one night a number of Iranians in Baghdad were involved in a brawl. They were arrested and spent the night in detention. The next day, Haji Ahmad Aqa, the chief of police, told them that, although he knew that none of them was a follower of Baha'u'llah, he was setting them free for the sake of Baha'u'llah because they were compatriots of his.

THE OPPOSITION TO BAHA'U'LLAH

In 1858, there arrived in Baghdad a prominent Iranian cleric named Shaykh 'Abdu'l-Husayn Tihrani, who had been commissioned by Nasiru'd-Din Shah to regild the domes of the Shi'i shrines in Iraq. He immediately became the centre of the opposition to Baha'u'llah and the Babis. He declared when he first arrived in Baghdad that the Babis were ignorant people and of no account and that should Baha'u'llah come out and debate his beliefs openly, it would be made evident to all that the views of the Babis were erroneous. One of those in Tihrani's circle, who also came to Baha'u'llah's house hoping to learn the secret of alchemy there, urged Tihrani to debate openly with Baha'u'llah and thereby make matters clear to everyone and he offered to make the arrangements for this. Tihrani agreed and so the man came to Baha'u'llah who also agreed to the debate at any place and any time within the next ten days. When this was relayed back to Tihrani, however, he began to create excuses and backed out. This affair became known among the Iranians in Baghdad and Kazimayn and greatly discomfitted Tihrani.

Then in 1860, Mirza Buzurg Khan Qazvini became the Iranian consul in Baghdad and he was also greatly opposed to Baha'u'llah. Even before he arrived in Baghdad, the word went about that he was going to have all the Babis arrested and sent back to Iran. He arrived with some thirty or forty men and joined forces with Tihrani. From the first, he tried to isolate the Babis by forbidding the Iranians in Baghdad and Kazimayn to meet with Baha'u'llah. However, shortly after Qazvini's arrival in Baghdad, one of the wealthy Iranian merchants of Baghdad who was devoted to Baha'u'llah gave a feast at his house in honour of Baha'u'llah that was so splendid that it became the talk of the town. This merchant died shortly afterwards having made Baha'u'llah the executor of his will. Then another prominent wealthy Iranian merchant died, having made Baha'u'llah the executor of his will. Thus far from Qazvini's aim of reducing Baha'u'llah's influence among the Iranian community, the latter's skilful handling of the disputes among the families of these deceased men over their inheritance greatly increased his prestige.

The next ploy of Qazvini was to go to the governor Mustafa Nuri Pasha and say that there were a few people who had escaped from Iran and come to Baghdad and he wanted to send them back to Iran. The governor had been forewarned of what Qazvini was plotting by 'Abdu'llah Pasha Baban and so he pretended ignorance and told Qazvini that he had no objection. Then Qazvini said that he needed the governor's assistance for this. The governor replied that, if it was just a few runaways he wanted to arrest, why did he need the governor's assistance? Who was it that he wanted to arrest? In this way the governor got Qazvini to admit that it was Baha'u'llah that he intended to arrest. The governor expressed surprise, saying that this man was held in great honour by all of the scholars and dignitaries of Baghdad and was the pride of the Iranians in the city, so how was it that Qazvini was now calling him a runaway and was wanting to involve the governor in arresting him? Qazvini replied that this man was the enemy of the religion of both the governor and himself. To which the Governor responded by saying that evidently he and Qazvini followed different religions and angrily dismissed the Consul.

Having been unsuccessful in their efforts, and greatly embarrassed by the results, Tihrani and Qazvini next resolved to try to assassinate Baha'u'llah. They offered a substantial reward to the criminal fraternity in Baghdad if they should attack Baha'u'llah's house by night and kill him or assassinate him as he walked through the streets. Baha'u'llah's friends warned him of these threats to his safety and Mulla 'Ali Mardan Kirkuti, who was in charge of the customs-house in Baghdad and a great admirer of Baha'u'llah, suggested that Baha'u'llah move for a time to his house in Kirkuk, out of harm's way, and then return once the danger had passed. Baha'u'llah, however, declined this offer and even continued to walk through Baghdad at night. When he came across one of those who was waiting to attack him, he would joke with them and send them on their way. The Babis, however, fearing for Baha'u'llah's life, decided to accompany him at all times, forming a small bodyguard. One of the would-be assassins, in later years, described how he had been waiting for Baha'u'llah one night with a concealed pistol in his hand. But as soon as he saw Baha'u'llah coming, a great consternation overtook him and the pistol fell from his hand. Baha'u'llah had instructed his brother Kalim to pick up the pistol, return it to the would-be assassin and show him the way back to his house as he looked lost.

Tihrani then convened a gathering of Shi'i clerics in Kazimayn to discuss how to deal with Baha'u'llah (this meeting probably occurred in July 1861). They decided to declare *jihad*, holy war, against the Babis and Baha'u'llah. One night, a certain cleric named Sayyid Husayn Rawdih-khan, who had been at these meetings and who had been on friendly terms with Baha'u'llah in Tehran, came in disguise to the latter's house, in a state of agitation with the news. On the following night, a group of one hundred or more Shi'i Kurds would come past Baha'u'llah's house performing the Muharram ritual of beating their chests and lamenting the martyrdom of the Shi'i holy figure, the Imam Husayn. It was planned that as they passed the house of Baha'u'llah, they would attack the house and kill all the occupants. Baha'u'llah calmed the man down, gave him some tea and told him to be assured that everything would be all right. Some of the Babis who heard this news came to the outer apartments of Baha'u'llah's house the next day fully armed but he sent them away. Then that night, when the Kurds arrived, Baha'u'llah ordered his brother Kalim to open the door and let them into the outer apartment and to give them refreshments. Baha'u'llah then entered and sat down and spoke to them in such a way that they left amazed at the way their enmity and anger had been transformed into affection and acquiescence.

The attack by the Kurds having failed, the clerics gathered at Kazimayn decided to issue a joint declaration to the effect that Baha'u'llah and the Babis were infidels and should be killed. They thought that with this, all of the Shi'is in Iraq would rise up against the Babis and kill them. For this to be effective, however, they need the signature of the most senior cleric of all, Shaykh Murtada Ansari. He was invited to come from Najaf and join them. When he heard what they had to say, however, he left the meeting and refused to listen to their entreaties. He returned to Najaf. On the way back, he sent a message to Baha'u'llah, saying that he had been unaware of the purpose of the gathering and that had he known, he would never have left Najaf. He asked for God's protection for Baha'u'llah from the evil planned against him. With this key support missing, the plan for a joint declaration fell through. 'Abdu'l-Baha, the son of Baha'u'llah, has described what happened after Shaykh Murtada left the gathering of clerics at Kazimayn:

> Those gathered in Kázimayn then arranged to come two days later and attack us. We were only forty-six in all, and our strong man was Áqá Asadu'lláh-i-Káshí (Káshání), whose dagger, even when worn above his *shál* [the cloth used as a girdle], would dangle and touch the ground. Now there was a certain Siyyid Hasan from Shiraz. He was not a believer, but he was a very good man. One morning, when the Blessed Perfection had been up and about, this Áqá Siyyid Hasan came knocking at our door. Our black maid opened the door, Áqá Siyyid Hasan came in and, much agitated, asked, 'Where is the Áqá [Bahá'u'lláh]?' I said, 'He has gone to the riverside.' 'What is it that you say?' he responded. I offered him tea and said, 'He will come back.' He replied, 'Áqá! The world has been turned upside down . . . It has become turbulent . . . Do you know that last night they held a council in the presence of Shaykh 'Abdu'l-Husayn and the Consul? They have also reached some sort of agreement with the Válí [governor]. How is it that the Blessed Perfection

has gone to the riverside? They have decided to start their attack tomorrow.' Whilst he was telling me what had happened, the Blessed Perfection came in. Áqá Siyyid Hasan wanted immediately to express his anxiety. But the Blessed Perfection said, 'Let us talk of other matters', and went on speaking. Later, Áqá Siyyid Hasan insisted on unburdening himself. However, the Blessed Perfection told him, 'It is of no consequence.' So Áqá Siyyid Hasan stayed to lunch and then went home.

Late in the afternoon the Blessed Perfection came out. The friends gathered round Him. Amongst them were two who were double-faced: Hájí 'Abdu'l-Hamíd and Áqá Muhammad-Javád-i-Isfahání. The Blessed Perfection was walking up and down. Then He turned to the Friends and said, 'Have you heard the news? The mujtahids [senior Shi'i clerics] and the Consul have come together and gathered ten to twenty thousand people round them to wage *jihád* against Us.' Then He addressed the two double-faced men, 'Go and tell them, by the One God, the Lord of all, I will send two men to drive them away, all the way to Kazimayn. If they are capable of accepting a challenge, let them come.' The two hurried away and repeated what they had heard.[42]

The governor was angry when he heard what the gathering of clerics had been planning and commented: 'This is not Iran and if they intend to foment public disorder and civil commotion, they will not be permitted to do that.'[43] Then he wrote to them and said that, if they genuinely wanted to resolve the issue, then he would gather a meeting of the religious leaders of all communities, Baha'u'llah would come also and there could then be a public debate. Each side could put their case and it would become clearwho was in the right and who was not. And if they tried to do something else, he would have them all drowned in the Tigris. When the clerics heard the governor's message, they realised that they could not pursue their plan.

Then the clerics gathered at Kazimayn decided to send to Baha'u'llah one of their number, Haji Mulla Hasan Tihrani, known as 'Amú, in order to put to Baha'u'llah a proposition that they thought he would never accept. The son of Baha'u'llah, 'Abdu'l-Bahá, writes of this episode thus:

> . . . the Persian 'ulamá [clerics] who were at Karbilá and Najaf chose a wise man whom they sent on a mission to Him [Bahá'u'lláh]; his name was Mullá Hasan 'Amú. He came into the Holy Presence, and proposed a number of questions on behalf of the 'ulamá, to which Bahá'u'lláh replied. Then Hasan 'Amú said, 'The 'ulamá recognize without hesitation and confess the knowledge and virtue of Bahá'u'lláh, and they are unanimously convinced that in all learning he has no peer or equal; and it is also evident that he has never studied or acquired this learning; but still the 'ulamá say, "We are not contented with this; we do not acknowledge the reality of his mission by virtue of his wisdom and righteousness. Therefore, we ask him to show us a miracle in order to satisfy and tranquilize our hearts."'
>
> Bahá'u'lláh replied, 'Although you have no right to ask this, for God should test His creatures, and they should not test God, still I allow and accept this request. But the Cause of God is not a theatrical display that is presented every hour, of which some new diversion may be asked for every day. If it were thus, the Cause of God would become mere child's play.
>
> 'The 'ulamá must, therefore, assemble, and, with one accord, choose one miracle, and write that, after the performance of this miracle they will no longer entertain doubts about Me, and that all will acknowledge and confess the truth of My Cause. Let them seal this paper, and bring it to Me. This must be the accepted criterion: if the miracle is performed, no doubt will remain for them; and if not, We shall be convicted of imposture.' The learned man, Hasan 'Amú, rose and replied, 'There is no more to be said'; he then kissed the knee of the Blessed One although he was not a believer, and went. He gathered the 'ulamá and gave them the sacred message. They consulted together and said, 'This man is an enchanter; perhaps he will perform an enchantment, and then we shall have nothing more to say.' Acting on this belief, they did not dare to push the matter further.
>
> This man, Hasan 'Amú, mentioned this fact at many meetings. After leaving Karbilá he went to Kirmánsháh and Tihrán

and spread a detailed account of it everywhere, laying emphasis on the fear and the withdrawal of the 'ulamá.[44]

Qazvini was pressing the governor hard to have Baha'u'llah and the Babis delivered to the Iranian government at the border. Rumours spread in the town that this was going to happen and the Babis feared for their lives and property. Baha'u'llah wrote to Mirza Sa'íd Khan, the Minister for Foreign Affairs of the Iranian government, but that produced no response. Eventually, Baha'u'llah decided that the Babis should apply for Ottoman citizenship in order to escape the clutches of the Iranian consul. The governor agreed and over a twenty day period some 120 men, women and children went to the government house and received Ottoman papers. Regarding these events, Baha'u'llah wrote to the shah in later years:

> By the leave and permission of the King of the Age [the shah], this Servant journeyed from the Seat of Sovereignty [Tihran] to 'Iráq, and dwelt for twelve years in that land. Throughout the entire course of this period no account of Our condition was submitted to the court of thy presence, and no representation ever made to foreign powers. Placing Our whole trust in God, We resided in that land until there came to 'Iráq a certain official [Qazvini] who, upon his arrival, undertook to harass this poor company of exiles. Day after day, at the instigation of some of the outwardly learned [Tihrani and others] and of other individuals, he would stir up trouble for these servants, although they had at no time committed any act detrimental to the state and its people or contrary to the rules and customs of the citizens of the realm.
>
> Fearing lest the actions of these transgressors should produce some outcome at variance with thy world-adorning judgement, this Servant despatched a brief account of the matter to Mírzá Sa'íd Khán at the Foreign Ministry, so that he might submit it to the royal presence and that whatever thou shouldst please to decree in this respect might be obeyed. A long while elapsed, and no decree was issued. Finally matters came to such a pass that there loomed the threat of imminent strife and bloodshed.

Of necessity, therefore, and for the protection of the servants of God, a few of them appealed to the Governor of 'Iráq.[45]

DEPARTURE OF BAHA'U'LLAH FROM BAGHDAD

As part of their strategy against Baha'u'llah and the Babis, for some time Tihrani and Qazvini had been sending reports to the Shah and his government in Iran and to Mushiru'd-Dawlih, the Iranian ambassador in Istanbul. They claimed, for example, that some of the tribes in the area had been converted to the Babi religion and that Baha'u'llah was now in a position to lead 100,000 men against Iran. The reality was that there were about forty or fifty Babi men (who with their families probably numbered 150 in all) in Baghdad and less than that number in nearby Kazimayn. Such reports, ridiculous as they were and despite Mushiru'd-Dawlih's attempts to point out their falsity, were sufficient to alarm the Shah. The Iranian government asked that Baha'u'llah be either handed over to the Iranian authorities at the Iranian border or else removed far from the Ottoman provinces that border Iran. The Ottoman government rejected these suggestions saying that Baha'u'llah had come to their territory as a guest and they would not ill-treat their guests. Then in June 1861, the Sultan 'Abdu'l-Majid died and a new Sultan, 'Abdu'l-Aziz, came to the throne. The Iranian government saw this as a good opportunity to renew its request on the basis of the goodwill between the two governments. In May 1862, the Foreign Minister of Iran wrote to Mushiru'd-Dawlih to renew their request to the Ottoman government.

At first, the Ottoman government refused to countenance any action against Baha'u'llah since they had had such favourable reports about him from their own governors and officials in Baghdad. The last two governors in particular, Mustafa Nuri Pasha and Namiq (Namık) Pasha, had had the greatest respect for Baha'u'llah. The former was especially grateful to Baha'u'llah for the moral support that he had given him when he was dismissed as governor for a short time in 1861 on account of false charges that had been laid against him. After prolonged pressure over a period of a year, the Ottoman government eventually gave in and agreed to the Iranian government's demands to remove Baha'u'llah from proximity to the border with Iran. Instructions were sent to Namiq Pasha but he was reluctant to act on them. It was not until three months passed, during which he had received five successive instructions from the Prime Minister, that he could bring himself to act.

Within the Babi community there had been signs that affairs were about to enter a new phase. During the years in Baghdad, it had been the custom of the Babis to gather together in the evenings and chant their holy writings. One night they would chant the words of the Bab, the next those of Quddus, the foremost disciple of the Bab, and the next the writings of Baha'u'llah. Sometimes these recitals would go on until dawn. Then in about January 1863, Baha'u'llah began to give the Babis tablets of his own, full of yearning and sorrow, to recite every evening. Baha'u'llah's brother Kalim had rented a farm on the banks of the Tigris about three kilometres south of Baghdad and the family and all of the Babis would often go there. They had repaired there for the celebration of Naw-Ruz (New Year, 21 March 1863). During these celebrations, however, Baha'u'llah caused to be read a new tablet, called the Tablet of the Holy Mariner (See pp. 165–6), which contained gloomy foreboding of an upheaval in the state of affairs.

On 24 March, Baha'u'llah's brother Mirza Musa and his son, 'Abdu'l-Baha went to call on the governor to offer the customary greetings on the third day after the completion of the Muslim fast of the month of Ramadan. The governor asked that Baha'u'llah call upon him. Baha'u'llah replied that he never went to the governorate but that he would meet the governor in the mosque nearby. Baha'u'llah went to the mosque as arranged but at the last minute, Namiq Pasha changed his mind and sent a representative. Baha'u'llah was shown the communications received from Istanbul asking him to proceed to that city. It was phrased as an invitation but such invitations were in effect orders from the Sultan's government. In any case, Baha'u'llah agreed to go.

The Babi community was thrown into turmoil at the thought of Baha'u'llah's departure. Baha'u'llah had insisted that he had responsibilities towards his family and others in Baghdad and could not just set off for Istanbul of a sudden, since it was clear that this was to be a permanent removal and there was no prospect of him returning. After negotiations, it was agreed that there would be one month for preparation for departure and that his family and some twenty-five of the Babis could accompany him. Baha'u'llah was much occupied with consoling those who were to be left behind and there was such a stream of visitors that it became clear that the preparations for the journey would not be complete in time if matters continued thus. Then Najib Pasha offered the use of his garden just to the north of the city and it was decided that Baha'u'llah would go and camp there and receive the crowds of people who had come to say farewell, and that would leave family free to complete the preparations for the journey.

When it came time for Baha'u'llah to leave on 22 April 1863, there were great scenes of commotion outside his house as people lamented his departure. The poor were particularly distraught as he was the main supply of their food and clothing. One old lady who lived in a hovel used to greet Baha'u'llah every day as he passed to go to the coffee-shop. She would kiss his hand and he would give her a few coins to support her. Now that he was going, Baha'u'llah arranged for a daily allowance to be given her until she died.

EVENTS AT THE GARDEN OF RIDVAN

The garden of Najib Pasha is now known by Baha'is as the Garden of Ridván (paradise, pronounced Rezvaan) because it was during the twelve days that Baha'u'llah spent in that garden that he first openly declared his mission and his station. He told a select number of his companions that he was 'He whom God shall make manifest', the messianic figure promised by the Bab. This

Print of Baghdad showing the River Tigris that runs through the city
and the bridges of boats that was the main way of crossing the river

event is commemorated annually by Baha'is as the twelve days of
Ridván and this festival is the holiest of the Baha'i holy days.

On 22 April 1863, Baha'u'llah was rowed across the river
Tigris and set up his tent in this garden. Five or six other tents
were set up for other Babis, some of whom cooked and served
tea. It was springtime and the roses were in bloom. The garden-
ers would cut these and pile them high in the main tent every day
such that those sitting around the tent could scarcely see each
other across it. Crowds of people came out from the city to bid
farewell to Baha'u'llah: notables, religious leaders, wealthy merchants and the ordinary people of the city. Baha'u'llah received
them in the main tent, had tea and refreshments served and then
saw them off back to Baghdad. Food was sent from Baghdad and
cooked at the garden. Baha'u'llah went to Baghdad to the public
baths there on one day. On the eighth or ninth day, Baha'u'llah's
family joined him in the garden.

The governor, Namiq Pasha, came himself and expressed his
sorrow that such a distinguished person was leaving Baghdad.

Namiq Pasha had arranged for officials to accompany the party and had sent word that at every stage of the journey, food and whatever else was needed should be provided (Baha'u'llah however preferred not to take advantage of this and purchased food at every stage so as not to be a cause of hardship to the inhabitants of each place he stopped). Namiq Pasha commented also on the fact that previously the enemies of Baha'u'llah had been adamant that he should go and were jubilant when they learned of it – some had said that Baha'u'llah and all the Babis were about to be handed over to the Iranian authorities while others had said they would be drowned in the Tigris. When the enemies of Baha'u'llah learned of the respect that Baha'u'llah had been shown and of the money he had been offered as expenses for the journey, their joy had turned to frustration. Namiq Pasha commented wryly: 'Formerly they insisted upon your departure. Now, however, they are even more insistent that you should remain.'[46]

One of those present in the garden, Nabil Zarandi, has recorded the following account of Baha'u'llah during those days in the garden:

> One night, the ninth night of the waxing moon, I happened to be one of those who watched beside His [Baha'u'llah's] blessed tent. As the hour of midnight approached, I saw Him issue from His tent, pass by the places where some of His companions were sleeping, and begin to pace up and down the moonlit, flower-bordered avenues of the garden. So loud was the singing of the nightingales on every side that only those who were near Him could hear distinctly His voice. He continued to walk until, pausing in the midst of one of these avenues, He observed: 'Consider these nightingales. So great is their love for these roses, that sleepless from dusk till dawn, they warble their melodies and commune with burning passion with the object of their adoration. How then can those who claim to be afire with the rose-like beauty of the Beloved choose to sleep?' For three successive nights I watched and circled round His blessed tent. Every time I passed by the couch whereon He lay, I would find

Him wakeful, and every day, from morn till eventide, I would see Him ceaselessly engaged in conversing with the stream of visitors who kept flowing in from Baghdád.[47]

However, of the exact details of the declaration that Baha'u'llah made during these twelve days we have little information. Ustad Muhammad 'Ali Salmani was one of the Babis who was present. He records:

> After some days, Bahá'u'lláh proceeded to a garden outside the city, and there His tent was pitched. This was the garden of Najíb Páshá [later known as the Garden of Ridvan] and it was here in this garden that He openly declared His Mission. That is, He spoke of the manifestation of the Exalted One, the Báb, saying that He was the Qá'im [the expected messianic figure in Shi'i Islam], that the Cause was His Cause – and at the same time, with certain intimations, He also declared His own Mission. During the twelve days of His sojourn in that garden, every morning and every afternoon He would speak of the Báb's Cause and declare His own.[48]

The daughter of Baha'u'llah, Bahiyyih Khanum, who would have been among the family members who joined Baha'u'llah in the garden on the eighth or ninth day, has left this account:

> Four days before the caravan was to set out, the Blessed Perfection called 'Abbás Effendi ['Abdu'l-Baha, his son] into his tent and told him that he himself was the one whose coming had been promised by the Báb – the Chosen of God, the Centre of the Covenant. A little later, and before leaving the garden, he selected from among his disciples four others, to whom he made the same declaration. He further said to these five that for the present he enjoined upon them secrecy as to this communication, as the time had not come for a public declaration; but that there were reasons which caused him to deem it necessary to make it at that time to a few whom he could trust. These reasons he did not state.[49]

However, 'Abdu'l-Baha, who was also present, appears to indicate that it was on the very first day of his arrival in the garden that Baha'u'llah first proclaimed that he was 'He Whom God shall make manifest' and declared Ridvan as a festival:

> Bahá'u'lláh with the utmost glory, might and honour, proceeded from his house to the side of the Tigris River with a great crowd accompanying him. He crossed the Tigris and took up residence in the garden of Najíb Páshá. In that garden, the tent of Bahá'u'lláh was pitched and at that very hour, in spite of the efforts of his enemies, he proclaimed the Ridván festival. At such a time, when he appeared to have been vanquished and the Bábís were in fear and grief, Bahá'u'lláh, with great authority, on the afternoon [of the first day of Ridvan], as soon as he had entered the garden of Ridván, proclaimed the Ridván festival and declared his mission explicitly and unambiguously. Until that day, he had not claimed to be He Whom God shall make manifest. On that day he claimed this.[50]

In a Tablet written about this Ridvan period and about the Ridvan festival years later, Baha'u'llah states:

> The Divine Springtime is come, O Most Exalted Pen, for the Festival of the All-Merciful is fast approaching. Bestir thyself, and magnify, before the entire creation, the name of God, and celebrate His praise, in such wise that all created things may be regenerated and made new. Speak, and hold not thy peace . . . This is the Day whereon naught can be seen except the splendours of the Light that shineth from the face of Thy Lord, the Gracious, the Most Bountiful . . . This is the Day whereon the unseen world crieth out: 'Great is thy blessedness, O earth, for thou hast been made the foot-stool of thy God, and been chosen as the seat of His mighty throne' . . . This is the Day whereon every sweet smelling thing hath derived its fragrance from the smell of My garment – a garment that hath shed its perfume upon the whole of creation. This is the Day whereon the rushing waters of everlasting life have gushed out of the Will of the All-Merciful. Haste ye, with your hearts and souls, and quaff your fill, O Concourse of the realms above! . . .
>
> Say: He it is Who is the Manifestation of Him Who is the Unknowable, the Invisible of the Invisibles, could ye but perceive it. He it is Who hath laid bare before you the hidden and treasured

Gem, were ye to seek it. He it is Who is the one Beloved of all
things, whether of the past or of the future. Would that ye might
set your hearts and hopes upon Him![51]

Baha'u'llah himself states that during those days, he made three
important statements to his followers. The first was to forbid the
use of the sword – in other words to cancel the ordinance of holy
war. The second was that, having declared himself a recipient of
a divine message, or in Baha'i terminology, a Manifestation of
God, no other Manifestation of God would appear for one thousand years. Baha'u'llah's third statement was that on that day
and through that declaration, all of the names and attributes of
God were fully manifested.

When Namiq Pasha visited Baha'u'llah in the garden and saw
the throngs of people that were streaming out of the town to bid
farewell to Baha'u'llah, he suggested that Baha'u'llah move to
Firayjat, five kilometres further north. On the twelfth day after he
entered the garden, on 3 May 1863, Baha'u'llah and his retinue
set off on their journey. The crowds who had come to see them
off expressed their distress by lamenting and some even threw
themselves in front of Baha'u'llah's horse. On that day, the
people saw two signs of his newly assumed authority. Baha'u'llah
rode for the first time a horse – he had always ridden a mule
before – and he now wore different headgear – a *táj*.[52]

By evening they reached Firayjat and set up camp there for a
further week while affairs in Baghdad were completed. Even
here many people from Baghdad came out to see Baha'u'llah
daily. Then they finally set off on the three-month journey to
Istanbul.

THE JOURNEY TO ISTANBUL

Baha'ullah's caravan wended its way northward from Baghdad.
Some days the party camped in the open countryside, other
days, they would arrive at a town by nightfall and camp outside
the town. At each town on the journey, the party would be met

by town officials and accorded every respect by virtue of the government edict and Namiq Pasha's instructions.

Azal (Mirza Yahya) did not at first join the party and was not one of the people on the official list to go to Istanbul. In fact, as Baha'u'llah records, he was supposed to have been going to Iran to disseminate the writings of the Bab there, when instead he turned up at Mosul:

> We especially appointed certain ones to collect the writings of the Primal Point. When this was accomplished, We summoned Mírzá Yahyá and Mírzá Vahháb-i-Khurásání, known as Mírzá Javád, to meet in a certain place. Conforming with Our instructions, they completed the task of transcribing two copies of the works of the Primal Point . . . When We departed, these writings were in the possession of these two persons. It was agreed that Mírzá Yahyá should be entrusted with them, and proceed to Persia, and disseminate them throughout that land. This Wronged One proceeded, at the request of the Ministers of the Ottoman Government to their capital. When We arrived in Mosul, We found that Mírzá Yahyá had left before Us for that city, and was awaiting Us there. Briefly, the books and writings were left in Baghdád, while he himself proceeded to Constantinople and joined these servants.[53]

It appears that Azal had not wanted to join the party before Mosul since he was afraid that the real intention of the Ottoman authorities was to hand them over to the Iranian government at the border. And so he shadowed the party, keeping his distance. By the time they got to Mosul, however, they were clearly moving away from the Iranian border and so Azal felt safe enough to reveal his presence to a few of the party. Most however did not even know what he looked like, so assiduously had he kept himself hidden during the whole of the period in Baghdad.

As the caravan progressed each person in the party had their allotted tasks. Some were responsible for grooming the horses, some for feeding them, some for preparing the food for the party, some for purchasing provisions, some for pitching and looking after the tents, one was responsible for making tea, another for contacting the local people and so on. They usually managed forty to fifty kilometres a day.

The journey was full of incident. Because they usually travelled by night to avoid the heat, it happened on several occasions that either one of the mules or even people would get detached from the party and a party had to be sent out to search for them. As they tried to cross the Zab River near Irbil, two of the mules accompanying the party were swept away and lost. As they approached Mardin, an Arab muleteer who was travelling with them had his three mules stolen during the night. He seized the hem of Baha'u'llah's robe and pleaded with Baha'u'llah to help him get his mules back. The local officials said that this would be impossible since the area was swarming with thieves and robbers and shortly before a load of silk belonging to the provincial governor himself had been stolen and despite all his efforts, the governor had been unable to retrieve this. Baha'u'llah nevertheless insisted that they looked for the stolen mules and when they arrived in Mardin, he again told the governor there and his officials that the mules must be found. They sent horsemen out in all directions and eventually the mules were found and returned. Baha'u'llah's son 'Abdu'l-Baha tells of another incident on the way.

In those days a famine raged all along the road. When we reached a station Mirza Jafar Yazdi and I would ride from one village to another, from one Arab or Kurdish tent to another trying to get food, straw, barley, etc., for men and animals. Many a time we were out till midnight.

One day we happened to call on a Turk who was harvesting. Seeing his large pile of straw we thought we had come to the end of our search. I approached the Turk politely, and said, 'We are your guests and one of the conditions of (religious) Faith is to honour the newly arrived guests. I have heard that you are a very liberal people, very generous, and that whenever you entertain a guest you kill and cook for him a whole sheep. Now, we desire such and such a thing, and are ready to pay any price that you demand. We hope this is sufficiently reasonable.'

He thought for a moment, and then said, 'Open your sack.'

Mirza Jafar opened it and he put into it a few handfuls of straw.

I was amused, and said, 'Oh, my friend! What can we do with this straw? We have thirty-six animals and we want feed for every one of them!'

In brief, everywhere we encountered many difficulties, until we arrived in Karpout. Here, we saw that our animals had become lean, and walked with great difficulty. But we could not get straw and barley for them.

At Karpout the Acting Governor-General came to call on us – and with him brought ten cart-loads of rice, ten sacks of barley, ten sheep, several baskets of rice, several bags of sugar, many pounds of butter, etc. These were sent as gifts by the Governor-General, Ezzat Pasha, to the Blessed Perfection [Baha'u'llah].

After our experiences, and knowing how difficult it was to get anything from the farmers along the way – when I looked at these things I knew that they were sent from God, and they were gladly accepted . . .

We stayed at Karpout one week and had a good rest. For two days and nights I did nothing but sleep. The Governor-General, Ezzat Pasha, called on the Blessed Perfection. He was a very good man and showed much love and service.[54]

Eventually, travelling northwards, they reached the coast of the Black Sea at the port of Samsun. Here they boarded a ship and sailed to Istanbul where they arrived on 16 August 1863.

FOUR

Istanbul and Edirne (1863–1868)

Baha'u'llah's three-month stay in Istanbul (Constantinople) and five-year stay in Edirne mark a very important stage in the development of his claims and position. At the beginning of this period, he could be said to have been a leading Babi. By the end, he was the founder and leader of an independent religion.

BAHA'U'LLAH IN ISTANBUL

As they had been invited to the capital by the Ottoman government, Baha'u'llah and his party were met on their arrival by a government official and escorted to a government guest-house which had been designated for them and where another official was appointed to look after their needs. A representative of the Iranian ambassador Mushiru'd-Dawlih and several other dignitaries came to call on Baha'u'llah. They advised him that it was customary for prominent new arrivals in the city to call on such persons as the Foreign Minister and ingratiate themselves with them thus gaining access to the Prime Minister (the Grand Vizier) and perhaps even the Sultan himself. Baha'u'llah, however, said that he had come to Istanbul

View of Istanbul

at the invitation of the Ottoman government and if they had anything that they wished to communicate with him, they could do so, but he had no favours to ask and had not come to the capital with some scheme to push forward as others did and so saw no reason to scurry about the capital seeking favours. Baha'u'llah later referred to this matter thus:

> Call Thou to remembrance Thine arrival in the City (Constantinople), how the Ministers of the Sultán thought Thee to be unacquainted with their laws and regulations, and believed Thee to be one of the ignorant. Say: Yes, by My Lord! I am ignorant of all things except what God hath, through His bountiful favor, been pleased to teach Me. To this We assuredly testify, and unhesitatingly confess it.[55]

An infant daughter of Baha'u'llah died during these three months that he spent in the city. Among the places that Baha'u'llah visited in Istanbul were the Khirqih-yi Sharif Mosque (Hırka-yı Şerif Camii), the Sultan Mehmet Mosque and the shrine of Ayyub Ansari (Eyyûb-i Ensarî). One of his companions has noted something of his usual routine in those days: 'It was common during those days for the Blessed Beauty to have both lunch and dinner in the *bírúní* (outer quarters) of the house which had been provided for His use, when both believers and friends would often join Him and partake of those meals.'[56]

After a time, word came that Baha'u'llah and his family and companions were to be sent to Edirne, an ancient city formerly known as Adrianople, in the province of Rumelia (now in European Turkey). It was clear that this was now a formal decree of exile, brought about at the instigation of the government of Iran. Having arrived in Istanbul as a guest of the government, he was being sent to Edirne as an exile. Baha'u'llah was angry and declared that he had done nothing wrong and to treat him thus was manifestly unjust. His initial response was that they would refuse to submit to this order and all die a martyr's death there in the heart of the capital of the Ottoman Empire, making a stand for truth and justice. Such a stand needed unity and resolve on the part of everyone, however, and when it became clear that Azal and those who associated with him were not united with the others in this, Baha'u'llah decided to submit to the order. He did however send a stern reply to the Sultan and his ministers. Unfortunately the text of this reply has been lost but we can get an inkling of what it contained from some of Baha'u'llah's other writings of a few years later addressed to the same Sultan and ministers:

> Be fair in your judgement, O ye Ministers of State! What is it that We have committed that could justify Our banishment? What is the offence that hath warranted Our expulsion? . . . By God! This is a sore injustice that ye have perpetrated – an injustice with which no earthly injustice can measure. To this the Almighty is Himself a witness.
>
> Have I at any time transgressed your laws, or disobeyed any of your ministers in 'Iráq? Inquire of them, that ye may act with discernment towards Us and be numbered with those who are well-informed. Hath anyone ever brought before them a plaint

against Us? Hath anyone amongst them ever heard from Us a word contrary to that which God hath revealed in His Book? Bring forth, then, your evidence, that We may approve your actions and acknowledge your claims! . . .

By God! Ye dealt with Us neither in accordance with your own principles and standards, nor with those of any man living, but in accordance with the promptings of your evil and wayward passions, O ye concourse of the froward and the arrogant!. . .

Beware, O King, that thou gather not around thee such ministers as follow the desires of a corrupt inclination, as have cast behind their backs that which hath been committed into their hands and manifestly betrayed their trust. Be bounteous to others as God hath been bounteous to thee, and abandon not the interests of thy people to the mercy of such ministers as these. Lay not aside the fear of God, and be thou of them that act uprightly. Gather around thee those ministers from whom thou canst perceive the fragrance of faith and of justice, and take thou counsel with them, and choose whatever is best in thy sight, and be of them that act generously . . .

Let thine ear be attentive, O King, to the words We have addressed to thee. Let the oppressor desist from his tyranny, and cut off the perpetrators of injustice from among them that profess thy faith . . .

Have I, O King, ever disobeyed thee? Have I, at any time, transgressed any of thy laws? Can any of thy ministers that represented thee in 'Iraq produce any proof that can establish My disloyalty to thee? Nay, by Him Who is the Lord of all worlds! Not for one short moment did We rebel against thee, or against any of thy ministers. Never, God willing, shall We revolt against thee, though We be exposed to trials more severe than any We suffered in the past.[57]

Whatever the content of Baha'u'llah's reply was, the government official who had brought Baha'u'llah the order for exile and had taken back Baha'u'llah's response reported that the colour of the Grand Vizier turned dark with anger as he read the words addressed to him by Baha'u'llah and the official thought it prudent to back surreptitiously out of the room.

Baha'u'llah also sent a message to the Iranian ambassador Mushiru'd-Dawlih:

> What did it profit thee, and such as are like thee, to slay, year after year, so many of the oppressed, and to inflict upon them manifold afflictions, when they have increased a hundredfold, and ye find yourselves in complete bewilderment, knowing not how to relieve your minds of this oppressive thought . . . His Cause transcends any and every plan ye devise. Know this much: Were all the governments on earth to unite and take My life and the lives of all who bear this Name, this Divine Fire would never be quenched. His Cause will rather encompass all the kings of the earth, nay all that hath been created from water and clay . . . Whatever may yet befall Us, great shall be our gain, and manifest the loss wherewith they shall be afflicted.[58]

ARRIVAL IN EDIRNE AND THE OPEN PROCLAMATION OF BAHA'U'LLAH'S CLAIM

Baha'u'llah sent some of his followers off to Baghdad and Iran and set off with the remainder to Edirne (Adrianople) on 1 December 1863. The journey, although much shorter than the journey from Baghdad to Istanbul, was undertaken in winter and the exiles suffered greatly as they had become used to the warmth of Iraq and did not have clothes suitable for the cold. It was the coldest winter in living memory that year. The ice was so dense that to obtain water, a fire had to be lit near springs of water and kept burning for a couple of hours before they thawed out. Upon their arrival in Edirne, they were at first lodged in a caravanserai before being dispersed to a number of houses in the town. These houses were not suitable for the cold weather either and it is reported that a carafe of water froze in Baha'u'llah's own room from the cold. Baha'u'llah's daughter, Bahiyyih Khanum, remembers the journey and the early days in Edirne thus:

> The journey to Adrianople . . . was the most terrible experience of travel we thus far had. It was the beginning of winter, and very cold; heavy snow fell most of the time; and destitute as we

were of proper clothing or food, it was a miracle that we survived it. We arrived at Adrianople all sick – even the young and strong. My brother again had his feet frozen on this journey.

Our family, numbering eleven persons, was lodged in a house of three rooms just outside the city of Adrianople. It was like a prison; without comforts and surrounded by a guard of soldiers. Our only food was the prison fare allowed us, which was unsuitable for the children and the sick.

That winter was a period of intense suffering, due to cold, hunger, and, above all, to the torments of vermin, with which the house was swarming. These made even the days horrible, and the nights still more so. When they were so intolerable that it was impossible to sleep, my brother would light a lamp (which somewhat intimidated the vermin) and by singing and laughing seek to restore the spirits of the family. In the spring, on the appeal of the Blessed Perfection to the governor, we were removed to somewhat more comfortable quarters within the city. Our family was given the second story of a house, of which some of the believers occupied the ground floor.[59]

Baha'u'llah comments on his journey from Istanbul to Edirne and his arrival there in a passage addressed to the Ottoman Sultan:

When they expelled Us from thy city [Istanbul], they placed Us in such conveyances as the people use to carry baggage and the like. Such was the treatment We received at their hands, shouldst thou wish to know the truth. Thus were We sent away, and thus were We brought to the city which they regard as the abode of rebels. Upon our arrival, We could find no house in which to dwell, and perforce resided in a place where none would enter save the most indigent stranger. There We lodged for a time, after which, suffering increasingly from the confined space, We sought and rented houses which by reason of the extreme cold had been vacated by their occupants. Thus in the depth of winter we were constrained to make our abode in houses wherein none dwell except in the heat of summer. Neither My family, nor those who accompanied Me, had the necessary raiment to protect them from the cold in that freezing weather.[60]

THE SPLIT WITH AZAL

Soon after the arrival of the exiles in Edirne, it became clear that large numbers of the Babis were allying themselves with Baha'u'llah, responding to increasingly open allusions to a claim of leadership that were being made in the writings of Baha'u'llah. This greatly increased the jealously and hatred that had been welling up inside Azal since the days of Baghdad. He was further incensed at what occurred when Shaykh Salman, who was Baha'u'llah's courier to Iran, asked Azal to compose a commentary on a verse of the famous Iranian poet Sa'di. Azal's reply drew derision even from Sayyid Muhammad Isfahani, his own supporter. Thus as the respect and affection shown to Baha'u'llah increased, so too did the efforts of Azal to undermine this claim. Goaded on by Sayyid Muhammad Isfahani and a few others, Azal began, about one year after their arrival in Edirne, to plan to poison Baha'u'llah. Baha'u'llah's brother, Kalim, had knowledge of medicine and Azal questioned him surreptitiously about the effects of certain medicines and poisons. When he had accumulated sufficient knowledge, he invited Baha'u'llah to his home one day and served him tea in a cup which he had smeared with a poison which was probably sublimate of mercury (mercury chloride). The result left Baha'u'llah gravely ill for a month and with a tremor of the hand for the rest of his life. Having failed in this, Azal tried to deflect blame by saying that it is was Baha'u'llah who had tried to poison him and had mistakenly taken some of his own poison. Next Azal tried poisoning the well from which Baha'u'llah's family drew water – this fact was revealed by one of Azal's wives who temporarily deserted him and came to seek refuge with Baha'u'llah. Azal also tried to induce Baha'u'llah's barber, Ustad Muhammad 'Ali Salmani, to cut Baha'u'llah's throat as he was shaving him. This suggestion so infuriated Salmani that he nearly did away with Azal on the spot. Salmani himself tells the story thus:

> When the bath day arrived, Azal came in first. He washed his head and body and used the henna. I sat beside him to help.

View of Edirne. In the background is the Sultan Selim (Selimiyyih)
Mosque which was the place appointed for the meeting
between Baha'u'llah and Azal

The house in Edirne occupied by Baha'u'llah after the split with Azal

He began to talk, and to give me advice. He said: 'There was at
one time a Mirza Na'ím who was the governor of Nayríz. He
persecuted the believers, and killed them, and greatly harmed

the Cause.' Next, he began to extol the virtues of boldness and courage. He said that some are courageous by nature, and that when the moment came, they would prove themselves brave. Then he went back to the story of Mirza Naʻím: he said that of all the Nayríz believers' children, one had survived – a boy of eleven or twelve. One day Mirza Naʻím went into the bath, and this boy went there as well, and had brought along a knife with a handle made of horn. When the governor started to come up out of the water tank, the boy plunged the knife into his stomach and ripped it open . . .

Having said this, Azal started in again, praising the virtue of courage. 'How fine a thing it is,' he said, 'for a man to be brave. Now see what they are doing to the Cause of God! Every one harming the Faith. Every one risen up against me! Even my own brother! And I, never allowed a moment's peace! Never a tranquil breath!'

He managed his tones in such a way as to say: 'I, the appointee; I, the helpless victim – and my brother (God forgive me for repeating this!) a tyrant, a usurper!'

'How wonderful is courage,' he went on. 'How much needed now, to save the Cause of God'

Taken all together – the tone of his voice, the story of Mirza Naʻím, the praise of courage, the urging me onward – all this meant only one thing: 'Kill my brother!' That is, kill the Blessed Beauty.

When these words were uttered I was overcome by nausea, and sicker than I had ever been in my whole life. I felt as if the walls of the bath were falling in on me. I was unhinged. Not able to speak, I went away outside the bath, and sat down on a bench. And in my awful inward turmoil, I thought to myself, I will go back into the bath, and I will cut off his head. Then let whatever happens, happen. Then I thought: It would be easy enough to kill him. But suppose when I stood before the Blessed Beauty I should be condemned? Coming before Him in that condition? I went on, thinking it out: After murdering this fellow, if I should go and stand in the presence of Baháʼuʼlláh, and if He should say to me, 'Why did you kill him?' what answer could I give? It was this thought that stopped me.[61]

These events brought matters to a head and so Baha'u'llah directly confronted and challenged Azal. He composed a work called the Tablet of Command in which he put forward his claims unequivocally and ordered that it be taken to Azal and a response demanded. Azal eventually responded by issuing a claim of his own.

Azal's response precipitated what Baha'u'llah, who had up to this point concealed Azal's doings from the Babis, called the 'Days of Stress' and the 'most great separation.' On 10 March 1866, Baha'u'llah withdrew to a house in the city and refused to meet with anyone. He ordered that, in his absence, the Babis must choose between himself and Azal. Everything that Baha'u'llah possessed was divided into two and half was sent to Azal. All the money received from the government and from Iran was also divided and Azal's fair share sent to him. The Babis were thrown into consternation. Many of them had not known of the extent of Azal's enmity towards Baha'u'llah and now they were being asked to make a choice between the two. For two months Baha'u'llah remained secluded hoping that by thus withdrawing himself, the fire of animosity in Azal would be subdued. Instead, Azal resorted to writing a letter to Iran filled with lies about Baha'u'llah and to complaining to the governor that Baha'u'llah was depriving him and his family of their share of the government subvention and that they were starving – this occurred shortly after a considerable amount of money which had come from Qazvin in Iran had all been sent to Azal. These actions merely drove those few Babis who were still wavering into the camp of Baha'u'llah, Azal being left with just three or four supporters in Edirne.

There was a new governor in Edirne, Khurshid (Hurşid) Pasha, and he soon became a great admirer of Baha'u'llah and 'Abdu'l-Baha. He had invited Baha'u'llah to a banquet as the guest of honour and frequently asked 'Abdu'l-Baha to spend evenings with him. When the letters of Azal with false accusations about Baha'u'llah arrived at the governor's offices, he showed them to Baha'u'llah. Since Baha'u'llah saw that secluding himself had had no effect on Azal's behaviour, he reemerged into the Babi community. Baha'u'llah also began in early 1866 to write works addressed to the Babis in Iran in which he revealed his claim to be the promised one of the Bab. A handful of dedicated messengers took news of the claim and some of these writings of Baha'u'llah to the cities of Iran. As word of this spread among the Babis in Iraq and Iran, almost all of the Babis who heard it accepted Baha'u'llah's claim.

Baha'u'llah was, however, greatly saddened by Azal's actions. Quite apart from the physical harm done by the poison, that his own half-brother, whom he had cared for and brought up since their father's death when Azal was only eight years old, should now manifest such hatred and animosity towards him, was one of the gravest blows that Baha'u'llah had to endure in his lifetime. And the dissension caused in the Babi community was also a source of sorrow to one to whom disunity among the members of the new religion caused greater pain that any persecution.

In September 1867, a certain Babi named Mir Muhammad Shirazi proposed that Baha'u'llah and Azal should meet face to face and debate their differences so that all could judge the matter for themselves. Mirza Yahya agreed to this and set the place of the meeting as the Mosque of Sultan Selim (Selimiye) in the centre of the town. Baha'u'llah proceeded to this location but Azal failed to appear and sent a message asking that the meeting be postponed for a few days. Baha'u'llah wrote to Azal asking him to arrange a new date and everyone waited for Azal to do this. But days passed and no new date was fixed. As a result Azal's prestige sank to a new low among the Babi community.

By this time, word of Baha'u'llah's claim had spread throughout Iran and the number of pilgrims coming from that country increased greatly. Baha'u'llah sent these pilgrims back to Iran with writings of his, enthused to spread the new religion among both Babis and Muslims. It was at this time that the Baha'i community can be said to have come into existence, in that the followers of Baha'u'llah started to call themselves Baha'is, rather than Babis, and began to use the greeting 'Alláhu Abhá' (God is most glorious). Most of the prominent Babis had already visited Baha'u'llah in Baghdad or Edirne and required little convincing of the truth of Baha'u'llah's claim. They immediately began to spread word of this to their fellow Babis and many of them also wrote treatises in proof of the claim of Baha'u'llah.

The debate between supporters of Baha'u'llah and those of Azal was fierce throughout Iran and, in places, even violent. The Azalis protested that the dispensation of the Bab was only just over two decades old and many of the laws given by the Bab had not even had a chance to be applied. The Baha'is answered by pointing out that the Bab himself had foreseen that he was but a forerunner of a much greater figure who would inaugurate a new age and that he had warned Azal that should this figure appear in his lifetime, he should unhesitatingly submit to his authority. The Bab had even said that if anyone claimed to be this prophesied figure, He Whom God shall make manifest, none were to doubt this and none should oppose him. Eventually, only a very small number (probably less than 5%) of the Babis refused to commit to Baha'u'llah; some of these became followers of Azal, Azalis, while others declined to commit to either side.

Baha'u'llah began at this time a series of letters to the kings and leaders of the world announcing his claim to be the one promised in the scriptures of all of the religions of the world and laying down the conditions for peace in the world. One of these, a letter to the French Emperor Napoleon III, was sent through the Comte de Gobineau who had been the French Ambassador in Tehran and had been in correspondence with Baha'u'llah; another, written to the Shah of Iran was written at this time but not sent until later from 'Akka. It was also at this time that the Baha'i Faith spread to the Caucasus and a Baha'i community was established at Baku.

A group of the family and companions of Baha'u'llah in Edirne. Among those mentioned in this book are: Seated L to R: Mirza Muhammad Javad Qazvini, Mirza Mahdi (the Purest Branch), 'Abdu'l-Baha, Mirza Muhammad Quli (half-brother of Baha'u'llah), Mirza Mahdi Dihaji. Seated on the ground to the right: Mirza Muhammad 'Ali ('Abdu'l-Baha's half-brother). Standing at the back: third from L: Nabil Zarandi; fourth from L: Mirza Aqa Jan; fifth from L: Mishkin Qalam; sixth: Sayyah

BANISHMENT FROM EDIRNE

Seeing that they could not influence the governor of Edirne, Azal and his supporters decided on a new tactic. Sayyid Muhammad Isfahani and another follower of Azal named Aqa Jan Big Kaj-kulah (skew-cap) were sent to Istanbul to see if they could influence the Ottoman government against Baha'u'llah. They began to spread rumours among the personnel in the Iranian embassy and among the officials of the Ottoman government, exaggerating the number of followers gathered around Baha'u'llah in Edirne and claiming that Baha'u'llah was making converts among the Turkish population of Edirne and intended to raise a revolt in that area. Suggestions were made that Baha'u'llah was in contact with Bulgarian revolutionaries. Unsigned letters were thrown into the homes of prominent government officials in Istanbul, purporting to have been written by Baha'is and boasting of their numbers and power. Matters were not helped by three of Baha'u'llah's followers who also went to Istanbul to pursue their trade and were somewhat indiscreet in the statements they made. It may seem ridiculous that such rumours were taken seriously but the province of Rumelia, in which Edirne lay, was embroiled in the general unrest that was sweeping the Balkans and threatened to break apart the Ottoman Empire. The Ottoman authorities were very nervous about any disturbances in this area. Furthermore, Fu'ad Pasha (Keçecizade Mehmed Fuad Paşa), the Foreign Minister, passed through Edirne at this time and saw for himself the high esteem in which Baha'u'llah was held by all the notables of the town. The Iranian government, through its ambassador Mushiru'd-Dawlih, was also at this juncture pressing for Baha'u'llah's activities to be more tightly controlled.

It was a combination of these events, the circumstances in the Balkans and the rumours being spread by Sayyid Muhammad Isfahani of Baha'u'llah's activities in Edirne, that caused the Ottoman government to act. The file of letters from the governor of Edirne and from Azal and his supporters were all sent to the Police Department in Istanbul in April 1868 and a Commission of Investigation was set up. Some seven of Baha'u'llah's followers in Istanbul were arrested and interrogated about Baha'u'llah's activities in Edirne. Questions about the exact claim that Baha'u'llah was making and why so many people were coming from Iran to Edirne were asked. The Baha'is in Edirne were summoned to the government offices and questioned, spied upon and their numbers and names recorded. The letters of complaint and accusation that Azal had sent were carefully scrutinized. Although the Commission of Investigation found no evidence of any wrong-doing on the part of Baha'u'llah and his followers, it concluded that the fact that Baha'u'llah had advanced religious claims was in itself a cause of potential disorder in the area and therefore recommended that he and his family and companions be banished from that area and imprisoned.[62]

In the meantime, seeing an ideal opportunity, the Iranian ambassador Mushiru'd-Dawlih wrote to the Iranian consuls in different parts of the Ottoman Empire telling them that the Ottoman government was displeased with the Baha'is and would no longer take their part, therefore now was the time to act against them. A number of Baha'is who had earlier been arrested in Egypt by the Iranian consul were handed over to the authorities and exiled to Khartum in the Sudan. There had been altercations between the followers of Baha'u'llah and the followers of Azal in Baghdad and it was probably as a result of this, the conversion of Turkish subjects to the Baha'i Faith, and the actions of the Iranian consul that all of the Baha'is of Baghdad were rounded up and exiled to Mosul in July 1868.

The Sultan gave his approval to the recommendations of the Commission of Investigation and orders were sent to Edirne. Khurshid Pasha, the governor of Edirne, was unwilling to carry out such an unjust order and left the city, leaving the implementation to his subordinates. One day, the house of Baha'u'llah was surrounded by troops and all of the Baha'is arrested. The Baha'is were taken to the government house and each was questioned to ascertain whether they were indeed followers of Baha'u'llah. They were all then informed that their possessions and businesses must be sold or auctioned off immediately and they must prepare themselves for departure within three days. The actions of Azal and his supporters had however redounded upon them and they were also included in the edict of banishment.

Needless to say there was great consternation among the Baha'is in Edirne. Pandemonium reigned as people hurriedly tried to put their affairs in order, sell their possessions, and prepare for departure. The decree that was sent to the governor of Edirne did not specify where they were to be sent and rumours had circulated that they would be handed over to the Iranian authorities or separated and imprisoned in different locations or killed, all of which added to the consternation among the Baha'is. One of the Baha'is, believing that he was to be separated from Baha'u'llah, was so distraught that he cut his own throat. Baha'u'llah's daughter Bahiyyih Khanum recollects that when they heard the tumult raised as a result of this attempted suicide, they rushed to the scene and at first thought it was her brother 'Abdu'l-Baha who had cut his own throat. Then they heard 'Abdu'l-Baha's voice raised from the middle of the crowd speaking with great force:

> On hearing him, two things amazed us. First, he seemed to be wrought up to the highest pitch of anger and indignation. Never before had we heard him speak an angry word. We had known him sometimes impatient and preemptory, but never angry. And then, his great excitement had apparently given him command of the Turkish language, which no one had ever heard him speak before. He was, in Turkish, and in the most impassioned and vehement manner, protesting against, and denouncing, the treatment of the officers and demanding the presence of the governor, who in the meantime had returned to the city. The officers seemed cowed by his vehemence, and the governor was sent for. He came, and seeing the situation said, 'It is impossible, we cannot separate these people.'[63]

Telegrams were sent back and forth to Istanbul urging that Baha'u'llah's family and companions be kept together and eventually the Ottoman government agreed to this. The people of the city were also incensed at the unfairness of the edict. Some of the European Christian missionaries in the town tried to intervene on behalf of Baha'u'llah as did the foreign consuls in the town. The British Consul in Edirne, John Blunt, reported these events and commented:

> All I can say is that the Shek [Shaykh, i.e. Baha'u'llah] in question has led a most exemplary life in this city; that he is regarded with sympathy, mingled with respect and esteem, by the native Mahomedans and has received good treatment at the hands of

the Ottoman Authorities; and that the general impression here is that the persecution [of which] he is now made the object originates with the Persian Government and its Legation at Constantinople . . .

The Babees during their residence at Adrianople have done nothing that I know of to warrant the suspicion, much less the conviction, of the Porte that they were occupied in fomenting religious dissensions in Roumelia. They may have been indirectly engaged in the propagation of their tenets in Persia, but during the Six years they remained in this City they led a very retired life; mixed up very little with the Mahomedan element and appear to have studiously avoided doing anything which might create the suspicion that they abused the hospitality accorded to them by the Porte.

With reference to their alleged ill-treatment by the authorities of Adrianople, I have every reason to believe that the Governor General and most of the members of the local administration regarded their Chief Mirza Hussein Ali [Baha'u'llah] with respect and consideration; and that till the order to deport them reached this place they were not subjected to persecution.

The Defterdar who is acting as Governor General during the absence of Hourschid [Khurshid] Pasha and who received the above order, displayed, from all I am told, unnecessary haste and much harshness and severity in carrying it out, to a degree which excited the sympathy and compassion of all classes of the population.[64]

Describing these events in a letter sent to the Ottoman Prime Minister, 'Álí Pasha (Mehmed Emin Âli Paşa), Baha'u'llah wrote:

Know thou, O servant, that one day, upon awakening, We found the beloved of God at the mercy of Our adversaries. Sentinels were posted at every gate and no one was permitted to enter or leave. Indeed, they perpetrated a sore injustice, for the loved ones of God and His kindred were left on the first night without food . . .

The people surrounded the house, and Muslims and Christians wept over Us, and the voice of lamentation was upraised between earth and heaven by reason of what the hands of the oppressors had wrought. We perceived that the weeping of the people of the Son [the Christians] exceeded the weeping of others – a sign for such as ponder.

One of My companions offered up his life, cutting his throat with his own hands for the love of God, an act unheard of in bygone centuries and which God hath set apart for this Revelation as an evidence of the power of His might. He, verily, is the Unconstrained, the All-Subduing.[65]

Some of the Baha'is who were not on the original list of exiles from Baghdad were told that if they wished to accompany Baha'u'llah they would have to pay for the journey themselves. The citizens of Edirne were amazed that people would voluntarily pay to go into banishment and imprisonment. Baha'u'llah writes about this in a later letter to 'Álí Pasha, the Ottoman Prime Minister:

Ye have plundered and unjustly despoiled a group of people who have never rebelled in your domains, nor disobeyed your government, but rather kept to themselves and engaged day and night in the remembrance of God. Later, when the order was issued to banish this Youth, all were filled with dismay. The officials in charge of My expulsion declared, however: 'These others have not been charged with any offence and have not been expelled by the government. Should they desire to accompany you, no one will oppose them.' These hapless souls therefore paid their own expenses, forsook all their possessions, and, contenting themselves with Our presence and placing their whole trust in God, journeyed once again with Him . . .[66]

Eventually all was ready and Baha'u'llah and his companions left Edirne on 12 August 1868 accompanied by a small military escort. Baha'u'llah's concern for his companions is revealed in the following report from one of those who accompanied him:

Whenever any of the believers would lament their separation from Bahá'u'lláh, tears would flow down His cheeks, and if any of them [during the four-day journey to Gallipoli], strayed away from the group, fell asleep and was left behind or became lost, the Blessed Beauty [Baha'u'llah] would dispatch horsemen in all directions to search for him, refusing meanwhile to proceed until he was found.[67]

After five days they reached Gallipoli. Here they were dismayed to find that the previous hard-won concession had been reversed and they were again to be separated from each other and sent to different destinations. Baha'u'llah's daughter Bahiyyih Khanum recalls:

> On our arrival at this town we were met with the information that the governor had a telegraphic order from the sultan's government directing our separation; that my father with one servant was to go to one place, my brother with one servant to another, the family to Constantinople, the other followers to various places. This sudden and unexplained withdrawal of the hard-won concession we had so recently obtained exhausted our patience. We unhesitatingly declared that we would not be separated, and a repetition, in substance, of the events of the last days in Adrianople followed. My brother went to the governor and told him that we would not submit to separation. 'Do this,' said he, 'take us out on a steamer and drown us in the ocean. You can thus end at once our sufferings and your perplexities. But we refuse to be separated.'
>
> We remained in Gallipoli for a week, in the same terrible suspense which we had experienced at Adrianople. Finally my brother, by his eloquence in argument and power of will, succeeded in gaining for a second time from the Constantinople government the concession that we should remain together.[68]

Baha'u'llah states that he addressed 'Umar Effendi Bigbáshí (Ömer Efendi Beybaşı), the official who was in charge of arrangements for their departure, saying:

> From the outset, a gathering should have been convened at which the learned men of this age could have met with this Youth in order to determine what offence these servants have committed. But now the matter hath gone beyond such considerations,

and, according to thine own assertion, thou art charged with incarcerating Us in the most desolate of cities. There is a matter, which, if thou findest it possible, I request thee to submit to His Majesty the Sultán, that for ten minutes this Youth be enabled to meet him, so that he may demand whatsoever he deemeth as a sufficient testimony and regardeth as proof of the veracity of Him Who is the Truth. Should God enable Him to produce it, let him, then, release these wronged ones, and leave them to themselves.[69]

Although 'Umar Effendi promised to convey the message and to bring back a reply, he was not heard from again. Baha'u'llah warned his companions of the hardships ahead and said that if anyone did not feel strong enough to withstand these, they should leave. None did however. After three days in Gallipoli, on 21 August 1868, Baha'u'llah and his companions were put aboard an Austrian-Lloyd liner bound for Egypt.

Baha'u'llah, in several of his writings, severely condemns the injustice of the actions of the Ottoman authorities. He and his followers had done nothing wrong and to be banished and imprisoned thus was manifestly unfair. As he travelled from Edirne to Gallipoli, Baha'u'llah wrote to the Ottoman Prime Minister, 'Álí Pasha:

> Thou hast, O Chief, committed that which hath caused Muhammad, the Apostle of God, to lament in the most sublime Paradise. The world hath made thee proud, so much so that thou hast turned away from the Face through whose brightness the Concourse on high hath been illumined. Soon thou shalt find thyself in manifest loss! Thou didst conspire with the Persian Ambassador to harm Me, though I had come unto you from the source of majesty and grandeur with a Revelation that hath solaced the eyes of the favoured ones of God . . .
>
> Hast thou imagined thyself capable of extinguishing the fire which God hath kindled in the heart of creation? Nay, by Him Who is the Eternal Truth, couldst thou but know it. Rather, on account of what thy hands have wrought, it blazed higher and burned more fiercely. Erelong will it encompass the earth and all

that dwell therein. Thus hath it been decreed by God, and the powers of earth and heaven are unable to thwart His purpose.[70]

Despite the actions of the Iranian ambassador, Mushíru'd-Dawlih, in bringing about stage after stage of the exile of Baha'u'llah, from Baghdad to Istanbul, from Istanbul to Edirne and now this latest exile from Edirne, Baha'u'llah displayed his sense of justice in testifying to the personal integrity of this man, who was to go on to become one of the greatest reforming Prime Ministers of Iran:

> I testify that he [Mushíru'd-Dawlih] was so faithful in his service to his Government that dishonesty played no part, and was held in contempt, in the domain of his activities. It was he who was responsible for the arrival of these wronged ones in the Most Great Prison ('Akká). As he was faithful, however, in the discharge of his duty, he deserveth Our commendation. This Wronged One hath, at all times, aimed and striven to exalt and advance the interests of both the government and the people, not to elevate His own station.[71]

FIVE

The Early 'Akka Period (1868–1877)

Akka was to be the last place of exile for Baha'u'llah. The ship carrying Baha'u'llah and his companions docked at Alexandria and they were transferred to another ship going to Haifa. They arrived off Haifa on 31 August 1868. Here Baha'u'llah and most of the Baha'is were taken off the ship in small boats to the landing-stage at Haifa. The decree of the Ottoman government had been, however, that four of Baha'u'llah's supporters should be sent on with Azal to Famagusta in Cyprus, while two of Azal's supporters should be kept with Baha'u'llah and his supporters. The two Azalis chosen to remain in 'Akka were Sayyid Muhammad Isfahani, the main supporter of Azal, and Aqa Jan Big Kaj-kulah. As Baha'u'llah left the ship one of his followers who had been selected to remain with Azal was distraught and threw himself into the sea. He was rescued but put back onto the ship to depart to Cyprus. After a few hours on the shore at Haifa, Baha'u'llah's party were rowed across the bay to 'Akka which had been specified as their place of confinement in the imperial decree.

'Akka was a walled city on the Mediterranean coast of the Ottoman province of Syria. It had been the capital of an

The Citadel of 'Akka where Baha'u'llah was imprisoned for two years (1868–1871). His cell is on the far right of the top floor

Ottoman province three decades previously but no longer. Its port had silted up and so ships were now using Haifa across the bay. The city was in decline. Its population fell from 40,000 to under 10,000 during the course of the nineteenth century. The aqueduct which a former governor had built to bring fresh water to the city had fallen into disrepair and water had to be carried into the city and was thus scarce. The air had grown foul and there was no vegetation within the city walls. 'Akka was now used as a place of confinement for political prisoners of the Ottoman empire. Because of the poor conditions in the town, it was confidently felt that most prisoners condemned to confinement in 'Akka would soon die. Thus for example, of seventy-six Bulgarian political prisoners who arrived in 'Akka in January 1878, twenty-five (i.e. one third of their number) had died within one month, despite medical facilities being extended to them through the intervention of the British consular agent.[72]

IMPRISONMENT IN THE CITADEL

As Baha'u'llah and his companions entered the city by the sea-gate, there was a hostile crowd gathered to gape and jeer at the one who was being called 'the God of the Persians'. The party and its escort stopped at the police station in the centre of the city where it was proposed that they be held but this was mani-festly too small to accommodate them. They were moved on to the citadel in the north-west corner of the city. Baha'u'llah and his family were housed on the upper floor and the rest of the Baha'is spread throughout the rest of this building. The two Azalis were, however, lodged in another part of the city, in rooms over the *limán* (city prison), rooms that overlooked the single landgate of the city, thus enabling them to report to the authorities any Baha'is who tried to enter the city.

On the first night of their arrival, the prisoners suffered greatly from lack of water. The ration for each person was three loaves of salty and inedible bread each day. Over the next few days, typhoid fever and dysentery broke out among the prison-ers and lasted four months. Three of the prisoners died, two of them brothers, on the same night. Baha'u'llah wrote about these experiences to 'Álí Pasha, the Ottoman Prime Minister:

> Upon our arrival, we were surrounded by guards and confined together, men and women, young and old alike, in the army bar-racks. The first night all were deprived of either food or drink, for the sentries were guarding the gate of the barracks and per-mitted no one to leave. No one gave a thought to the plight of these wronged ones. They even begged for water, and were refused.
>
> Most of Our companions now lie sick in this prison, and none knoweth what befell Us, except God, the Almighty, the All-Knowing. In the days following Our arrival, two of these servants hastened to the realms above. For an entire day the guards insisted that, until they were paid for the shrouds and burial, those blessed bodies could not be removed, although no one had requested any help from them. At that time we were devoid of earthly means, and pleaded that they leave the matter

unto us and allow those present to carry the bodies, but they refused. Finally, a carpet was taken to the bazaar to be sold, and the sum obtained was delivered to the guards. Later, it was learned that they had merely dug a shallow grave into which they had placed both blessed bodies, although they had taken twice the amount required for shrouds and burial.[73]

Baha'u'llah's daughter, Bahiyyih Khanum, recalls their arrival in 'Akka in similar terms:

All the townspeople had assembled to see the arrival of the prisoners. Having been told that we were infidels, criminals, and sowers of sedition, the attitude of the crowd was threatening. Their yelling of curses and execrations filled us with fresh misery. We were terrified of the unknown! We knew not what the fate of our party, the friends and ourselves would be.

We were taken to the old fortress of 'Akká, where we were crowded together. There was no air; a small quantity of very bad coarse bread was provided; we were unable to get fresh water to drink; our sufferings were not diminished. Then an epidemic of typhoid broke out. Nearly all became ill.[74]

Speaking about the first night of their imprisonment in 'Akka on another occasion, Bahiyyih Khanum said:

Then came another time of heart-sickening suffering. The mothers who had babes at breast had no milk for them, for lack of food and drink, so the babes could not be pacified or quieted. The larger children were screaming for food and water, and could not sleep or be soothed. The women were fainting.

Under these conditions, my brother ['Abdu'l-Baha] spent the first part of the night in passing about among the distressed people, trying to pacify them, and in appealing to the soldiers not to be so heartless as to allow women and children to suffer so. About midnight he succeeded in getting a message to the governor. We were then sent a little water and some cooked rice; but the latter was so full of grit and smelled so badly that only the strongest stomach could retain it. The water the children drank; but the rice only the strongest could eat. Later on, some of our people in unpacking their goods found some pieces of the bread which had been brought from Gallipoli, and a little sugar. With these a dish was prepared for the Blessed Perfection [Baha'u'llah], who was very ill. When it was taken to him, he said: 'I command you to take this to the children.' So it was given to them, and they were somewhat quieted.

The next morning conditions were no better; there was neither water nor food that could be eaten. My brother sent message after message to the governor, appealing in behalf of the women and children. At length he sent us water and some prisoners' bread; but the latter was worse even than the rice – appearing and tasting as though earth had been mixed with the flour.[75]

The decree of Baha'u'llah's banishment was publicised in the city and read out in the mosques. According to the explicit text of the decree, Baha'u'llah and his party had been investigated and found guilty of rebellion and of corrupting the thoughts and morals of the people and had been sentenced to be 'sent to 'Akka to be confined by the military powers in perpetual banishment' and the governor of 'Akka and the religious judge (*qádí*) there were to arrange that upon their arrival there, Baha'u'llah and his party were to be 'lodged in the citadel and not to be allowed to meet with or communicate with anyone.' Furthermore, 'the officials are to be very careful to ensure that these people are kept under constant surveillance so that they do not take even one step without permission.'[76] The rumours that went around the town called them 'enemies of God'. Bahiyyih Khanum recalls:

When we were first brought to the barracks we had no knowledge as to the manner of life to which we were to be consigned. We feared that the Blessed Perfection [Baha'u'llah], my brother, and perhaps others would be placed in dungeons and chained. The only information about it which we could obtain was that our sentence would be read on Friday – our arrival being early in the week. This uncertainty was an additional horror. When the sentence was read to us, we learned that it stated that we were political prisoners, nihilists, murderers, and thieves; that wherever we went, we corrupted the morals of the people; that we had leagued to overthrow the Ottoman Empire; that we could be given no leniency, and that the orders to keep us under bolt and bar must not be broken. It was because of this evil reputation, which had doubtless been given to the government by those who had reasons for desiring our destruction . . . that we were subjected to such stern treatment and were given no more latitude or aid.[77]

The edict of the government was strictly applied to the prisoners. They were under rigorous surveillance and even when a barber came to call on them, he was accompanied by a policeman. The Iranian consul in Damascus was instructed to proceed to 'Akka, to confer with the governor of the city regarding the measures needed to maintain the strict terms of their confinement and to appoint a representative in the city who would keep this matter under observation and report back to him.

Gradually some concessions were made. The rations of inedible food were changed to a sum of money and one of the Baha'is was allowed to leave the citadel, accompanied by a guard, and make purchases in the town. They were permitted to go to the public baths once a week. After a year or so of these difficult conditions, the people of 'Akka gradually began to realise that the Baha'is were not the evil people they have been led to believe and conditions eased. It was 'Abdu'l-Baha above all who, through his knowledge and wisdom, gradually won the affection of many people. A certain Dr Petro who visited the prisoners as a physician soon became a friend and was able to reassure the governor. He also acted as a courier taking messages in and out of the citadel in the lining of his hat. Another who was won over was a cleric, Shaykh Mahmud al-'Arrábí (from the village of 'Arrába, some thirty kilometres east of 'Akka). He had been angry when he had heard of the arrival of the prisoners and had at first intended to harm Baha'u'llah, but eventually he was won over after meeting Baha'u'llah in the citadel.

Word of Baha'u'llah's location gradually filtered back to Iran and the Baha'is there started to come to visit him. The strict surveillance at the gates meant that most were not even able to get into the city and had to content themselves with seeing a wave of Baha'u'llah's hand from his window in the citadel as they stood outside the city walls. Some of the first Baha'is to make contact with the prisoners in 'Akka were Haji Amin and Shaykh Salman, who acted as couriers, taking the writings of Baha'u'llah to Iran and distributing these and bringing back from Iran the letters of the Baha'is and their gifts to Baha'u'llah. Haji Amin was able to meet Baha'u'llah in the public baths to which Baha'u'llah was taken every week. The story of one of the Baha'is who made the journey to 'Akka at this time is here told:

Haji Amin, the courier of Baha'u'llah who would take Baha'u'llah writings to the Baha'is in Iran and return with their letters and gifts

Áqá 'Abdu'r-Rahím-i-Bushrú'í, one of the early believers, reached 'Akká after an arduous six-month trek which took him through Baghdad, Diyárbakr and Mosul on his way to the Holy Land. At that time the Ancient Beauty [Baha'u'lláh] was imprisoned in the military barracks, which was closely guarded. 'Abdu'r-Rahím encountered Nabíl-i-Zarandí in 'Akká and told him of his longing to attain the presence of Bahá'u'lláh. 'I myself have been wandering within sight of this prison for no less than nine months,' Nabíl replied, 'and still the portals of meeting with the Blessed Beauty have remained closed to me.'

After hearing these words, 'Abdu'r-Rahím left Nabíl and made his way to the seashore where he washed the clothes he had been wearing, let them dry, and put them back on. He had just begun to circumambulate the prison fortifications when he noticed someone on the upper floor of the prison beckoning him from a window. He realized at once that it was the Ancient Beauty summoning him to His presence. In great haste he reached the outer gate of the barracks, passed by the armed guards and fearlessly strode into the prison. No one tried to stop him. In a state of reverence and humility, he attained the presence of the Blessed Beauty [Baha'u'lláh]. 'Although you underwent countless hardships,' Bahá'u'lláh addressed him, 'nevertheless you have attained the Treasure. Verily, we have closed the eyes of the guards that you might behold the Countenance of God and bear witness, with your own eyes, to His power and greatness. Relate to the Friends of God all that you have seen.' . . .

When the time came for Áqá 'Abdu'r-Rahím to leave His presence, the Blessed Beauty entrusted him with several Tablets to be delivered to certain persons in Persia. While passing through Baghdad however, he aroused the suspicions of several government officials who began to follow him. Passing by a shop, he carefully removed the parcel of Tablets from beneath his arm, and relying upon God threw it into the shop and continued walking. Before long the officials overtook him and conducted him to the police superintendent who, after a number of questions, was well pleased with him and even provided some money for his journey.

As sunset approached, 'Abdu'r-Rahím wandered back towards that same shop and cautiously passed in front of it. As he did so, the owner beckoned him to enter. Greeting him with the words, 'Alláh'u'Abhá' [the Baha'i greeting], he returned the parcel to him.

'Abdu'r-Rahím spent several days in Baghdad staying at the home of that man and meeting other believers. He then journeyed to Búshihr and went on to Yazd, Isfahán and Mashhad delivering the Tablets to their intended recipients.[78]

One of the Baha'is, Mirza Hadi, known as 'Abdu'l-Ahad Shirazi, had been detailed by Baha'u'llah to settle in 'Akka secretly prior to Baha'u'llah's arrival but at first it was too dangerous even to establish contact with him. Later he acted as a contact for the Baha'is who travelled from Iran as pilgrims. He had a grocer's stall in the bazaar and the Baha'i sent out from the citadel to buy provisions would visit his stall and secretly pass messages backwards and forwards among the vegetables purchased. On occasions he would hide some of the visiting Baha'is in his home in the Khan-i 'Avamid, one of the caravanserais of the town (also called Khan-i Jurayni or Khan al-'Umdan). Then another Baha'i obtained a commercial visa from the Iranian government and was able to obtain the assistance of the Iranian consular agent to settle in 'Akka, becoming a partner of Mirza 'Abdu'l-Ahad.

BADÍ, BAHA'U'LLAH'S COURIER TO NASIRU'D-DIN SHAH

One of those who did manage to get into 'Akka and meet Baha'u'llah in early 1869 was a nineteen-year-old youth who had travelled in stages from Khurasan in north-eastern Iran. He was so enraptured and transformed by meeting Baha'u'llah that Baha'u'llah named him Badí' (wondrous, new). During his interviews with Baha'u'llah, mention was made of the tablet to Nasiru'd-Din Shah which had been written in Edirne but had not yet been delivered, although many had vied for the honour of this task. Badi' now volunteered and Baha'u'llah accepted.

Picture of Badi', Baha'u'llah's messenger to Nasiru'd-Din Shah,
taken after his arrest and shortly before his execution
(he is in the centre with a chain around his neck)

Badi' was told to go to Haifa and there Baha'u'llah's letter to
Nasiru'd-Din Shah was delivered to him together with a second
letter from Baha'u'llah giving him his instructions and warning
of the danger of his task. The text of this second letter is as
follows:

> He is God, exalted is He.
>
> We ask God to send one of His servants, and to detach him
> from Contingent Being, and to adorn his heart with the decora-
> tion of strength and composure, that he may help his Lord
> amidst the concourse of creatures, and, when he becometh
> aware of what hath been revealed for His Majesty the King, that
> he may arise and take the Letter, by the permission of his Lord,
> the Mighty, the Bounteous, and go with speed to the abode of
> the King. And when he shall arrive at the place of his throne let

him alight in the inn, and let him hold converse with none till he goeth forth one day and standeth where he [i.e. the King] shall pass by. And when the Royal harbingers shall appear, let him raise up the Letter with the utmost humility and courtesy, and say, 'It hath been sent on the part of the Prisoner.' And it is incumbent upon him to be in such a mood that, should the King decree his death, he shall not be troubled within himself, and shall hasten to the place of sacrifice saying, 'O Lord, praise be to Thee because that Thou hast made me a helper to Thy religion, and hast decreed unto me martyrdom in Thy way! By Thy Glory, I would not exchange this cup for [all] the cups in the worlds, for Thou hast not ordained any equivalent to this . . .' But if he [i.e. the King] letteth him [i.e. the messenger] go, and interfereth not with him, let him say 'To Thee be praise, O Lord of the worlds! Verily I am content with Thy good pleasure and what Thou hast predestined unto me in Thy way, even though I did desire that the earth might be dyed with my blood for Thy love. But what Thou willest is best for me: verily Thou knowest what is in my soul, while I know not what is in Thy soul; and Thou art the All-knowing, the Informed.'[79]

Badi' faithfully carried out his mission. He walked all the way back to Iran and tracked down the shah on a hunting expedition. He boldly approached the shah and handed over Baha'u'llah's letter. When the shah realised what it was, he had Badi' arrested and tortured to make him reveal his associates. His torturer later related what had occurred:

At first I spoke to him kindly and gently; 'Give me a full account of all this. Who gave you this letter? From where have you brought it? How long ago was it? Who are your comrades?' He said 'This letter was given to me in 'Akka by Hadrat-i-Bahá'u'lláh [His Holiness Baha'u'llah]. He told me: "You will have to go to Iran, all alone, and somehow deliver this letter to the Shah of Iran. But your life may be endangered. If you accept that, go; otherwise I will send another messenger." I accepted the task. It is now three months since I left. I have been looking for an opportunity to give this letter into the hands of the Sháh and bring it to his notice. And thanks be to God that today I rendered my service. If you want Bahá'ís, they are numerous in Iran, and if you want my comrades, I was all alone and have none'. I pressed him to tell me the names of his comrades and the names of the Bahá'ís of Iran, particularly those of Tihrán. And he persisted with his denial: 'I have no comrade and I do not know the Bahá'ís of Iran.' I swore to him: 'If you tell me these names I will obtain your release from the Sháh and save you from death.' His reply to me was: 'I am longing to be put to death. Do you think that you frighten me?' Then I sent for the bastinado, and *farráshes* [footmen] (six at a time) started to beat him. No matter how much he was beaten he never cried out, nor did he implore. When I saw how it was I had him released from the bastinado and brought him to sit beside me and told him once again: 'Give me the names of your comrades.' He did not answer me at all and began to laugh. It seemed as if all that beating had not harmed him in any way. This made me angry. I ordered a branding-iron to be brought and a lighted brazier. While they were preparing the brazier I said: 'Come and speak the truth, else I will have you branded'; and at that I noticed that his laughter increased. Then I had him bastinadoed again. Beating him that much tired out the *farráshes*. I myself was also tired out. So I had him untied and taken to the back of another tent, and told the *farráshes* that by dint of branding they ought to get a confession from him. They applied red-hot iron several times to his back and chest. I could hear the sizzling noise of the burning flesh and smell it too. But no matter how hard we tried we could get nothing out of him. It was about sunset that the Sháh returned from hunting and summoned me. I went to him and related all that had happened. The Sháh insisted that I should make him confess and then put him to death. So I went back and had him branded once again. He laughed under the impact of the red-hot iron and never implored. I even consented that this fellow should say that what he had brought was a petition and make no mention of a letter. Even to that he did not consent. Then I lost my temper and ordered a plank to be brought. A *farrásh*, who wielded a pounder used for ramming in iron pegs, put this man's head on the plank, and stood over him with the raised pounder. I told him: 'If you divulge the names of your comrades you will be released, otherwise I will order them to bring that pounder down on your head.'

He began to laugh and give thanks for having gained his object. I consented that he should say it was a petition he had brought, not a letter. He even would not say that. And all those red-hot rods applied to his flesh caused him no anguish. So, in the end, I gave a sign to the *farrásh*, and he brought down the pounder on this fellow's head. His skull was smashed and his brain oozed through his nostrils. Then I went myself and reported it all to the Sháh.[80]

Over the next few years, Baha'u'llah wrote a series of letters to the major monarchs of Europe and to the Pope and these were dispatched using the consular agents of the various powers in 'Akka and other means. In these letters, Baha'u'llah both proclaims his mission and claims and also advises the rulers of the world on how to arrange their affairs so as to bring about peace and improve the condition of their subjects (see pp. 175–80). Louis Catafago, the French consular agent in 'Akka, for example, who had developed a close friendship with 'Abdu'l-Baha, translated a letter to the Emperor Napoleon III into French and transmitted this (this was the second letter, the first having been sent from Edirne, see p. 80).

THE DEATH OF MIRZA MAHDI, THE PUREST BRANCH

Some of the Baha'is who could not gain entry to 'Akka stayed in Haifa, Nazareth and other places in the vicinity hoping to gain access. One of them, for example, lived in a cave on Mount Carmel. Gradually arrangements were made for these pilgrims. One of the Baha'is, Khalil Mansur, a coppersmith, was instructed to set himself up in Haifa and look after the pilgrims. As each pilgrim arrived, he would report their presence to 'Akka and, whenever possible, arrangements would be made to take them to 'Akka and get them in to the citadel to see Baha'u'llah.

In Baghdad, Baha'u'llah had met with all and sundry, frequenting coffee houses where he could talk to people about the new religion. In Edirne, he had met with all who came to call and even accepted an invitation for a feast at the governor's residence. From the time that he reached 'Akka however, Baha'u'llah devoted himself to dictating his works and would only meet with the Baha'is, whether pilgrims or those resident in 'Akka. Bahiyyih Khanum states:

> Arriving at 'Akká, Bahá'u'lláh said to the Master ['Abdu'l-Baha]: 'Now I concentrate on My work of writing commands and counsels for the world of the future, to thee I leave the province of talking with and ministering to the people. Servitude is the essence of worship. I have finished with the outer world, henceforth I meet only the disciples.'[81]

On 23 June 1870, a tragedy occurred when Mirza Mahdi, a son of Baha'u'llah, who was given the title 'the Purest Branch', fell through a skylight when he was pacing the roof of the citadel, wrapt in meditation. His sister Bahiyyih Khanum recalls:

> We were imprisoned in the barracks, without any substantial change in our manner of life, for two years. During this time none of us left the prison – not even my brother or any of the children. The Blessed Perfection [Baha'u'llah] passed his time in his room, writing tablets, or rather dictating them to my younger brother [Mirza Mahdi], who was a rapid penman. 'Abbás Effendi ['Abdu'l-Baha] would copy them and send them out by the physician [Dr Petro].
>
> It was usual to carry on this work during the evening. One evening towards the end of the second year, my younger brother came, as was his habit, to write for his father. But as he was not very well, and as some others of the family were also ill, the Blessed Perfection told him to go and come later. So he went up to the flat roof of the barracks, where we were accustomed to walk, and which was our only recourse for fresh air and exercise. He was walking up and down, repeating tablets and gazing at the sky, when he stumbled, lost his balance, and fell through the opening to which the ladder from below led up. The room into which he fell had a lofty ceiling, it was the living room of the family. No one was in the room at the time, but, hearing his cries, some of the family rushed in and found him lying in a heap

on the floor with the blood pouring from his mouth. The Blessed Perfection, hearing the commotion, opened the door of his room and looked out. When he saw his son he turned back and reentered his room, saying 'Mihdí has gone.'

We took him up and laid him on his mat. He was perfectly conscious. Later the Blessed Perfection came and remained with him. The physician was sent for; he said that there was no hope.

My brother lived for about thirty hours. When he was about to pass away the Blessed Perfection said to him: 'What do you desire? Do you wish to live, or do you prefer to die? Tell me what you most wish for.' My brother replied: 'I don't care to live. I have but one wish. I want the believers to be admitted to see their Lord. If you will promise me this, it is all I ask.' The Blessed Perfection told him that it would be as he desired.

So, after much patient suffering, my brother's gentle spirit took its flight. As we could not leave the barracks, we could not bury our dead; nor had we the consolation of feeling that we could provide for him through others the grateful final tribute of a proper and fitting burial, as we had no means wherewith even to purchase a coffin. After some consideration and consultation among ourselves, finding that we had nothing to dispose of, and at a loss how to proceed, we told our Lord [Baha'u'llah] of the sad situation. He replied that there was a rug in his room which we could sell. At first we demurred, for in taking his rug we took the only comfort he had; but he insisted and we sold it. A coffin was then procured, and the remains of my deceased brother placed in it. It was carried out by our jailors and we did not even know whither it was taken.[82]

In one of his writings about this event, Baha'u'llah states: 'I have, O my Lord, offered up that which Thou hast given Me, that Thy servants may be quickened and all that dwell on earth be united.'[83] In Baha'i theology, this death is described as a martyrdom and is elevated to 'the rank of those great acts of atonement associated with Abraham's intended sacrifice of His son, with the crucifixion of Jesus Christ and the martyrdom of Imám Husayn.'[84] It was later ascertained that the remains of Mirza Mahdi were buried near the shrine of Nabi Salih, just outside the walls of 'Akka, from where they, together with his mother's remains, were transferred in 1939 to a shrine on Mount Carmel.

Following upon the dying request of Mirza Mahdi, Baha'u'llah requested an interview with the governor, at which he asked that his followers be given free access to him. The governor had been informed of Mirza Mahdi's last words and was inclined to grant this request. In any case, in October 1870, four months after the death of Mirza Mahdi, the mobilization of Ottoman troops meant that the citadel was needed as a barracks and so Baha'u'llah was moved into a house in the west of the city, the Christian quarter.

Bahiyyih Khanum, the daughter of Baha'u'llah, has recorded something of the personal life of Baha'u'llah at this time:

> I should perhaps here say a word about our relations, in the family, to the Blessed Perfection. After his declaration [of his mission and station] we all regarded him as one far above us, and tacitly gave him a corresponding position in our demeanor towards him. He was never called upon to consider, or take part in, any worldly matters. We felt no claim upon him because of family relationship – no more than that of his other followers. When we had but two rooms for all, one was set apart for him. The best of everything was always given to him. He would take it and then return it to us and do without. He slept upon the floor because his people had no beds, although he would have been furnished one had he wished it.[85]

Baha'u'llah gave to his followers the follow prayer, which mentions his being in the 'Most Great Prison' in the 'most desolate of . . . cities' ('Akka):

> Thou seest, O my God, how Thy servants have been cleaving fast to Thy names, and have been calling on them in the daytime and in the night season. No sooner, however, had He been made manifest through Whose word the kingdom of names and the heaven of eternity were created, than they broke away from Him and disbelieved in the greatest of Thy signs. They finally banished Him from the land of His birth, and caused Him to

dwell within the most desolate of Thy cities, though all the world had been built up by Thee for His sake. Within this, the Most Great Prison, He hath established His seat. Though sore tried by trials, the like of which the eye of creation hath not seen, He summoneth the people unto Thee, O Thou Who art the Fashioner of the universe!

I beseech Thee, O Thou the Shaper of all the nations and the Quickener of every moldering bone, to graciously enable Thy servants to recognize Him Who is the Manifestation of Thy Self and the Revealer of Thy transcendent might, that they may cut down, by Thy power, all the idols of their corrupt inclinations, and enter beneath the shadow of Thine all-encompassing mercy, which, by virtue of Thy name, the Most Exalted, the All-Glorious, hath surpassed the entire creation.[86]

RESIDENCE IN THE HOUSE OF 'UDI KHAMMAR

After leaving the citadel, Baha'u'llah was moved four times within a year but by September 1871, he was settled in the house of a Christian merchant named 'Udi Khammar (who had himself moved to a large mansion at Bahji, outside 'Akka). This house on the western seafront of the city was large enough for a family but completely inadequate for the number of people now squeezed into it. At one point thirteen people were sleeping in a room. There was now free access to Baha'u'llah for those who came to visit him and the family and companions were free to go about in the city as they wished. Baha'u'llah himself, however, was required to remain confined in the house, his only exercise being to pace the floor of his room, his only view being out of a window onto a small town square.

It was at this time that an English doctor, Dr Chaplin, who was working at a missionary hospital in Jerusalem, came to 'Akka, met the Baha'i exiles and wrote an account of this to the *Times* of London, which was published on 5 October 1871. He records his interview with 'Abdu'l-Baha, who at this time was 27 years of age, thus:

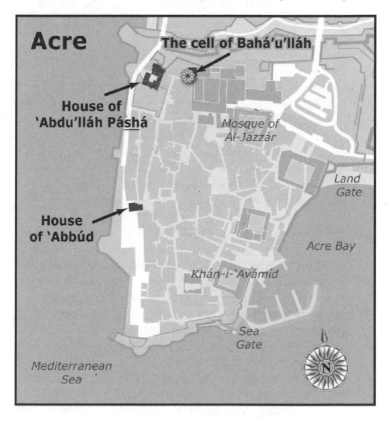

Map of 'Akka showing the main sites associated with Baha'i history

In the spring of the present year I had an opportunity of visiting the Babs in their place of confinement. Beheyah Allah [Baha'u'llah] himself does not readily concede an interview to strangers, and receives only such as are desirous of obtaining from him instruction in religious truth. We were received by his son, who is apparently about 30 years of age, and has a fine intellectual countenance, with black hair and beard, and that sallow, melancholic look which distinguishes nearly all Persians of the intelligent and religious class. He was dressed in a robe of white flannel, with a cap of the same material, and a small white turban. Over his shoulders was thrown a brown cloth abbai. He appeared pleased to see us, but objected to answer questions respecting the origin and history of the sect. 'Let us speak of things spiritual,' he said, 'what you are now asking me is of no importance.' But on our telling him that people in England would naturally be curious to know in what way so remarkable a religious movement had arisen, and who were the originators of it, he gave us the information here detailed. He had a remarkably earnest, almost solemn manner, spoke excellent Arabic fluently, and showed a minute and accurate knowledge of the Old and New Testaments, as well as an acquaintance with the history of religious thought in Europe. Our interview lasted two hours, during the whole of which time an animated conversation was maintained. Like a true Oriental, he seldom gave a direct answer to a question upon any point of doctrine, but replied by another question, or by an illustration, his object throughout apparently being to convince his questioners of what he considered to be truth. He seemed to speak as one conscious of possessing superior light – as a great teacher might speak to his disciples. 'Why,' he inquired, 'did not the Jews, who at the time of our Lord's advent were in expectation of their Messiah, believe on him?' And, assenting to our reply that it was because they misunderstood the Scriptures, he asked whether it might not be the case that Christians in like manner now misunderstood the Scripture – the inference (not expressed) being that his father was sent by God to teach the true doctrine . . .

Between 70 and 80 share the exile and imprisonment of their leader. They are allowed considerable liberty within the walls of the city, Beheyah alone being confined to his house . . . From all that I could learn, these people lead pure and harmless lives, and hold no political opinions which could render them dangerous.[87]

By this time, the tensions between some of Baha'u'llah's followers and the Azalis living in 'Akka were growing. One of those who had come to 'Akka as a follower of Baha'u'llah and who was a brother-in-law of Azal had joined the two Azalis, Sayyid Muhammad Isfahani and Aqa Jan Big Kaj-kulah. These three were harassing the Baha'is, preventing pilgrims who had

travelled from Iran from meeting Baha'u'llah by reporting them
to the authorities. 'Abdu'l-Baha recalls:

> In the days of Bahá'u'lláh, during the worst times in the Most
> Great Prison, they would not permit any of the friends either to
> leave the Fortress or to come in from the outside. 'Skew-Cap' and
> the Siyyid [Aqa Jan Big Kaj-kulah and Sayyid Muhammad, the
> two Azalis] lived by the second gate of the city, and watched
> there at all times, day and night. Whenever they spied a Bahá'í
> traveller they would hurry away to the Governor and tell him
> that the traveller was bringing in letters and would carry the
> answers back. The Governor would then arrest the traveller,
> seize his papers, jail him, and drive him out. This became an
> established custom with the authorities and went on for a long
> time . . .[88]

The Azalis were also feeding false information to the governor
and to the Iranian consular representative in 'Akka and even
forging letters said to be from Baha'u'llah and containing statements calculated to inflame the authorities against him. On one
occasion, they had caused to be arrested, as he left 'Akka, and
imprisoned for six months, a certain Na'im Effendi, who had
become a Baha'i in Cyprus as a result of the activities of the
Baha'is who had been exiled there with Azal.

Baha'u'llah could sense that trouble was brewing and he sent
away from 'Akka a hot-headed Arab Baha'i who was likely to
cause trouble. On several occasions, some of his followers came to
him and asked permission to eliminate the Azalis but he forbade
this and urged them to patience. In addition two Baha'is from
Kashan, who had been among those exiled from Edirne, fell out
with the other Baha'is and moved off to a separate residence. They
did not join the Azalis but did lodge a complaint with the Mufti
(highest religious official) of 'Akka about the Baha'is.[89]

Baha'u'llah was very distressed at the lies being spread by the
Azalis and the disunity among the Baha'is. He did as he had
done under similar circumstances previously in Baghdad and
Edirne. He cut off all communications with his followers (in

Baghdad, he had gone off to the mountains of Kurdistan, and in Edirne, he had shut himself away in his house). He shut himself away in his house and refused to meet anyone. He also wrote at this time a very moving tablet which is usually referred to in English as the Fire Tablet, in which he laments his circumstances (being surrounded by enemies who were attacking him and followers who failed to follow his teachings, see pp. 173–5).

Then on 22 January 1872, disaster struck as some seven of the followers of Baha'u'llah, despite all that Baha'u'llah had said, decided to put an end to the mischief that the Azalis were causing. They knew that if they asked permission, Baha'u'llah would forbid it, therefore they decided to act secretly. Bahiyyih Khanum describes their intentions and actions thus:

> [They] thought that they would settle the matter themselves, without taking counsel with the Blessed Perfection [Baha'u'llah] or my brother. They reasoned that if they should take such counsel, they would be forbidden to execute their plans, and, having been forbidden, they could not disobey. 'We will,' they said, 'do a wicked deed; but we will stop the evil doings of these people even if we are cursed for it. We will save our Lord though at the risk of our own souls.' They . . . proceeded to the house of the Azalís. Their intention was to demand of them a promise to stop their mischief, under threat of death; but they did not have the opportunity to get so far as that. Having called the Azalís out they asked them whether they intended to kill the Blessed Perfection and the Master; whereupon the Azalís attacked them fiercely with clubs and sticks. A general fight followed in which [the Azalis] were killed.[90]

The rooms of the Azalis were over the city prison and opposite the governor's offices. At the sound of the fighting, people came running and there was an immediate uproar. When it was realised what had happened, a group of officials and soldiers was sent to the house of Baha'u'llah accompanied by a mob armed with sticks and stones. Baha'u'llah, 'Abdu'l-Baha and most of the Baha'i men were arrested and brought before a court consisting of the governor and several senior officials.

Baha'u'llah remained silent until the military commander of the garrison asked him about the crime that had been committed. To which Baha'u'llah replied: 'Should a soldier under your command break a rule, would you be held responsible and punished for it?' 'Abdu'l-Baha, who was present, has narrated the gist of Baha'u'llah's replies to the interrogation that followed:

> I am innocent of any knowledge of this matter. How could I, who teach love and pity for every creature – who have given my life and that of my family to demonstrate that this is true religion – instigate this thing?
>
> You are trying to fasten upon me a guilt of which I am innocent; but I am ready to die. If you wish to execute me, I will sign any paper which you may prepare consenting to my execution; but I declare to you that I am innocent of this accusation.[91]

Baha'u'llah and most of the other Baha'is were placed in custody in a caravanserai adjoining the city prison while 'Abdu'l-Baha was chained up in the city prison itself for one night before joining his father. After three days, Baha'u'llah's innocence having been established to the satisfaction of the court, he was freed. The investigations and trial went on for some time during which some twenty-three of the Baha'is remained imprisoned. During these investigations, the question of what had happened to the two Baha'is of Kashan who had cut themselves off from the other Baha'is arose. There are differing accounts of the death of these two individuals. Cholera had appeared in 'Akka and, according to one account, the two died of cholera and had been buried secretly in the house where they lived in order to avoid the quarantine regulations. According to another account, they were killed but it is not stated who killed them or why. In any case their disappearance now came to light and the house where they lived was searched and their bodies found. This compounded the ill-feeling and suspicion towards the Baha'is.

Eventually after seven months, there was a new governor who was much impressed by the character of 'Abdu'l-Baha and asked to meet with Baha'u'llah. At this interview, Baha'u'llah asked the governor to complete the investigations which he did. The seven men guilty of killing the Azalis were sentenced to terms of between seven and fifteen years imprisonment and the remainder freed. Writing about this event at about this time, Baha'u'llah states in the Tablet to Dhabih:

> The imprisonment inflicted on this Wronged One, O Dhabíh, did to Him no harm nor can it ever do so; nor can the loss of all His earthly goods, His exile, or even His martyrdom and outward humiliation, do Him any hurt. That which can hurt Him are the evil deeds which the beloved of God commit, and which they impute to Him Who is the Sovereign Truth. This is the affliction from which I suffer, and to this He, Himself, Who is potent over all things, beareth Me witness.[92]

These murders had cancelled at one fell swoop all of the work that 'Abdu'l-Baha had been doing for the previous years in building up the trust of the citizens of 'Akka and reassuring them that the exiles were not the evil men that they had been depicted as being. Hatred and animosity returned and accusations of heresy, atheism and terrorism were freely and openly flung in the faces of the Baha'is. Even the children of the exiles, if they showed themselves in the streets, would be vilified and pelted with stones. Ilyás 'Abbúd, who lived in the other half of the building in which Baha'u'llah lived, was so alarmed that he strengthened the partition between the two residences. The great change in their circumstances was recorded by Rev. James Neil, an English missionary and a colleague of Dr Chaplin, who visited 'Akka in 1872, the year following Chaplin's visit and who also met with 'Abdu'l-Baha:

> We found almost all the members of this new and interesting sect of Babyum [sic] in prison, where they had been thrown just before our coming in consequence of a fracas in which two of their number had perished. Very contradictory accounts were abroad of this sad affair, the townspeople alleging that the members of the sect had murdered those who had died on account of their secession from the body, and they themselves

declaring that these two young men, who had long separated from them, instigated by the orthodox Mohammedans, had continued ever since the most insulting conduct towards their former brethren, which was on the occasion in question at last resented by certain rash young men, and led to fatal consequences. So great was the dislike or dread felt towards these apparently harmless and peaceful people that we could not induce any one to accompany us when we visited them in prison.

We had a long interview with the son of their prophet. It was indeed strange to find an Eastern in Syria so well educated, and to hear him speak so tolerantly and intelligibly of Christ and Christianity . . . We could not but deeply sympathise with this persecuted sect.[93]

Once more, 'Abdu'l-Baha began slowly and painstakingly to rebuild bridges and restore the reputation of the exiles. As the above accounts by Dr Chaplin and Rev. James Neal demonstrate, 'Abdu'l-Baha was remarkably suited to this role and had soon allayed the suspicions of the populace and turned many an enemy into a friend. His sister, Bahiyyih Khanum records an example of this:

The [Baha'is] needed fuel, but the people would not sell it to them. They regarded us as heretics and thought there was merit for them in harshness and unkindness towards us. 'Abbás Effendi ['Abdu'l-Baha] obtained permission to send out of the city for charcoal, and a camel-load was brought back. The driver was stopped by a Christian merchant. 'This is better charcoal than I can get,' he said, and without more ceremony took it for himself – nor would he return the money paid for it.

This was reported to my brother. He went to the merchant's shop and stood in the door. He was not noticed. Then he entered and sat down by the door. The merchant continuing to transact his business with those who came and paying him no attention, he waited in silence for three hours. At length, when the others had left and no more came, the merchant said to him: 'Are you one of those prisoners here?' 'Abbás Effendi assenting, he continued, 'What have you done that you are imprisoned?'

'Since you ask me,' replied 'Abbás Effendi, 'I will tell you. We have done nothing. We are persecuted as Christ was persecuted.'

'What do you know of Christ?' said the merchant.

My brother replied in such a manner that the merchant perceived that he was not ignorant of Christ and the Christian Bible. He then began to question him about the Bible and was interested in his replies, as my brother gave him explanations which he had never before heard.

Next he invited my brother to a seat beside him and continued the conversation for two hours. At its conclusion he seemed much pleased, and said 'The coal is gone, I cannot return you that, but here is the money.' He then escorted my brother to the door and down into the street, treating him with the greatest respect. Since that time he and 'Abbás Effendi have been fast friends, and the two families also.

Yet the prejudices and animosities of the people against us were so deep-rooted that much time and patience have been required to remove them.[94]

Baha'u'llah and his family and companions were at first confined to the back half of this house which belonged to 'Udi Khammar; later Baha'u'llah was also given access to the front half of the house which belonged to 'Abbud

Early in 1873, Baha'u'llah completed his most important book, the Kitab-i Aqdas, the Most Holy Book, in which are laid out the laws of the religion as well as many of the social teachings and institutions which would be the foundation of the social order envisaged by Baha'u'llah (see p. 180–6).

THE MARRIAGE OF 'ABDU'L-BAHA

It was in the summer of 1873 that 'Abdu'l-Baha was married to Munirih Khanum, the niece of two brothers who were devoted followers of Baha'u'llah in Isfahan. She had been brought to 'Akka by Baha'u'llah in early 1873, at a time when the situation was very difficult due to the murder of the Azalis and all other Baha'i pilgrims had been told to stay away. 'Abdu'l-Baha himself had been reluctant to marry, although a number of spouses had been proposed to him over the years. He felt he could serve his father better if he remained single, as indeed did his sister Bahiyyih Khanum who never married. Although he had turned down the other spouses who had been proposed to him, he was attracted to Munirih Khanum and agreed to marry her. The marriage was put off for a few months however because the tight accommodation in their place of residence meant that the couple could not have a room to themselves. Ilyas 'Abbud, their neighbour who lived in the other half of the same building and who had been so fearful of the Baha'is earlier, had by this time been won over by 'Abdu'l-Baha. Bahiyyih Khanum went to the wife of Ilyas 'Abbud and told her of the problem. When he was informed, 'Abbud immediately opened up a doorway between his residence and Baha'u'llah's and gave 'Abdu'l-Baha a room in his house for his use. Once this happened the marriage was able to proceed.

Four daughters were the surviving children from this marriage; the two sons who were born both died at about the age of two and three other daughters died in infancy. In later years, 'Abdu'l-Baha was put under a great deal of pressure to marry again so that he would have a son to succeed him, but he declined to do this. Bahiyyih Khanum explained many years later:

> Many influences, and those of the very strongest character, have been brought to induce my brother to take a second wife – a practice which the Blessed Perfection [Baha'u'llah] did not in terms forbid, but advised against. The believers have urged it strongly for several reasons. Very many of them wish to take a second wife themselves, but feel constrained from doing so by the Master's ['Abdu'l-Baha's] example. In Persia, except among believers, polygamy is a universal custom, and the restriction to one wife, which all believers feel and respect, seems very severe. Then there is a general wish that the Master might have a son to succeed him. Other arguments have been advanced; and the pressure brought to bear upon him has been, and still is, very great – greater than you can easily imagine.
>
> The general advice of the Blessed Perfection against a second marriage would in itself have had the effect with my brother of a command and have settled the question; but as regards him it was withdrawn by our Lord before his death. He said to 'Abbás Effendi ['Abdu'l-Baha] that he rather wished to lead the believers gradually to monogamy than to force them to adopt it, which they felt bound to do by reason of the Master's example; that therefore, and since it was much desired by all that the Master should have a son, he withdrew even the advice in his case, and desired him to consider himself free to follow his own desires and inclination.
>
> To this the Master replied that his own wishes and feelings were against a second marriage, though, if the Blessed Perfection should command it, he would obey. This, however, the Blessed Perfection never did.
>
> To all other appeals his reply has always been a firm refusal. He thinks that if it had been God's will that he should leave a son, the two who had been born to him would not have been taken away. He believes that the best and highest condition of life for a man is marriage to one wife, and that it is his duty to set that example to the world. ['Abdu'l-Baha later carried out his father's wish to make monogamy a binding law on the Baha'is].[95]

On the right is Bahiyyih Khanum, the daughter of Baha'u'llah, and on the left is Munirih Khanum, the wife of 'Abdu'l-Baha

Late in that same year, 1873, 'Abbud made the whole of his residence, which as mentioned above, adjoined the house where Baha'u'llah was living, available to Baha'u'llah. Baha'u'llah therefore moved to a room overlooking the sea in the House of 'Abbud.

LAST YEARS WITHIN 'AKKA

A number of governors came and went. Most were unfriendly towards the Baha'is upon arrival because of the information that they been given about them. Through the efforts of 'Abdu'l-Baha, however, several of them became friendly during the course of their tenure. Ahmad Big Tawfiq (Ahmed Bey Tevfik), who was governor from 1873 to 1874 and who was the governor who had completed the investigation of the murder of the Azalis and had set those who were innocent free, gradually became more and more attached to the Baha'is. At Baha'u'llah's suggestion he repaired the aqueduct which had brought water from the spring at Kabri to 'Akka, thus restoring a fresh water supply to 'Akka. One governor who remained unfriendly was 'Abdu'r-Rahman Pasha, who governed from 1874 to 1875. He sent reports to the central authorities in the province stating that although the decree of banishment had specified that the Baha'is were not to be in contact with anyone, they in fact had the freedom of the town, were meeting with whomever they liked and several of them had even set up shops. Orders came that the Baha'is had no right to open shops and engage in business. The governor decided to implement this order in a manner that would be of maximum embarrassment to the Baha'is. He planned to go into the bazaar in the middle of the day and order the Baha'is to shut their shops. 'Abdu'l-Baha heard of this however and told the Baha'is not to open their shops. Instead of discomfiting and harming the Baha'is, news of the governor's own dismissal came and he was discomfited. The next few governors were protective of the Baha'is and respectful towards Baha'u'llah.

Baha'u'llah's private apartments were in the front of the house overlooking the sea (the part formerly occupied by 'Abbud). One of the Baha'is who lived in 'Akka at this time states that Baha'u'llah's secretary, Mirza Aqa Jan, occupied a room at the back of the house:

> This room had a window facing east onto a small square, in which there was a covered water fountain. The people would carry water from this to their homes. There was just one seat next to this window which was specially for Baha'u'llah.
>
> Every day, towards the late afternoon, Baha'u'llah would come to this room and would give permission for those Baha'is who were resident in 'Akka or who were pilgrims to meet with him, either collectively or individually.[96]

Another Baha'i records an audience with Baha'u'llah in the House of 'Abbud:

> I was present at the blessed House in 'Akká one morning and heard Bahá'u'lláh explaining that 'man is not infallible', but

Khan-i 'Avamid. Many of the companions-in-exile of Baha'u'llah and the pilgrims who came to visit him stayed at this caravanserai in 'Akka

that 'God is the All-Forgiving'. 'In the same way that God is the "Concealer",' He added, 'so should the believers be forgiving if they find faults in one another. Tell them not to be concerned only with themselves, but to centre their attention on the Cause of God. That which is pleasing unto God is unity among the believers.' Later, He offered us some *nabát* (rock candy).[97]

Baha'u'llah even began to leave this house in which he had been confined and to visit the houses of his brother and some of the Baha'is, who had taken up residence in various localities in 'Akka, especially in the Khan-i 'Avamid, a caravanserai in the south-east corner of the city near the sea gate. In these years, the number of Baha'is coming as pilgrims from Iran increased although it took some six months to travel on foot to 'Akka. Among those who came was Sulayman Khan of Tunukabun in Mazandaran, who came to 'Akka in 1875 and was directed by Baha'u'llah to proceed to India and spread the Baha'i Faith there, a task which he carried out with success. These pilgrims were also lodged at the Khan-i 'Avamid as were many of the Baha'is. This caravanserai had been in a dilapidated state when the Baha'is first began to use it but they had gradually repaired it.

During these 'Akka years a number of prominent citizens of 'Akka and the surrounding citizens became Baha'is or close friends of the Baha'is. Among the most prominent were Shaykh 'Ali Miri, Mufti of 'Akka, who had come to Baha'u'llah while he was still in the citadel and had been a close friend ever since. It was he, for example, who had informed 'Abdu'l-Baha that 'Abdu'r-Rahman Pasha intended to close the shops of the Baha'is (see above). Among the Christians, a certain 'Abdullah had become an enthusiastic convert and was trying to persuade others of the truth of the Baha'i Faith.

When Mustafa Diya (Ziya) Pasha became governor in 1876, he let it be known that Baha'u'llah could leave the confines of the city if he wished. 'Abdu'l-Baha, knowing how much Baha'u'llah loved greenery, having grown up in the lush vegetation of Mazandaran in Iran, and how much he missed this in the dusty, barren streets of 'Akka, rented an island in the middle of a small river, which he developed into a beautiful garden and which Baha'u'llah later named the garden of Ridvan, in remembrance of the garden outside Baghdad where he had made the declaration of his mission. 'Abdu'l-Baha also rented and made some necessary repairs to a small mansion at Mazra'ih, some seven kilometres north of 'Akka. It was surrounded by gardens and had running water provided by the aqueduct to 'Akka. He then tested the situation by going out of the gates of the city to visit the mansion. The guards made no move to stop him as he passed out of the gates for the first time since his arrival nine years previously. To make absolutely sure, he hosted a picnic under some trees at Bahji and invited a number of the officials and notables of the town to it. Again no-one commented on the fact that someone who had been subjected to a strict government order of confinement was proceeding at will outside the walls of the city. This may partly have been due to the fact that Sultan

'Abdu'l-'Aziz, the Ottoman Sultan who had been responsible for the decree for the exile of Baha'u'llah to 'Akka and his confinement there, was overthrown and either committed suicide or was killed in 1876. His two principal ministers, Fu'ad Pasha and 'Álí Pasha, who had initiated and confirmed Baha'u'llah's exile and confinement had already died in 1869 and 1871 respectively.

Once 'Abdu'l-Baha had completed repairs to the mansion and had satisfied himself that there would be no government objections, he rented a carriage and asked Baha'ullah to visit the garden of Ridvan. Baha'u'llah refused, saying he was a prisoner. 'Abdu'l-Baha asked a second time and a third time but received the same reply. He then went to Shaykh 'Ali Miri, Mufti of 'Akka, and asked him to intervene with Baha'u'llah. Shaykh 'Ali Miri went but Baha'u'llah again refused, saying he was a prisoner. Shaykh 'Ali would not accept this reply and continued to plead with Baha'u'llah for a whole hour until the latter eventually agreed to leave the city. Thus finally in June 1877, Baha'u'llah left the city in which he had been strictly confined for nine years and visited the Garden of Ridvan. Immediately after this, he took up residence in Mazra'ih.

As an example of the wit and humour that characterised the Baha'i exile community in 'Akka, even in the midst of imprisonment and hardships, it is related that when the Garden of Ridvan was being prepared, all the Baha'is lent a hand in raising the level of the island so that it would not flood and then worked on the soil to develop it into a garden. One day, Nabil Zarandi came to this garden while the other Baha'is were busy at work. One of them called out to Nabil to take a spade and give them a hand. Nabil, whose given name was Mulla Muhammad and to whom Baha'u'llah had given the name Nabíl (meaning 'noble' in Arabic), replied that 'Baha'u'llah has prohibited me from working with a spade since he named me "na bíl" (which in Persian means "no spade").'[98]

Another example involved Aqa Muhammad 'Ali Isfahani who had a great sense of humour. On one occasion, Baha'u'llah attended a memorial meeting in 'Akka for one of the Baha'is who had died. Aqa Muhammad 'Ali noticed how graciously and beautifully Baha'u'llah spoke about the deceased. Longing for the same treatment, Aqa Muhammad 'Ali is reported to have said to Baha'u'llah, 'I shall be honoured if you would presume that I am dead also, and give me the privilege of inviting you to attend a memorial meeting for me!' Thereupon he arranged a memorial meeting for himself at which he entertained Baha'u'llah and the Baha'is of 'Akka.[99]

Baha'u'llah himself also often made jokes and witticisms. On one occasion when they were still in Baghdad, a rather rotund Iranian cleric came to visit Baha'u'llah and sat down pompously. 'I am the seal of the *mujtahids*', he announced upon his arrival. Mujtahids are the most senior grade of Shi'i clerics and the word seal (*khátam*) is usually connected with Muhammad being the seal, meaning the last, of the prophets. The word can also mean, as intended here, the most excellent. Baha'u'llah however, taking the first meaning (which would make what had been said mean 'I am the last of the *mujtahids*'), quipped: 'Let's hope so.'[100]

SIX

The Later 'Akka Period (1877–1892)

Baha'u'llah spent two years (1877–79) living in the small mansion of Mazra'ih with only a few members of his family, his secretary Mirza Aqa Jan and a doorman, accompanying him. He then moved to a larger mansion at Bahji, situated three kilometres north of 'Akka. This mansion had been constructed by 'Udi Khammar, the Christian merchant who had owned the house in 'Akka to which Baha'u'llah had moved in 1871. 'Udi Khammar died in an epidemic that raged through the area in 1879 and so the mansion became available for 'Abdu'l-Baha to rent for Baha'u'llah in September 1879. Most of his family and several of his companions moved there with him.

'Abdu'l-Baha was left behind in 'Akka at the House of 'Abbud with his mother, wife and sister. Here he was able to look after the affairs of the religion. He would interact with the government authorities and notables of the town, make arrangements for the pilgrims and arrange for food and supplies to be sent to Bahji. Baha'u'llah could therefore concentrate on his writings and on meeting the growing number of Baha'i pilgrims who came to 'Akka from Iran, the Ottoman domains, Egypt, Russia and India. Some of the Baha'is of Iran who had been forced to leave their homes by persecution settled in the Haifa–'Akka area.

When, in 1880, the 'Urabi Pasha revolt against British rule in Egypt caused much disorder, some of the Baha'is there lost their possessions, fled to 'Akka for safety and settled there. In addition, from about 1885 onwards, many of the Baha'is that had been exiled from Baghdad to Mosul in 1868 moved to 'Akka.

THE GARDEN OF RIDVAN

Baha'u'llah had been raised in the lush province of Mazandaran and always loved greenery and flowers. A few years after his arrival in Bahji he instructed one of the Baha'is to begin a small garden around the mansion. And now that he had some comparative freedom, he used to visit a number of gardens, such as the gardens of Junayna and Firdaws, but in particular the Ridvan garden, where he would sit on the benches by the water's edge. One of the daughters of 'Abdu'l-Baha has described what this garden meant to Baha'u'llah:

The Ridvan Garden: Baha'u'llah would frequently repair to this garden, situated near 'Akka, and would sit on these benches with the river flowing behind. This picture was taken in the early 1900s

Oh the joy of the day when Bahá'u'lláh went to the beautiful Ridván, which had been prepared for Him with such loving care by the Master ['Abdu'l-Baha], the friends, and the pilgrims!

The Master's heart was gladdened indeed to see the enjoyment of His beloved Father, resting under the big mulberry tree, by the side of the little river rippling by, the fountain which they had contrived splashing and gurgling in sounds refreshing indeed after the long years of confinement in the pestilential air of the penal fortress of 'Akká. Only those who were present there could realize in any degree what it meant to be surrounded by such profusion of flowers, their colours and the scents, after the dull walls and unfragrant odours of the prison city.

I remember well the greatest of our joys was to go with Bahá'u'lláh for the occasional picnics to the Ridván.[101]

Mirza Ahmad Yazdi recalls Baha'u'llah's early visits to the Garden of Ridvan thus:

When Baha'u'llah left the city of Acca he went first, not to Masraeh [Mazra'ih], but to the garden of Rizwan. The wide seats under the big mulberry trees were there then and Baha'u'llah had a mosquito curtain fixed up over a place on the wide bench and used to sleep there at nights. It was summer, and fine weather, and there was great happiness and rejoicing among the friends. The house in the garden, where Baha'u'llah afterwards had a room, was not then built. There was a hut or small building there, but not for sleeping purposes.[102]

Baha'u'llah himself has alluded to this garden in several of his writings:

On the morning of the blessed Friday we proceeded from the Mansion and entered the Garden. Every tree uttered a word, and every leaf sang a melody. The trees proclaimed: 'Behold the evidences of God's Mercy' and the twin streams recited in the eloquent tongue the sacred verse 'From us all things were made alive.' Glorified be God! Mysteries were voiced by them, which provoked wonderment. Methought: in which school were they educated, and from whose presence had they acquired their learning? Yea! This Wronged One knoweth and He saith: 'From God, the All-Encompassing, the Self Subsistent.'[103]

This garden was very beautiful, so much so that when Midhat Pasha the governor of the province of Syria visited 'Akka in May 1880, it was recommended that he camp there and permission for this was given by 'Abdu'l-Baha.[104] It was as a result of 'Abdu'l-Baha's meeting with Midhat Pasha on this occasion that an invitation was extended to 'Abdu'l-Baha to visit Midhat Pasha in Beirut, which he did the following month. On this trip to Beirut, 'Abdu'l-Baha was welcomed with great honours and met with such eminent Middle Eastern personalities as Shaykh Muhammad 'Abduh. Similar to this was the occasion a few years later in which 'Abdu'l-Baha met Shaykh Yusuf, the Mufti (highest religious official) of Nazareth, when the latter visited 'Akka and was then invited by the Mufti to visit him in Nazareth. The Mufti came out of Nazareth to welcome 'Abdu'l-Baha as he approached and extended every courtesy and honour to him.

Baha'u'llah often arranged outings. The following is a description of one of these outings that Baha'u'llah organized written by the son of Zaynu'l-Muqarrabin (who used to transcribe the tablets of Baha'u'llah) who participated in it:

> On one of the days when we were at Bahji, Baha'u'llah came down from the mansion during the morning, got into his white carriage and ordered his attendants to proceed to the place known as Nahr (which is today known as Nahariya). Several of those who were in the mansion including my father, myself, one of the Baha'is of Najafabad called Aqa Muhammad Baqir Júzání, whom Baha'u'llah had honoured with the title of Há'í, Mishkín Qalam and some others were invited to accompany him to this place.
>
> Nahr is a place north of 'Akka which consists of many springs of water, including the spring that feeds water to 'Akka, and numerous gardens and orchards. The owners of these gardens had built around each spring a large pool of water which they would use to irrigate their trees and their crops. Each of

these owners considered the coming of Baha'u'llah to their garden as their greatest desire and utmost honour and joy.
Baha'u'llah rested by one of these reservoirs and a small tent
was pitched for him and he remained there from morning until
the late afternoon. The Epistle to the Son of the Wolf (one of
Baha'u'llah's works), in which he repeatedly addresses the
recipient as 'O Shaykh', was begun on that day and in that
place.

Those who had accompanied him remained in a garden adjacent to the one that Baha'u'llah was in. It was a day of joy and
light, a time of bliss and incomparable delight, a moment of
immeasurable gladness and pleasure bright.

A sheep had previously been slaughtered, but all were
worried about how they were going to cook and feed those
gathered there. Eventually they gave the responsibility for
organising the cooking and preparing the food to my father
(Zaynu'l-Muqarrabin). He called for cooking utensils to be
brought from the nearby village and he began to prepare two
sorts of kebab. One was the sort known as Husayni, but which
from that day on became known as Kabab Zayni, the other
Kabab Barg.[105] All of this was done in a spirit of joy and
happiness.

When it came time to eat, a portion of the food was taken to
Baha'u'llah and it was said to him: 'This is what Zayn has
cooked.' He replied: 'Although it has been some time that I have
not partaken of meat, because Zayn has put himself to a lot of
trouble, I will take a small portion to eat.'[106]

Among other places that Baha'u'llah visited during these years
were the houses of some of the Baha'is in 'Akka (specially that of
his brother Mirza Musa Kalim), the Druse villages of Yirkih and
Abu-Sinan, and he also visited Haifa on three occasions and
pitched his tent on Mount Carmel. On his third visit to Haifa in
1891, he pointed out to 'Abdu'l-Baha a site for the Bab to be
buried and a mausoleum to be built. The remains of the Bab had
been concealed since the Bab's execution in 1850, only being
moved from time to time to preserve their concealment. 'Abdu'l-
Baha succeeded in having these remains brought to 'Akka

and then built a shrine and buried the remains there in 1909. Sayyid Asadu'llah Qumi wrote of these visits by Baha'u'llah to Haifa:

> He [Baha'u'llah] visited Haifa several times and I accompanied him on each occasion in order to serve him. Each afternoon he would stroll along the streets of the German [Templers] and the Baha'is would accompany him, with great joy. 'Abdu'l-Baha was also present on most occasions. A tent was pitched opposite the door of a house and Baha'u'llah would sit there and the others would circle around him. What pleasant days those were!
>
> At that time, He [Bahá'u'lláh] went to the monastery that has been built atop Mount Carmel. He ate lunch there and wrote some words in the guest-book (*daftar*) that was on the table of the visitor's room. In addition he revealed a lengthy tablet [the Tablet of Carmel, see pp. 189–90]. The priests and monks of the monastery asked him to make Himself at home in the monastery

Mount Carmel. This print from the nineteenth century shows the monastery on top of the mountain that Baha'u'llah visited. At the foot of the mountain is Haifa and across the bay, 'Akka can be seen

but he declined . . . Baha'u'llah was extraordinarily gracious to them. He shed his bounty and grace upon them. The only thing that was the cause of grief to Him were some statues that were depicting the body of Christ and were set up around the place, in particular a statue of that holy figure fallen upon the dust, drenched in red blood. He was so affected by this that he repeated a number of times in a majestic tone: This is not permissible. Any human being would find this extremely painful. These Christians do not know.[107]

SOME ACCOUNTS OF BAHA'U'LLAH

It was during Baha'u'llah's second visit to Haifa in 1890 that there arrived in Haifa, a young British scholar, Edward G. Browne, who was to go on to become one of the greatest British orientalists. He had come specifically to meet Baha'u'llah, having studied the Babi and Baha'i religions over the preceding three years and visited Iran. Baha'u'llah returned to Bahji and received him there. Browne has left the following account of his meeting with Baha'u'llah:

Of the culminating event of this my journey some few words at least must be said. During the morning of the day after my installation at *Behjé* one of Behá's younger sons entered the room where I was sitting and beckoned to me to follow him. I did so, and was conducted through passages and rooms at which I scarcely had time to glance to a spacious hall, paved, so far as I remember (for my mind was occupied with other thoughts) with a mosaic or marble. Before a curtain suspended from the wall of this great ante-chamber my conductor paused for a moment while I removed my shoes. Then, with a quick movement of the hand, he withdrew, and, as I passed, replaced the curtain; and I found myself in a large apartment, along the upper end of which ran a low divan, while on the side opposite to the door were placed two or three chairs. Though I dimly suspected whither I was going and whom I was to behold (for no distinct intimation had been given to me), a second or two elapsed ere, with a throb of wonder and awe, I became definitely conscious that the room was not untenanted. In the corner where the divan met the wall sat a wondrous and venerable figure, crowned with a felt head-dress of the kind called *táj* by dervishes (but of unusual height and make), round the base of which was wound a small white turban. The face of him on whom I gazed I can never forget, though I cannot describe it. Those piercing eyes seemed to read one's very soul; power and authority sat on that ample brow; while the deep lines on the forehead and face implied an age which the jet-black hair and beard flowing down in indistinguishable luxuriance almost to the waist seemed to belie. No need to ask in whose presence I stood, as I bowed myself before one who is the object of a devotion and love which kings might envy and emperors sigh for in vain!

A mild dignified voice bade me be seated, and then continued: – 'Praise be to God that thou hast attained! . . . Thou hast come to see a prisoner and an exile . . . We desire but the good of the world and the happiness of the nations; yet they deem us

The room of Baha'u'llah in Bahji. It is in this room that his interview with Prof. Edward G. Browne occurred and it is also in this room that Baha'u'llah passed away

a stirrer up of strife and sedition worthy of bondage and banishment . . . That all nations should become one in faith and all men as brothers; that the bonds of affection and unity between the sons of men should be strengthened; that diversity of religion should cease, and differences of race be annulled – what harm is there in this? . . . Yet so it 'shall be; these fruitless strifes, these ruinous wars shall pass away, and the 'Most Great Peace' shall come . . . Do not you in Europe need this, also? Is not this that which Christ foretold? . . . Yet do we see your kings and rulers lavishing their treasures more freely on means for the destruction of the human race than on that which would conduce to the happiness of mankind . . . These strifes and this bloodshed and discord must cease, and all men be as one kindred and one family . . . Let not a man glory in this, that he loves his country; let him rather glory in this, that he loves his kind . . .'

Such, so far as I call recall them, were the words which, besides many others, I heard from Behá. Let those who read them consider well with themselves whether such doctrines merit death and bonds, and whether the world is more likely to gain or lose by their diffusion.[108]

Another account of a visit to Baha'u'llah is by a Baha'i, Tarazu'llah Samandari, who was seventeen years old at the time. He recalled his visit many years later:

It was the first day of Ridván [21 April 1892, at the Mansion of Bahji] . . . To begin with, He [Baha'u'llah] gave us candies, which they brought down from upstairs and passed around. We ate all the candies . . . We were five people – the first group to come out and pay our respects on the Ridván Festival. I was one, and the late 'Andalíb, and Hájí Abu'l-Hasan Shírází, one of the companions of the Báb, . . . and there were two others that I cannot call to mind.

When we arrived, we knelt before Bahá'u'lláh and remained seated on the floor in that position. The Blessed Beauty was seated on a chair. His room was carpeted with a mat woven of marsh reeds; there was nothing else in the room. He addressed us lovingly. After His expressions of loving-kindness, which I am no longer able to recall, He began to chant the Lawh-i Sultán, the Tablet to the Sháh [see pp. 170–2] – some part of it.

Truthfully, at that time I did not have sufficient capacity to experience those delights which were there to enjoy; but according to my degree of comprehension, such capacity as I had, on that day, I too – from His chanting, from His ways . . . Today, when I am at this age of ninety-two years, I feel it all.

That day I witnessed in Him two states of being: one was His overwhelming meekness, and no meekness greater than His can be conceived – a condition of evanescence and meekness referred to by Him in many Tablets. The other was the condition of might, of the power and authority of the Supreme Pen. When He would address the king, with what might He intoned, 'Yá Sultán!' At times He would gesture with His hand, at times He would move His foot, and with all majesty and power He would pronounce the words, 'O King!' When He came to: 'The invisible King standeth revealed in a visible temple and saith, "Fear not. Relate unto His Majesty the Shah that which befell Thee . . . "' at that moment, as He unfolded the tale of His calamities and trials, He manifested in His Person the very essence and spirit of ineffable meekness.

Then He brought the reading to a close and said, with that heavenly music of His voice: 'Taráz Effendi, stand up!' I stood up. They had brought a quantity of roses from Junayna, red roses, fresh from the bush, perhaps thirty or forty in all, and placed them on a mat or cushion in His room, on a white cloth. He said, 'Give a rose to each one present here.'

I took them up, and I gave one rose to each. Then I stood waiting.

He said, 'And what about My share?'

I took one and offered it to Him.

Then He said, 'Take one yourself, as well.'

I took one myself. And He dismissed us, saying, 'Go in God's care – *Fí amánu'lláh*.'[109]

Some of the eminent Islamic scholars who met Baha'u'llah have written brief accounts of meeting him. Thus for example, Shaykh Mahdí al-Azharí recorded the following words of Fádil Mawlaví about Baha'u'llah:

I only met him once at which time I was able to examine all aspects of him. Seeing him was the equivalent for me of seeing half of the inhabitants of the world . . . Knowledge itself burst forth from him and wisdom and authority emanated from about him. I learned from just one session in his presence more than I learned from years with others.[110]

The eminent Lebanese Druse writer Amir Amin Arslan described the appearance of Baha'u'llah as he walked in the garden thus: 'His appearance struck my imagination in such a way that I cannot better represent it than by evoking the image of God the Father, commanding, in his majesty, the elements of nature, in the middle of clouds.'[111]

Many of the Baha'is who met Baha'u'llah were overcome by the experience and felt unable to write about it subsequently. The Iranian Baha'i historian, Fadil Mazandarani, has put together a composite of what has been written and said by those who met Baha'u'llah. This account of course contains some exaggerated language reminiscent of the language of lovers:

Baha'u'llah's matchless beauty, his heart-enthralling, sky-blue, shining eyes which saw and took note of the visible and the hidden, his high forehead and long eyebrows, his long black hair and beard, his imposing presence and great majesty were what most visitors and travellers, whether friend or stranger, commented upon. He wore firmly placed upon his head a light brown *táj*[112] of the type used by Sufis, somewhat taller than usual and of great beauty, embroidered with coloured threads, round the base of which was tied a small white turban, and also loosely-fitting clothes of white or of a grey colour, with a cloak (*abá*) over his shoulders. The majority of pilgrims however were, on account of being overwhelmed by the awe and ecstasy that they felt in his presence, unable to contemplate his face and clothes. He was of average build, neither tall, nor short, neither corpulent, nor thin. His appearance was of the utmost nobility, authority and might; his limbs of perfect proportions and beauty. He was indeed the very example and proof of the statement that God is 'the Best of Creators'.

There are two portraits in pen and one photograph of Baha'u'llah which are kept in the Archives in the Holy Land and shown to pilgrims. We have previously mentioned that Darvish Muhammad drew the portraits in Baghdad, one in the public baths and one outside, while the photograph was taken in Edirne with the *táj* and turban mentioned above. Out of respect, none of these is distributed but the pilgrims and visitors to the Holy Land can view them.

It was Baha'u'llah's custom to sit on a seat placed upon a platform.[113] Even in the garden of Ridvan, where he would stay sometimes for recreation, a seat was placed for him in the shade of the trees, the interwoven branches of which formed a green canopy, and the pilgrims with the utmost respect would line up and, when they had been given permission, would sit on the seats nearby. No-one, whether of the Baha'is or not, would arrive without first receiving permission to come into his presence and, when in his presence, they would be beside themselves with emotion and unable to speak.

Among the well-known characteristics of Baha'u'llah was his love of greenery, grass, flowers, fragrances, running water and morning breezes as well as the cleanliness and refinement which appeared in all aspects of his private and public life. Indeed, the perfect example of the verse revealed in the *Kitab-i Aqdas*, 'He, verily, desireth to see in you the manners of the inmates of Paradise in His mighty and most sublime Kingdom' [v. 46] could be seen in every particular of his life.

Then there is the matter of one's income, of being self-reliant and free from poverty and suffering and occupying oneself with a craft, a profession or with trade as it is written in the *Kitab-i Aqdas*: 'It is incumbent upon each one of you to engage in some occupation – such as a craft, a trade or the like. We have exalted your engagement in such work to the rank of worship of the one true God' [v.33]. In the early years of his residence in 'Akka, Baha'u'llah praised and emphasised the acquisition of a craft, profession or trade to such an extent that 'Abdu'l-Baha went to the home of Aqa 'Abdu'l-Ahad in the Khan [i-'Avamid] and learnt from him the craft of weaving straw mats, while Mirza Muhammad 'Ali [half brother of 'Abdu'l-Baha] went into partnership with Ustad Muhammad 'Ali Yazdi to open a dyer's shop. Baha'u'llah also had a great love of spreading the literary arts and of decorating and illuminating the borders of Persian calligraphy as indeed can be seen and taken pleasure from in the beauty of the pages and specimens of calligraphy of the writings of Baha'u'llah that are produced in this style and manner.

For the education of the children, a school was established, at Baha'u'llah's instructions, in 'Akka, where Aqa Sayyid Asadu'llah Qumi and some others occupied themselves with teaching reading and writing Persian. In this manner, the Persian language, composition and eloquence of style was preserved as it ought to be in the children of those Baha'is who had emigrated to the Holy Land.

Among the other manifest qualities of Baha'u'llah were his matchless moral and spiritual courage, his fortitude and joyfulness even in times of hardship and difficulties, his generosity and munificence, his sympathy and compassion towards the poor and misfortunate, and his paying no heed to the rich and powerful.[114]

Baha'u'llah greatly loved children. The following is a story illustrating his relationship with children:

Áqá Muhammad-i-Tabrízí has recounted how, as a child of four or five, he would go with his family to the Mansion of Bahjí each Friday, as was customary among the believers at that time, to attain the presence of the Blessed Beauty. They would stay all day, using the rooms on the lower floor of the Mansion.

During one of these visits the grown-ups were resting in their rooms at noontime; as it was a warm day, he left his room and wandered to the upper floor of the Mansion where he entered the large hall. Ambling about he eventually came to the room where food was stored, and here he noticed a bag filled with [crystallised] sugar. Instinctively he took a handful, put it in his mouth, then filled both hands before leaving the store-room. Back in the hall, he froze in his tracks upon seeing the Blessed Beauty pacing to and fro there. Slowly and in a gentle manner, Bahá'u'lláh came towards him, cast a loving glance at his hands and then led the little boy towards a large table in the middle of the hall. Picking up a plate of candies, He offered one to the child who, with closed fist, accepted it. 'It seems you like sweets,' Bahá'u'lláh said. 'Eat well! Goodbye. And may God protect you.'[115]

Baha'u'llah's concern for the education of children, especially girls, and his setting up a school for the Baha'i children in 'Akka (to which Baha'u'llah's grand-daughters were also sent) was mentioned above. One of the Baha'is who had come to live in 'Akka when she was a child, Rafieh Mansour, recalled that when she had been taken to see Baha'u'llah, he had particularly asked about her education:

> Mrs. Mansour recalled that on another occasion, which she believed to be a Holy Day, she accompanied her grandmother into the presence of Bahá'u'lláh. They made the trip together to Bahjí and waited for a few moments in a room adjoining that of the Blessed Perfection. It was a large room, and a curtain was drawn across the entrance to the room of Bahá'u'lláh.
>
> 'We were waiting for Bahá'u'lláh to give permission for us to enter,' she remembered. 'Suddenly the curtain was drawn back and Bahá'u'lláh Himself stood in the doorway. I remember the creamy colour of His garment. He began asking about everyone, and looking at me, standing beside my grandmother, He said: "Does this child go to school?" My grandmother answered that I was studying in a small class with a Bahá'í teacher, and this answer was accepted.'[116]

THE PROCESS OF 'REVELATION'

The number of letters arriving in 'Akka from Baha'is in Iran and throughout the Middle East increased greatly. It is not surprising then that, during these last years of his life, Baha'u'llah wrote a large number of tablets, most of them in reply to the letters that arrived, with some of the more important of them expounding on the social teachings of his religion. We have a few accounts of those who were permitted to be present when Baha'u'llah was composing his tablets – the process of revelation, as it is called by Baha'is:

Twice I had the honour of being present in His room during the revelation of the Holy Verses. No one was there except His secretary, Mírzá Áqá Ján, and another time, Mírzá Badí'u'lláh [one of Baha'u'llah's sons] was there copying Tablets. On these two precious occasions, as the Essence of Glory and Dignity [Baha'u'llah] paced the room and chanted verses, I could gaze upon Him and contemplate His luminous face, and behold the vision of the majesty of God and His divine Kingdom. This was indeed a great blessing. As He revealed the verses of God, His face was radiant. Sometimes, He would gesture with His hands while He looked through the window onto the sea.

It was His custom to drink water while revealing the verses when His lips became dry. Mírzá Áqá Ján was occupied in taking down the revealed words. The floor of the room was covered with papers from the dictation. One might guess that they amounted to about one-fifth of the Qur'án, revealed during those few hours.

The verses were revealed sometimes in a melodious voice, and sometimes with majesty and power – depending on the content of the revealed words. For instance, when the subject was prayer, a heavenly melody was heard; while admonitions and words of warning were uttered with the power of the Lord of lords!

Bahá'u'lláh Himself tells us that day and night the verses descended like torrential rain. From this, whoever is mindful will ask: What can He mean, that the verses descended like torrential rain? This means, without thought. This means, without deliberation. This means that, first the revelation comes down – and only then is it read . . . The rule always was that when the letters came in from the friends, Khádim [Mirza Aqa Jan] would be directed by Bahá'u'lláh to read Him the letters. Then, at Bahá'u'lláh's direction, he would make ready paper and pen, and an answer would be vouchsafed. To one after the other, upon each of those who had written, He would bestow an answer.

As to this question of revelation, I am unable to record what one then observes. At the highest possible speed, without any premeditation, these utterances would be revealed [by Baha'u'llah]. At such a speed that it would be impossible to conceive any swifter, he [Mirza Aqa Jan] would write them down. No one could read that 'Revelation-writing,' with the exception of a very, very few early believers who had some familiarity with it. Perhaps they could read some of the verses so recorded – but not the whole. Even Mírzá Áqá Ján, the Revelation scribe himself, was sometimes unable to read this writing, and he would then take it to Bahá'u'lláh, and Bahá'u'lláh would solve the problem.[117]

Another visitor has described that:

We saw Him several times at dawn and early morning, while He was speaking the revealed Word and Mírzá Aqá Ján was writing it down as He spoke it. Mírzá Aqá Ján used to have several [reed] pens well cut and pointed, with ink and paper ready. The flow of verses from the heaven of Revelation was swift. It was indeed like unto a fast-billowing ocean. Mírzá Aqá Ján wrote as quickly as he could – so quickly that the pen at times jumped out of his hand. He would immediately take up another pen. There were times when he could not keep up and would say: 'I am incapable of writing.' Then the Blessed Perfection would repeat what He had spoken.[118]

Another account is from 'Azizu'llah Varqa, who as a nine-year old boy had come with his father and brother as a pilgrim from Iran in about 1891. He has related:

One day I was in Bahá'u'lláh's Presence with the whole family and He called for the secretary to bring ink and paper quickly and in the same moment He requested us all to go. I was just a child, but seeing this haste to send every one away, I had a great longing to be present sometime when a Tablet is revealed. I had asked from one of the members of His family to ask Bahá'u'lláh if I could come, please, to see a Tablet revealed. A few weeks later in the Garden at Bahji, when I was playing with some children, the door of the home was opened and one member of the family called me and said that Bahá'u'lláh wished to see me. I ran to His room and entering I saw that He was chanting revealed Tablets and poems. So entering His room that day, I thought everything was the same as on other days, that

Bahá'u'lláh was only chanting. I stood near the door which I had entered, and was only a few moments in the room when I began trembling in my whole body. I felt I could not stand any more on my feet. His Holiness Bahá'u'lláh turning to me said 'Good-bye'. As I lifted the curtain to go out, I fell on the threshold and was unconscious. They took me to the room of the wife of His Holiness Bahá'u'lláh where they poured rose water and cold water on my face until I revived. The members of the Family asked me what had happened and I told them about going to Bahá'u'lláh to hear the chanting. When I was relating this, the lady who had called me first, came in, and she said to me: 'You, yourself, had asked me to permit you to be present, now that was the time when a Tablet was being revealed.'

Then I understood why Bahá'u'lláh in haste dismissed everybody. It is because the people cannot endure it, there is such a Power in the room.[119]

CONTACTS WITH STATESMEN AND REFORMERS

Throughout his ministry, there were many statesmen and reformers who contacted Baha'u'llah. Some were only advancing their self-interest. These included Malkam Khan, who was mentioned above (see p. 50), and Zillu's-Sultan, the son of Nasiru'd-Din Shah who sent an emissary to Baha'u'llah in 1884 to try to gain Baha'u'llah's support in his attempt to seize the throne. Baha'u'llah sent such individuals away disappointed.

There were others however, individuals who were genuinely interested in social reform and the modernization of the Middle East, with whom Baha'u'llah and Abdu'l-Baha were in contact and whom they tried to influence towards an understanding that political and social reform would not succeed without an underlying spiritual and moral reform. 'Abdu'l-Baha, for example, on the instructions of Baha'u'llah, wrote a treatise on the question of economic and social development which was published in India in 1882 as a contribution to this debate, *The Secret of Divine Civilization.*

Midhat Pasha, who has been mentioned above, was one of those who was attempting to bring reform to the Ottoman Empire and who was in touch with Baha'u'llah and 'Abdu'l-Baha. Other prominent Ottoman reformers included Namik Kemal, who was in contact with both Baha'u'llah and 'Abdu'l-Baha. Nuri Bey and Berketzade Ismail Hakki Effendi, who had been exiled by the Ottoman authorities to 'Akka, were also in contact with the Baha'i exiles. Of the later generation of Ottoman reformers, Ishak Sukuti and Suleyman Nazif were in close contact with Baha'u'llah and 'Abdu'l-Baha. Among the reformers in the Arab world, we have already mentioned above that Muhammad 'Abduh met 'Abdu'l-Baha in Beirut in 1880 and became a warm admirer of his, and Amir Amin Arslan was in close contact.

A number of these reformers even became to one extent or another followers of Baha'u'llah. These included such figures as Hajji Shaykhu'r-Ra'is who, although a Qajar prince, had become a cleric and was to become a leader of the Iranian constitutional movement. Another leading figure in the constitutional movement, Muhammad Vali Khan Tunukabuni Sipahsalar-i A'zam appears to have been secretly a Baha'i. Among the later Ottoman reformers who are said to have been Baha'is was Abdullah Cevdet.

These statements that various prominent statesmen and reformers were Baha'is is difficult to prove irrefutably because it was necessary for such prominent men to keep their belief in Baha'u'llah secret. Any public disclosure of their beliefs would have led to an immediate fall from their social position and perhaps even a death sentence. It will therefore take a great deal more research to uncover the true extent of the influence of Baha'u'llah and his teaching in this period.

LIFE AT BAHJI

The following account by the son of Zaynu'l-Muqarrabin relates some of the usual programme that Baha'u'llah followed during these years at Bahji:

The Mansion of Bahji as it appeared in the 1900s on approaching it
from 'Akka. Baha'u'llah's room is on the upper floor at the far left
of the balcony. The Shrine of Baha'u'llah is the building behind
and immediately to the left of the Mansion

Baha'u'llah would usually spend the spring, summer and part of
autumn at the mansion of Bahji, but would spend the winter
season in 'Akka. Some of the Baha'is who resided in the area
had a particular day of the week on which they had permanent
permission to call on Baha'u'llah at the mansion. Others would
seek permission whenever they wished to come and it would be
given them.

I do not now recall what the time interval was between my
father asking for permission to call on Baha'u'llah and that permission being given. But in any case, whenever he went to the
mansion, I would also go. On Baha'u'llah's orders, we remained
for several days in the room that is in the shadow of
Baha'u'llah's room and is called the Pilgrim House. Every day,
in the late afternoon, my father and whoever else of the 'Akka
residents or pilgrims was present would be summoned to
Baha'u'llah's room and would benefit from his presence. We
would take tea in his presence.[120]

Another account of Baha'u'llah's routine when he was living at
Bahji is given by Mirza Ahmad Yazdi:

He [Yazdi] told us that Jamali Mobarek [the Blessed Beauty, a
title of Baha'u'llah] was very methodical and punctual – had
appointed times for seeing believers, etc., and adhered strictly to

these times. When receiving believers he would sit in the corner furthest from the door, by the window, while the believers sat near the door. Rarely did any of them approach him closely. Occasionally, when receiving something from his hand they would kiss his hand, or the hem of his robe. Ahmad Yazdi, as a boy, was often in His room acting as servant; Jamali Mobarek would distribute sweets, etc. to the believers, taking one piece at a time in his fingers and naming one of his guests, to whom Ahmad Yazdi would then carry it. Jamali Mobarek used to have meals with his own family when at home, but when out always had meals by Himself. He had tea specially prepared for Himself . . .

Believers who had come long distances would be seen only once or twice a week for a few minutes. Baha'u'llah would seldom consent to see non-believers. It was a very rare favour for a non-believer to obtain an interview . . .

Although so majestic, Baha'u'llah was exceedingly loving, kind, courteous and generous. When out walking with some of the believers He would chat with them very affably. He frequently made jokes and humorous remarks and would laugh heartily on occasion, but none of the believers would dare to laugh in His presence, although they could not help smiling broadly.[121]

There were a number of Baha'i holy days that were special occasions at Bahji. The following is a description of a celebration of the Ridván festival:

For example, the days of the most mighty festival of Ridván, whether in the days that Baha'u'llah was resident in Bahji or in the days when he was in 'Akka, would be celebrated with great dignity and splendour. A large table would be laid in the room of Baha'u'llah during the entire twelve days. It would be laden with many different varieties of the best Iranian sweetmeats and confectionery prepared by Aqa Rida Shirazi who was one of those who were resident in 'Akka and who prepared these specially for Baha'u'llah on these particular days. As the Baha'is, both residents and pilgrims came into Baha'u'llah's presence, he would personally, standing at the head of the table, give to each person individually, in a clean handkerchief that each person would have in their hand, some of the sweets, smiling graciously and saying, '*Marhabá! Marhabá!*' [Welcome! Welcome!]. And when they left his presence, he would say '*Fí amáni'lláh wa hifz-ihi* [Go in the care and protection of God]" and would call the next group into his presence.[122]

Some may imagine that this phase of Baha'u'llah's life was, compared to previous phases, much more pleasant and comfortable, given that Bahji was considered one of the most prestigious and elegant residences in the area. This may not be a correct assessment however. If we consider the people whom Baha'u'llah surrounded himself with in Bahji, we find that these are the very people who were already showing signs of rebellion and disaffection and who were to rebel openly against Baha'u'llah's successor, 'Abdu'l-Baha, and to try to split the Baha'i community. Foremost among these was Mirza Muhammad 'Ali, 'Abdu'l-Baha's half-brother. Already he had, since the Edirne period, tried to create a following for himself and had claimed revelation for himself, then he had tried to interpolate some words into the text of some of Baha'u'llah's writings in order to elevate his status. Also at Bahji were Muhammad 'Ali's brothers and sisters, who supported him, and his mother, who never ceased to denigrate 'Abdu'l-Baha and to try to persuade Baha'u'llah to promote the position of her son. Mirza Aqa Jan, Baha'u'llah's secretary since the Baghdad days, was also at Bahji. He fell into disfavour with Baha'u'llah in these later years when he appeared to indicate that the material dictated to him by Baha'u'llah was in fact his own words. Five years after the passing of Baha'u'llah, he was to come out in open rebellion against 'Abdu'l-Baha. Living adjacent to Bahji was Sayyid 'Ali Afnan who had broken his promise to the wife of the Bab that he would bring her to 'Akka in 1882, an event that caused great sorrow to that lady and possibly precipitated her death which occurred a few months later. Mirza Muhammad Javad Qazvini was another individual who took up residence in Bahji and Mirza Mahdi Dihaji stayed there for a time also. All of these individuals would, after the passing of Baha'u'llah, support the rebellion of Mirza Muhammad 'Ali against 'Abdu'l-Baha. Many were already showing their disaffection and rebelliousness, and Baha'u'llah chose to gather all of these people under his wing at Bahji. Partly, this may have been to protect 'Abdu'l-Baha and leave him free to interact with the authorities and notables of 'Akka; partly it may have been to protect the Baha'i pilgrims, who were accommodated in 'Akka, from the divisiveness and rebelliousness beginning to manifest itself in those at Bahji. In any case, it is difficult to see that Baha'u'llah enjoyed his time at Bahji with the presence of such individuals around him. His feelings about the situation in Bahji can be gathered from a comment he made to one of his disciples that he wished that the pilgrims would just go to 'Akka and not come to Bahji:

> One day Bahá'u'lláh was very sad. His sadness was caused by the behaviour of a few of the believers who lived in His household. In great sorrow He said, 'Were it possible, We would recommend that the pilgrims who enter the city of 'Akká go directly to the presence of the Most Great Branch ['Abdu'l-Baha], listen to Him, then meet some of the steadfast believers, and immediately afterwards leave 'Akká and return to their homes. This would be most conducive to their spiritual development. The reason is this: In the Master's presence the friends are not subjected to tainted human thoughts and deeds. All they experience is heavenly sanctity. If the people would open their eyes, they would see clearly the difference between the heavenly perfections of the Master and the human frailties and faults of others. Then, even if they witness odious deeds committed in My household, they will only utter words of praise about the greatness and patience of the True One Who is glorious, mighty, and compassionate. We are aware of their false words and lies. We know. But We must remain silent and cover their sins. Unfortunately, the liars think that We do not know the truth.'[123]

One of the Baha'is, Sayyid Asadu'llah Qumi, who was engaged in teaching the children, records:

One day we were in the presence of Baha'u'llah and he was pacing, when suddenly I burst out sobbing uncontrollably because I saw that around that exalted being there circled souls whose actions and character were shameful and disreputable. Baha'u'llah said: 'Sayyid Asad, we manifested ourselves in order that feuding, disputes, tyranny and injustice should be removed and eliminated from the world . . . Some from among the Baha'is obey whatever God commands them to do; others hear and obey whatever appears to benefit them; while some pay no attention at all, whether it benefits them or not. But since they have come to this place because of this Cause, they are content and safe under the protection of the Cause of God. You should be joyful, but unless you pass beyond the Khalíj of Names, you will not enter the Most Great Ocean. Do you know what Khalíj means?' I said 'I do not know.' He said: 'A Khalíj is waters that branch out from an ocean.' I understood his meaning, the problem was solved. These individuals [here Qumi names some of those, such as Mirza Muhammad Javad Qazvini and Mirza Mahdi Dihaji, who had caused his distress] are the Khalíj and block the path of those who are seeking their Beloved.[124]

Although Bahji was a large mansion, it should not be thought that Baha'u'llah lived in great opulence and luxury. Writing about her grandmother Asiyih Khanum, during this period, Baha'u'llah's granddaughter has recorded, for example, that: 'Bahá'u'lláh had only two coats (made of Barak, a Persian woollen cloth); they were apt to wear out, and much of her [Asiyih Khanum's] time was spent, as I remember her, in patching and darning them and His stockings.'[125]

She has also recorded how the children in the family regarded Baha'u'llah:

We children looked upon Bahá'u'lláh as another loving Father; to Him we carried all our little difficulties and troubles. He took an interest in everything which concerned us.

He was always punctual, and loved daintiness and order. He was very particular and refined in his personal arrangements, and liked to see everybody well groomed, and as neatly

dressed as possible. Above all things, cleanliness was desirable
to Him.

'Why not put on your prettiest frocks?' He would say to
us.

All our holidays, all our treats and our happiness came from
Him in those days; when boxes of sweets were brought to Him
He would set some aside for us.

'Put that box of sweets over there, or Áqá ['Abdu'l-Baha] will
give it away to the people,' He would say in fun. 'Let the dear
children come in, and have some dessert,' He often said, when
we were being sent off to bed – my Father and my mother not
wishing that we should disturb Him – but He always welcomed
us with loving words. How we adored Him!

'Now children, tomorrow you shall come with Me for a picnic to the Ridván [garden],' He would say, and our night was so
full of joy we could scarcely sleep.[126]

As the years went by, Baha'u'llah showed ever greater regard for
the abilities of his eldest son. Several pilgrims have recorded that
on days when 'Abdu'l-Baha was to visit Bahji, Baha'u'llah would
pace the balcony anxiously looking in the direction of 'Akka, and
when he saw the figure of 'Abdu'l-Baha in the distance, he would
order all those in his company to go out and greet 'Abdu'l-Baha
and escort him to the mansion.[127] On one occasion, one of the
Baha'is who had come from Iran was unable to visit Bahji for a
time because of illness. He has recorded what occurred when he
was eventually able to visit Baha'u'llah at Bahji:

Then He asked how I was, and after that He said, 'In 'Akká, do
you not seek out the presence of Sarkár Áqá, the Master
('Abdu'l-Baha)?'. . .

I answered: 'I attend upon Him day and night . . .'

He smiled. 'Then why do you complain,' He said, 'that you
have not been in My presence? Why do you complain that you
have not been in My presence?'[128]

The appellation of Sarkar Aqa or Aqa (usually translated as 'the
Master'), although common enough as a term of respect among
Iranians, was one that was particular to 'Abdu'l-Baha since

Baha'u'llah forbade its being used in relation to anyone else. An eye-witness has recorded that:

> On another occasion, when they were in the presence of Bahá'u'lláh, Mírzá Díyá'u'lláh [one of the brothers of Mirza Muhammad 'Ali] came in to say: 'Áqá supplicates for permission that we all may go with the Friends to the Garden of Junaynih.' 'Who has said so?' Bahá'u'lláh enquired, to which Mírzá Diyá'u'lláh replied: 'Áqáy-i-Ghusn-i-Akbar' (the Greater Branch [a designation of Mirza Muhammad 'Ali]). Angrily, Bahá'u'lláh spoke: 'There is only one Áqá (Master, without specification), all the others have names; that one Áqá is "He round Whom all Names revolve", the Ghusn-i-A'zam (the Most Mighty Branch [a designation of 'Abdu'l-Baha]).'[129]

Baha'u'llah also had great regard for his daughter Bahiyyih Khanum. In many of his writings, Baha'u'llah refers to himself as the Tree of Life or the Tree beyond which there is no passing (see p. 172). Extending this analogy, he referred to 'Abdu'l-Baha as the Most Mighty Branch of that tree and to Bahiyyih Khanum as the Greatest Holy Leaf. This analogy can be seen in the following passage addressed to Bahiyyih Khanum:

> Verily, We have elevated thee to the rank of one of the most distinguished among thy sex, and granted thee, in My court, a station such as none other woman hath surpassed. Thus have We preferred thee and raised thee above the rest, as a sign of grace from Him Who is the Lord of the throne on high and earth below. We have created thine eyes to behold the light of My countenance, thine ears to hearken unto the melody of My words, thy body to pay homage before My throne. Do thou render thanks unto God, thy Lord, the Lord of all the world.
>
> How high is the testimony of the Sadratu'l-Muntahá [Tree beyond which there is no passing] for its leaf; how exalted the witness of the Tree of Life unto its fruit! Through My remembrance of her a fragrance laden with the perfume of musk hath been diffused; well is it with him that hath inhaled it and exclaimed: 'All praise be to Thee, O God, my Lord the most glorious!' How sweet thy presence before Me; how sweet to gaze

upon thy face, to bestow upon thee My loving-kindness, to favour thee with My tender care, to make mention of thee in this, My Tablet – a Tablet which I have ordained as a token of My hidden and manifest grace unto thee.[130]

Regarding Asiyih Khanum, the mother of 'Abdu'l-Baha and Bahiyyih Khanum, Baha'u'llah wrote many tender and loving words. It was his custom to write a tablet for the visitation of the grave of many of his prominent followers. The following is part of the tablet of visitation that he wrote for Asiyih Khanum, who is here referred to as the Most Exalted Leaf:

O faithful ones! Should ye visit the resting-place of the Most Exalted Leaf, who hath ascended unto the Glorious Companion, stand ye and say: 'Salutation and blessing and glory upon thee, O Holy Leaf that hath sprung from the Divine Lote-Tree! I bear witness that thou hast believed in God and in His signs, and answered His Call, and turned unto Him, and held fast unto His cord, and clung to the hem of His grace, and fled thy home in His path, and chosen to live as a stranger, out of love for His presence and in thy longing to serve Him. May God have mercy upon him that draweth nigh unto thee, and remembereth thee through the things which My Pen hath voiced in this, the most great station. We pray God that He may forgive us, and forgive them that have turned unto thee, and grant their desires, and bestow upon them, through His wondrous grace, whatever be their wish. He, verily, is the Bountiful, the Generous. Praise be to God, He Who is the Desire of all worlds; and the Beloved of all who recognize Him.'[131]

Asiyih Khanum died in 1886 and a very large funeral was held in her honour. She was soon followed by Mirza Musa Kalim, Baha'u'llah's faithful brother, who died in 1887; both of these had shared with Baha'u'llah all of his years of exile and imprisonment. Another death that caused great sorrow in 1887 was that of Husayn, the two-year-old son of 'Abdu'l-Baha, and Baha'u'llah's grandson. These deaths came at a particularly difficult time for the exiles as an unfriendly governor of 'Akka, Muhammad Yusuf Pasha, was making incessant demands, which 'Abdu'l-Baha tried hard to meet so as to protect Baha'u'llah. Eventually however, that governor was dismissed for embezzling government funds.

EVENTS IN IRAN

Events in Iran also caused Baha'u'llah grief. His followers were relentlessly persecuted throughout that land. In 1879, for example, two brothers in Isfahan (uncles of 'Abdu'l-Baha's wife Munirih) who were devoted Baha'is were arrested at the instigation of a senior cleric of that city who owed them a large sum of money and who had them killed on the accusation of being Baha'is in order to avoid repayment of his debt. In 1882, many of Baha'u'llah's most prominent followers were arrested in Tehran and kept in prison for up to nineteen months. In 1883, there were arrests in Yazd, Sarvistan, Rasht and Qazvin and the execution of a prominent Baha'i of Mazandaran. In 1885, a leading Baha'i in Khurasan was killed. From 1888 to 1891, there were several episodes of persecution, imprisonment and executions of Baha'is in the Isfahan area and the murder of a prominent Baha'i in Ashkhabad in Russian Turkistan. This latter episode was the first occasion in which those persecuting the Baha'is were arrested, tried and sentenced. Baha'u'llah was particularly pleased with the fact that when the death sentences were announced, the Baha'is of Ashkhabad intervened with the authorities to have the death sentences commuted to imprisonment. In 1891, seven Baha'is were executed in Yazd and there were further arrests in Tehran.

In addition, enemies of the Baha'i Faith, and in particular the Azalis, were spreading false rumours and accusations about Baha'u'llah and the Baha'is and even publishing these in newspapers published in Istanbul and elsewhere. The Azalis in Istanbul were constantly intriguing against the Baha'is and had enlisted the support of the Iranian Embassy there. Eventually this caused so much grief to the Baha'is in that city that it caused one of the prominent Baha'is there to commit suicide.

Baha'u'llah refers extensively to these matters in his last major work, the Epistle to the Son of the Wolf; for example:

> O Shaykh! My Pen is abashed to recount what actually took place. In the land of Sád (Isfahán) the fire of tyranny burned with such a hot flame that every fair-minded person groaned aloud. By thy life! The cities of knowledge and of understanding wept with such a weeping that the souls of the pious and of the God-fearing were melted . . .
>
> On the one hand, tidings have reached Us that Our loved ones have been arrested in the land of Tá (Tihrán) and this notwithstanding that the sun, and the moon, and the land, and the sea all testify that this people are adorned with the adornment of fidelity, and have clung and will cling to naught except that which can ensure the exaltation of the government, and the maintenance of order within the nation, and the tranquillity of the people . . .
>
> On the other hand, the officials of the Persian Embassy in the Great City [Istanbul] are energetically and assiduously seeking to exterminate these wronged ones. They desire one thing, and God desireth another. Consider now what hath befallen the trusted ones of God in every land. At one time they have been accused of theft and larceny; at another they have been calumniated in a manner without parallel in this world. Answer thou fairly. What could be the results and consequences, in foreign countries, of the accusation of theft brought by the Persian Embassy against its own subjects? If this Wronged One was ashamed, it was not because of the humiliation it brought this servant, but rather because of the shame of its becoming known to the Ambassadors of foreign countries how incompetent and lacking in understanding are several eminent officials of the Persian Embassy.[132]

Despite these problems and persecution, the Baha'is of Iran were striving to develop their communities. Initial moves towards the education of children were being made. The consciousness of the need to advance the role of women in communal affairs was arising. Baha'u'llah also took a keen interest in agriculture and stressed its importance in his writings. He suggested to some of the Baha'i pilgrims from the village of Saysan in Adharbayjan (north-west Iran), for example, that they take potatoes back with them and grow them there – the first time that potatoes had been grown in Adharbayjan. Some of the community institutions envisaged in Baha'u'llah's writings were also established during Baha'u'llah's lifetime.

At this time, the Baha'i Faith was being spread among the Zoroastrian and Jewish minorities in Iran and to new areas both within Iran and outside. Particularly important was the establishment of the Baha'i community in Ashkhabad in Russian Turkistan from 1882 onwards and the subsequent spread into Central Asia. In Ashkhabad, free from the persecutions in Iran, the Baha'i community was able to start to build the Mashriqu'l-Adhkar, the House of Worship which Baha'u'llah has ordained as being the spiritual heart of every Baha'i community, and also later the social institutions such as schools, medical facilities,

The Shrine of Baha'u'llah. The entrance to the shrine is in the centre of the photograph; the shrine itself is in the room at the far right of this building. The Mansion of Bahji is behind the row of trees to the left of the picture

homes for the aged and orphans, which must surround the central prayer-hall of the Mashriqu'l-Adhkar.

Baha'u'llah also encouraged the Baha'is to start to make their decisions, both individual and communal, through the process of Baha'i consultation (this is described in more detail on p. 208). When one of the most eminent Baha'is, Ibn Abhar, was in 'Akka, he asked Baha'u'llah where he should establish his residence. Rather than give him instructions, Baha'u'llah told him to return to Iran and consult with the Baha'is about the matter.

THE PASSING OF BAHA'U'LLAH

Baha'u'llah had alluded to his own passing from this world on many occasions. In the *Kitab-i Aqdas*, for example, he had written:

> Let not your hearts be perturbed, O people, when the glory of My Presence is withdrawn, and the ocean of My utterance is stilled. In My presence amongst you there is a wisdom, and in My absence there is yet another, inscrutable to all but God, the Incomparable, the All-Knowing. Verily, We behold you from Our realm of glory, and shall aid whosoever will arise for the triumph of Our Cause with the hosts of the Concourse on high and a company of Our favoured angels.[133]

In the last nine months of his earthly life, however, Baha'u'llah began to allude more regularly to his departure from the world in his writings and his audiences with the Baha'is. In early May 1892, he held a series of three meetings on three successive days in a tent pitched adjacent to Bahji commemorating the deaths of two male and one female Baha'i. A few days later, on 8 May, he was taken ill with a fever although he did not mention it to anyone. He continued to receive the Baha'is who wished to meet with him for a further twenty-four hours but then audiences ceased as his condition worsened. Doctors were summoned but they could only find a steady pulse and a fever. On 16 May,

'Abdu'l-Baha visited Bahji and then conveyed the following words from Baha'u'llah to the Baha'is in 'Akka: 'All the friends must remain patient and steadfast, and arise for the promotion of the Cause of God. They should not become perturbed, because I shall always be with them, and will remember and care for them.'[134] These words plunged the Baha'is into grief because they realised that the end was near. This was followed by great joy on the following day when 'Abdu'l-Baha visited Bahji again and brought news to the Baha'is in 'Akka that Baha'u'llah was much improved. On 22 May, all those who were resident in Bahji were summoned into Baha'u'llah's presence. They found him very weak. One of those present has recorded:

> The Blessed Beauty lay in His bed. Two were seated, one to either side of Him, and He leaned against them. They had fans in their hands, and they were fanning him. Then, He Himself began to speak. He addressed gracious and loving words to those about Him, spoke of His indisposition and recited some verses from the *Kitáb-i Aqdas*:
>
> *Be not dismayed, O peoples of the world, when the day-star of My beauty is set, and the heaven of My tabernacle is concealed from your eyes. Arise to further My Cause, and to exalt My Word amongst men.* [v. 38]
>
> Since He recited these verses, it became clear to us that He would ascend. Following these utterances, He vehemently counselled us to abstain from dissension and strife. Although His blessed body was feeble, He voiced this with great power, distinctly measuring out the words: 'Shun disharmony. Strive that no discord should arise among the friends. Let the friends avoid contention.' . . .
>
> And suddenly Jináb-i 'Andalíb could endure no more. He broke down, and Bahá'u'lláh dismissed us saying, 'Go, in God's care.'
>
> 'Abdu'l-Bahá was present too; as I recall He was standing. He directed us to circumambulate the bed. Those of us in our group simply walked around Bahá'u'lláh's bed, and He said to us: '*Fí amánu'lláh* – go in God's care.' We went out of the room.[135]

That was the last audience that Baha'u'llah gave. On the evening of Saturday, 29 May 1892, the twenty-first day after contracting his illness, Baha'u'llah passed away, eight hours after sunset. The next day, when the news broke, a throng of Baha'is and inhabitants of 'Akka filled the fields surrounding the mansion of Bahji. Shortly after sunset on that day, after the Sultan himself had been consulted by telegram and had agreed, Baha'u'llah was interred in a room in the most northerly of three houses that lay west of and close to the mansion. For seven days, everyone who came was fed by the family of Baha'u'llah as they expressed their sorrow and their condolences to 'Abdu'l-Baha. Notables from among the Muslims, Christians, Jews and Druse of the are expressed their sorrow and some composed tributes to Baha'u'llah in prose and verse. Similar tributes were received from as far afield as Damascus, Aleppo, Beirut and Cairo. On the ninth day after Baha'u'llah's passing, the seals on his will, the Kitab Ahdi (see p. 190), were broken and the contents, appointing 'Abdu'l-Baha as his successor, were read out before a gathering of Baha'is.

There were many distinguished citizens of 'Akka, Haifa and Beirut, Muslims and Christians, who composed poetry and recited elegies both at the funeral and later. The famous Baha'i poet 'Andalib was also present in 'Akka at the time of Baha'u'llah's passing and wrote a poem on that occasion of which this is a free translation:

> Today the cupbearer, by God's design,
>   poured bile into the cup of life, not wine.
> Every wound has its balm, each ache a cure –
>   except this wound! this endless ache of mine!
> The nightingales refuse to sing. No trees.
>   The world's gone dark, and every eye is blind.
> Calamity! The universe unbuilt.
>   Calamity! The reign of God undone.
> On the Sea of Mercy all waves lie still.
>   But waves of woe rise high! The storm's begun.

The banner of God's Name collapsed. Such grief,
    such grief that heaven will be overrun.
Through Him the Day of Resurrection dawned:
    Now earth quakes at the setting of His Sun.
From Sinai He called, 'Come see!' Now Moses
    hears these final words: 'You shall never see.'
On the Most Great Ocean the Crimson Ark
    has sunk. The tears of Noah drown the sea.
Look west! The Sun of Holiness has set.
    Look up! and in His placeless place He'll be.
We'll never hear His voice again, but there
    the Nightingale of Paradise flies free.[136]

SEVEN

The Writings of Baha'u'llah

The writings of Baha'u'llah are voluminous. They are loosely described by Baha'u'llah as comprising 100 volumes.[137] However only a few of these are self-contained books. Most of Baha'u'llah's writings consist of letters addressed mainly to his followers. These are known by Baha'is as 'Tablets' and over 7000 of them have been collected and fully authenticated by the Baha'i World Centre;[138] there are copies of many thousands of other tablets and work on authentication will continue for years to come. Only a small proportion of these have been published and an even smaller amount translated. Some of the better known tablets have names, such as the Tablet of the World, the Tablet of the Holy Mariner and the Tablet of Wisdom.

Although throughout this book the phrase 'Baha'u'llah wrote' and 'Baha'u'llah's writings' have been used, most of Baha'u'llah's writings were, as described in the preceding chapter, in fact, dictated. He wrote both in Persian and Arabic. Some of his Arabic writings, such as parts of the Tablet to the Shah, are in a very eloquent and correct Arabic while most of it has an innovative style and syntax. Many of his Persian works contain a heavy admixture of Arabic words and phrases which are also very eloquent but may be difficult for contemporary Iranians who do not have the educational background to comprehend them. Some of his works, however, are in a very pure Persian, with no Arabic words at all. In many of his works, he changes backwards and forwards between Arabic and Persian. Apart from his poetry, many of his prose writings in both Persian and Arabic have a rhyme and rhythm that adds to their eloquence and means that the favoured method for reciting his writings in their original language is to chant them.

The impact of Baha'u'llah's writings was mixed. Many of the Babis became attached to him during the Baghdad period as a result of reading his writings and without ever meeting him. In subsequent years too, many converts record that it was the beauty and penetrating power of his words that was the cause of their conversion. They became convinced that these words were the word of God. On the other hand, many read his writings and were unaffected by them and some, including even a few of the Babis, rose up in opposition to them and wrote books refuting them.

The standard Baha'i style for translating Baha'u'llah's writings into English was set by Shoghi Effendi, Baha'u'llah's second successor, in the 1920s and 1930s. He chose a style based on the English of the King James Authorized Version of the Bible as the best method for conveying something of the authority and gravitas appropriate for what Baha'is believe to be divine revelation.

THE BAGHDAD PERIOD

We have very little of Baha'u'llah's writings from the time that he was in Iran: a poem and one or two letters. It is therefore not until the Baghdad period of his life that we have any substantial writings. Probably the first important writing of Baha'u'llah from the Baghdad period to have survived is called the Tablet of All Food (see p. 37). It is a commentary on the Quranic verse 'All food was allowed to the children of Israel . . . (3:93).' In it Baha'u'llah identifies the children of Israel with the Babis spiritually and relates the word 'food' to spiritual nourishment in five metaphysical realms.

During Baha'u'llah's stay in Kurdistan, he came into contact with the Sufis of that region and remained in touch with them even after his return to Baghdad. This resulted in the Ode of the Dove, a poem in Arabic written in the style of one of the great Sufi poems of all time, which was written while he was still in Sulaymaniyyih for the Sufis there, and two mystical treatises written in the Sufi style for two prominent Sufis. These were named the Seven Valleys and the Four Valleys. The first describes the journey of the soul as it progresses through seven successive stages in its progresses towards the object of its existence; the second describes four modes of progress for the soul. There were also several pieces of poetry in Persian that expressed mystical themes as well as several tablets, such as the Tablet of the Maid of Heaven, the Tablet of the Eternal Youth and the Tablet of the Holy Mariner, which are highly mystical and some of them are written in a rhythmic style clearly intended for incantation. As an example of his mystical works, the following is a passage from the Seven Valleys:

> There was once a lover who had sighed for long years in separation from his beloved, and wasted in the fire of remoteness. From the rule of love, his heart was empty of patience, and his body weary of his spirit; he reckoned life without her as a mockery, and time consumed him away. How many a day he found no rest in longing for her; how many a night the pain of her kept him from sleep; his body was worn to a sigh, his heart's wound had turned him to a cry of sorrow. He had given a thousand lives for one taste of the cup of her presence, but it availed him not. The doctors knew no cure for him, and companions avoided his company; yea, physicians have no medicine for one sick of love, unless the favour of the beloved one deliver him.
>
> At last, the tree of his longing yielded the fruit of despair, and the fire of his hope fell to ashes. Then one night he could live no more, and he went out of his house and made for the

marketplace. On a sudden, a watchman followed after him. He broke into a run, with the watchman following; then other watchmen came together, and barred every passage to the weary one. And the wretched one cried from his heart, and ran here and there, and moaned to himself: 'Surely this watchman is 'Izrá'íl, my angel of death, following so fast upon me; or he is a tyrant of men, seeking to harm me.' His feet carried him on, the one bleeding with the arrow of love, and his heart lamented. Then he came to a garden wall, and with untold pain he scaled it, for it proved very high; and forgetting his life, he threw himself down to the garden.

And there he beheld his beloved with a lamp in her hand, searching for a ring she had lost. When the heart-surrendered lover looked on his ravishing love, he drew a great breath and raised up his hands in prayer, crying: 'O God! Give Thou glory to the watchman, and riches and long life. For the watchman was Gabriel, guiding this poor one; or he was Isráfíl, bringing life to this wretched one!'

Indeed, his words were true, for he had found many a secret justice in this seeming tyranny of the watchman, and seen how many a mercy lay hid behind the veil. Out of wrath, the guard had led him who was athirst in love's desert to the sea of his loved one, and lit up the dark night of absence with the light of reunion. He had driven one who was afar, into the garden of nearness, had guided an ailing soul to the heart's physician.

Now if the lover could have looked ahead, he would have blessed the watchman at the start, and prayed on his behalf, and he would have seen that tyranny as justice; but since the end was veiled to him, he moaned and made his plaint in the beginning. Yet those who journey in the garden land of knowledge, because they see the end in the beginning, see peace in war and friendliness in anger.

Such is the state of the wayfarers in this Valley . . . [139]

In the later Baghdad period when the Iranian clerics had gathered in Kazimayn to decide what to do about Baha'u'llah and danger threatened on all sides, a certain Sayyid Husayn Mutavalli Qumi, who was a Babi but had betrayed his co-religionists on more than one occasion, wrote to Baha'u'llah, urging him to leave Baghdad for a time as his life was in danger. Baha'u'llah's response is contained in a tablet that begins with a couplet from the Persian poet Hafiz:

> Sweetened become the mouths of India's parrots withal
> From this Persian candy that has gone forth to Bengal

In the tablet itself Baha'u'llah describes all of the schemes that had been hatched against him and responds to these thus:

> We are incandescent as a candle . . . We have burnt all the veils,
> We have lighted the fire of love . . . We shall not run away, We
> shall not endeavour to repel the stranger, We pray for calamity
> . . . What doth a soul celestial care if the physical frame is
> destroyed; indeed, this body is for it a prison . . . Until the time
> ordained cometh no one hath power over Us, and when the
> ordained time cometh it will find Our whole being longing
> for it.[140]

One of Baha'u'llah's most well known books is a series of epigrams known as the Hidden Words. The opening words of this book proclaim it to be a condensation of the spiritual teachings of the previous prophets of God:

> He is the Glory of Glories
> That is that which hath descended from the realm of glory,
> uttered by the tongue of power and might, and revealed unto the
> Prophets of old. We have taken the inner essence thereof and
> clothed it in the garment of brevity, as a token of grace unto the
> righteous, that they may stand faithful unto the Covenant of
> God, may fulfill in their lives His trust, and in the realm of spirit
> obtain the gem of Divine virtue.

The individual Hidden Words are mainly on mystical and ethical themes and are written in Arabic and Persian. The book is from about 1857–8 (Baha'u'llah was inspired with these words while walking the banks of the Tigris) and the following are the first three of the Arabic Hidden Words and the first of the Persian Hidden Words to give some idea of their style:

The Hidden Words. This page has the opening words of the
Hidden Words: "He is the Glory of Glories! This is that which
hath descended . . ." and most of the first of the Arabic Hidden
Words: "O Son of Spirit! My first counsel is this . . ."
(see p. 162). The calligraphy is that of Mishkin Qalam,
one of the companions-in-exile of Baha'u'llah and among
the finest calligraphers of his time

O Son of Spirit!
My first counsel is this: Possess a pure, kindly and radiant heart, that thine may be a sovereignty ancient, imperishable and ever-lasting.

O Son of Spirit!
The best beloved of all things in My sight is Justice; turn not away therefrom if thou desirest Me, and neglect it not that I may confide in thee. By its aid thou shalt see with thine own eyes and not through the eyes of others, and shalt know of thine own knowledge and not through the knowledge of thy neighbour. Ponder this in thy heart; how it behooveth thee to be. Verily justice is My gift to thee and the sign of My loving-kindness. Set it then before thine eyes.

O Son of Man!
Veiled in My immemorial being and in the ancient eternity of My essence, I knew My love for thee; therefore I created thee, have engraved on thee Mine image and revealed to thee My beauty.

O Ye People That Have Minds to Know and Ears to Hear!
The first call of the Beloved is this: O mystic nightingale! Abide not but in the rose-garden of the spirit. O messenger of the Solomon of love! Seek thou no shelter except in the Sheba of the well-beloved, and O immortal phoenix! Dwell not save on the mount of faithfulness. Therein is thy habitation, if on the wings of thy soul thou soarest to the realm of the infinite and seekest to attain thy goal.[141]

The most important work of Baha'u'llah from this period was however the Kitáb-i Íqán (Book of Certitude). This book was written in January 1861 for the uncle of the Bab who like most of the other kinsmen of the Bab had never become a Babi. This uncle of the Bab was visiting Baghdad and came to see Baha'u'llah. Baha'u'llah asked him what it was that prevented his belief in the mission of his nephew. The Bab's uncle responded with a list of points mainly revolving around the ful-filment of prophecy and the finality of the prophethood of Muhammad. Within forty-eight hours, Baha'u'llah had composed this book in response. In it, Baha'u'llah sets forth the proofs for the truth of the Bab's claim; although in fact exactly the same proofs apply to his own claim which he advanced just over two years after this book was produced. He explains that the prophecies contained in the scriptures of the world must be understood to be referring to spiritual truths and not literal physical reality and that moreover these spiritual truths have multifaceted meanings and can be understood at many different levels. For example, he explains the prophecy that appears in the Gospels, 'Immediately after the oppression of those days shall the sun be darkened, and the moon shall not give her light, and the stars shall fall from heaven, and the powers of the earth shall be shaken: and then shall appear the sign of the Son of man in heaven . . .'[142] thus:

> As to the words – 'Immediately after the oppression of those days' – they refer to the time when men shall become oppressed and afflicted, the time when the lingering traces of the Sun of Truth and the fruit of the Tree of knowledge and wisdom will have vanished from the midst of men, when the reins of mankind will have fallen into the grasp of the foolish and igno-rant, when the portals of divine unity and understanding – the essential and highest purpose in creation – will have been closed, when certain knowledge will have given way to idle fancy, and corruption will have usurped the station of right-eousness. Such a condition as this is witnessed in this day when the reins of every community have fallen into the grasp of fool-ish leaders, who lead after their own whims and desire. On their tongue the mention of God hath become an empty name; in their midst His holy Word a dead letter . . . in spite of all these manifold revelations of divine knowledge, which have encom-passed the world, they still vainly imagine the door of knowl-edge to be closed, and the showers of mercy to be stilled . . .
>
> What 'oppression' is greater than that which hath been recounted? What 'oppression' is more grievous than that a soul seeking the truth, and wishing to attain unto the knowledge of God, should know not where to go for it and from whom to seek it? For opinions have sorely differed, and the ways unto the

attainment of God have multiplied. This 'oppression' is the essential feature of every Revelation. Unless it cometh to pass, the Sun of Truth will not be made manifest. For the break of the morn of divine guidance must needs follow the darkness of the night of error. For this reason, in all chronicles and traditions reference hath been made unto these things, namely that iniquity shall cover the surface of the earth and darkness shall envelop mankind.[143]

Baha'u'llah then goes on to give several explanations of the words 'sun' and 'moon' and their 'darkening' in this prophecy: that they refer to the prophets and saints of each religious dispensation who are superceded with the coming of the next dispensation; that they refer to the teachings and laws of each of the founders of the world's religions that are 'darkened' because they no longer act as guides for humanity; that they refer to the clerics and divines of each religion who with the coming of the next teacher from God pass from being the sources of spiritual guidance to being the main obstacle that prevents the people from recognizing the new teacher and are thus 'darkened'. Baha'u'llah continues with similar interpretations of the other words of this prophecy and other significant terms such as 'Day of Resurrection' and 'return'. He states that these abstruse and hidden meanings are intended as Divine tests for humanity to determine who is following the true spirit of the teachings of God (and thus discerns the new teaching when it comes) and who is only following the outward form of religion (and rejects the new revelation when it comes). In particular, Baha'u'llah demonstrates that each religion has thought that its scriptures and teaching represent the final and highest level of Divine truth whereas in fact they are all part of an evolving and progressive revelation of God's Will.

Another of Baha'u'llah's works from this period, the Gems of Divine Mysteries, repeats some of the themes of the Book of Certitude as well as of the Seven Valleys. It was written at the request of an Iranian cleric resident in Karbala[144] who had come to hear of Baha'u'llah's fame and asked for a treatise on the signs of the expected messianic figure of Islam, the Mahdi. Here and there in this work as well as other works from this period, Baha'u'llah hints at the claim that he is at this stage concealing but which he will at the end of this period reveal:

> Gracious God! But for fear of the Nimrod of tyranny and for the protection of the Abraham of justice, I would reveal unto thee that which, wert thou to abandon self and desire, would enable thee to dispense with aught else and to draw nigh unto this city. Be patient, however, until such time as God will have proclaimed His Cause. He, verily, rewardeth beyond measure them that endure with patience.[145]

Finally from this period, we will briefly quote from a tablet of Baha'u'llah that, despite the limitations of translation, gives some hint of the rhyming and incantatory nature of many of Baha'u'llah's writings from this period. The Tablet of the Holy Mariner portrays in mystical form the call of the Manifestations of God, who are in this tablet portrayed as the Holy Mariner, and humanity's opposition to this call, more specifically the opposition that arises within the ranks of the followers of the Manifestation (individuals such as Judas Iscariot in Christianity and Devadatta in Buddhism). Given that it was written a few weeks before Baha'u'llah's own declaration of his claim in the Garden of Ridvan, it is interpreted by Baha'is as a prophesy of what would happen to Baha'u'llah himself when he raised his call and was opposed by Azal:

> O Holy Mariner! Bid thine ark of eternity appear before the Celestial Concourse,
> Glorified be my Lord, the All-Glorious! Launch it upon the ancient sea, in His Name, the Most Wondrous,
> Glorified be my Lord, the All-Glorious! And let the angelic spirits enter, in the Name of God, the Most High.
> Glorified be my Lord, the All-Glorious! Unmoor it, then, that it may sail upon the ocean of glory,
> Glorified be my Lord, the All-Glorious! Haply the dwellers therein may attain the retreats of nearness in the everlasting realm.

Glorified be my Lord, the All-Glorious! Having reached the sacred strand, the shore of the crimson seas,

Glorified be my Lord, the All-Glorious! Bid them issue forth and attain this ethereal invisible station, . . .

Glorified be my Lord, the All-Glorious! They passed the grades of worldly limitations and reached that of the divine unity, the centre of heavenly guidance.

Glorified be my Lord, the All-Glorious! They have desired to ascend unto that state which the Lord hath ordained to be above their stations.

Glorified be my Lord, the All-Glorious! Whereupon the burning meteor cast them out from them that abide in the Kingdom of His Presence,

Glorified be my Lord, the All-Glorious! And they heard the Voice of Grandeur raised from behind the unseen pavilion upon the Height of Glory:

Glorified be my Lord, the All-Glorious! 'O guardian angels! Return them to their abode in the world below,'

Glorified be my Lord, the All-Glorious! 'Inasmuch as they have purposed to rise to that sphere which the wings of the celestial dove have never attained;'

Glorified be my Lord, the All-Glorious! 'Whereupon the ship of fancy standeth still which the minds of them that comprehend cannot grasp.'[146]

ISTANBUL AND EDIRNE

There are several works that date from the three months that Baha'u'llah spent in Istanbul. The best know of these is the Tablet of the Bell. This is another incantatory work with much rhyme and rhythm, written on the anniversary of the Declaration of the Bab and announcing Baha'u'llah's own claims (albeit in ambiguous language such that one is uncertain whether he is referring to the Bab or himself). No translations of the Tablets from this period have been published as yet.

The writings of Baha'u'llah from the Edirne period are mainly concerned with Baha'u'llah's open proclamation of his claim. This was made in the first place to Azal. In later years,

Baha'u'llah was repeatedly to issue similar challenges to Azal in words such as these:

> Say: O Yahyá [Azal], produce a single verse, if thou dost possess divinely-inspired knowledge. These words were formerly spoken by My Herald [the Bab] Who at this hour proclaimeth: 'Verily, verily, I am the first to adore Him.' Be fair, O My brother. Art thou able to express thyself when brought face to face with the billowing ocean of Mine utterance? Canst thou unloose thy tongue when confronted with the shrill voice of My Pen? Hast thou any power before the revelations of Mine omnipotence? Judge thou fairly, I adjure thee by God, and call to mind when thou didst stand in the presence of this Wronged One and We dictated to thee the verses of God, the Help in Peril, the Self-Subsisting. Beware lest the source of falsehood withhold thee from the manifest Truth.[147]

Next, Baha'u'llah challenged the Babi community with his claim. In many of his tablets from this period, Baha'u'llah brings forward proofs based on the writings of the Bab and addresses the objections raised by the followers of Azal to his claims. His sole book from this period, the Kitáb-i Badí', the Wondrous Book, is also largely taken up with this theme. In the following passage from the Tablet to Ashraf, Baha'u'llah addresses the Babis who failed to follow him as 'the people of the Bayan' (the Bayan was the principal scripture of the Bab):

> Say: The first and foremost testimony establishing His truth is His own Self. Next to this testimony is His Revelation. For whoso faileth to recognize either the one or the other He hath established the words He hath revealed as proof of His reality and truth. This is, verily, an evidence of His tender mercy unto men. He hath endowed every soul with the capacity to recognize the signs of God. How could He, otherwise, have fulfilled His testimony unto men, if ye be of them that ponder His Cause in their hearts. He will never deal unjustly with any one, neither will He task a soul beyond its power. He, verily, is the Compassionate, the All-Merciful.

Say: So great is the glory of the Cause of God that even the blind can perceive it, how much more they whose sight is sharp, whose vision is pure ... The blind in heart, however, among the people of the Bayán – and to this God is My witness – are impotent, no matter how long the Sun may shine upon them, either to perceive the radiance of its glory, or to appreciate the warmth of its rays.

Say: O people of the Bayán! We have chosen you out of the world to know and recognize Our Self. We have caused you to draw nigh unto the right side of Paradise – the Spot out of which the undying Fire crieth in manifold accents: 'There is none other God besides Me, the All-Powerful, the Most High!' Take heed lest ye allow yourselves to be shut out as by a veil from this Day Star that shineth above the dayspring of the Will of your Lord, the All-Merciful, and whose light hath encompassed both the small and the great. Purge your sight, that ye may perceive its glory with your own eyes, and depend not on the sight of any one except your self, for God hath never burdened any soul beyond its power.[148]

To one of the Babis who opposed him, named Mirza Ahmad Kashani, Baha'u'llah addressed the following words (in the Persian Tablet of Ahmad), admonishing him:

Thine eye is My trust, suffer not the dust of vain desires to becloud its lustre. Thine ear is a sign of My bounty, let not the tumult of unseemly motives turn it away from My Word that encompasseth all creation. Thine heart is My treasury, allow not the treacherous hand of self to rob thee of the pearls which I have treasured therein. Thine hand is a symbol of My loving-kindness, hinder it not from holding fast unto My guarded and hidden Tablets ... Unasked, I have showered upon thee My grace. Unpetitioned, I have fulfilled thy wish. In spite of thy undeserving, I have singled thee out for My richest, My incalculable favours.[149]

Finally, during this period in Edirne, Baha'u'llah continued the process of addressing the kings and leaders of the world (this process was began in Istanbul and completed in 'Akka). In these tablets Baha'u'llah puts forward his claim to be the representative of God on earth and calls on the monarchs and religious leaders of the world to abandon their arms race and make moves towards peace. He warns them that the consequences of ignoring this message will be that they will sink ever deeper into conflict and burden their subjects with more than they can bear. Thus, for example, in the Surih-yi Muluk (Tablet to the Kings) that was written in the Edirne period and addressed to the kings in general, Baha'u'llah writes:

> O kings of the earth! Give ear unto the Voice of God, calling from this sublime, this fruit-laden Tree, that hath sprung out of the Crimson Hill, upon the holy Plain, intoning the words: 'There is none other God but He, the Mighty, the All-Powerful, the All-Wise.' This is a Spot which hath been sanctified by God for those who approach it, a Spot wherein His Voice may be heard from the celestial Tree of Holiness. Fear God, O concourse of kings, and suffer not yourselves to be deprived of this most sublime grace. Fling away, then, the things ye possess, and take fast hold on the Handle of God, the Exalted, the Great . . .
>
> . . . Follow, therefore, that which I speak unto you, and hearken unto it with your hearts, and be not of such as have turned aside. For your glory consisteth not in your sovereignty, but rather in your nearness unto God and your observance of His command as sent down in His holy and preserved Tablets. Should any one of you rule over the whole earth, and over all that lieth within it and upon it, its seas, its lands, its mountains, and its plains, and yet be not remembered by God, all these would profit him not, could ye but know it.
>
> Compose your differences and reduce your armaments, that the burden of your expenditures may be lightened, and that your minds and hearts may be tranquillized. Heal the dissensions that divide you, and ye will no longer be in need of any armaments except what the protection of your cities and territories demandeth. Fear ye God, and take heed not to outstrip the bounds of moderation and be numbered among the extravagant.
>
> We have learned that ye are increasing your outlay every year, and are laying the burden thereof on your subjects. This, verily, is more than they can bear, and is a grievous injustice . . .

Beware not to deal unjustly with anyone that appealeth to you and entereth beneath your shadow. Walk ye in the fear of God, and be ye of them that lead a godly life. Rest not on your power, your armies, and treasures. Put your whole trust and confidence in God, Who hath created you, and seek ye His help in all your affairs. Succour cometh from Him alone. He succoureth whom He willeth with the hosts of the heavens and of the earth.

Know ye that the poor are the trust of God in your midst. Watch that ye betray not His trust, that ye deal not unjustly with them and that ye walk not in the ways of the treacherous. Ye will most certainly be called upon to answer for His trust on the day when the Balance of Justice shall be set, the day when unto everyone shall be rendered his due, when the doings of all men, be they rich or poor, shall be weighed . . .

O kings of Christendom! Heard ye not the saying of Jesus, the Spirit of God, 'I go away, and come again unto you'? Wherefore, then, did ye fail, when He did come again unto you in the clouds of heaven, to draw nigh unto Him, that ye might behold His face, and be of them that attained His Presence? In another passage He saith: 'When He, the Spirit of Truth, is come, He will guide you into all truth.' And yet behold how, when He did bring the truth, ye refused to turn your faces towards Him, and persisted in disporting yourselves with your pastimes and fancies.[150]

The Tablet to Nasiru'd-Din Shah of Iran was also written during this period although it was not sent until the 'Akka period. In this Baha'u'llah asserts that his message is not from him but from God. He also refutes some of the allegations that had been made against him:

O King! I was but a man like others, asleep upon My couch, when lo, the breezes of the All-Glorious were wafted over Me, and taught Me the knowledge of all that hath been. This thing is not from Me, but from One Who is Almighty and All-Knowing. And He bade Me lift up My voice between earth and heaven, and for this there befell Me what hath caused the tears of every man of understanding to flow. The learning current amongst men I studied not; their schools I entered not. Ask of the city wherein I dwelt, that thou mayest be well assured that I am not of them who speak falsely. This is but a leaf which the winds of the will of thy Lord, the Almighty, the All-Praised, have stirred. Can it be still when the tempestuous winds are blowing? Nay, by Him Who is the Lord of all Names and Attributes! They move it as they list . . .

Amongst the people are those who allege that this Youth hath had no purpose but to perpetuate His name, whilst others claim that He hath sought for Himself the vanities of the world – this, notwithstanding that never, throughout all My days, have I found a place of safety, be it to the extent of a single foothold. At all times have I been immersed in an ocean of tribulations, whose full measure none can fathom but God. He, truly, is aware of what I say. How many the days in which My loved ones have been sorely shaken by reason of My afflictions, and how many the nights during which My kindred, fearing for My life, have bitterly wept and lamented! And this none can deny save them that are bereft of truthfulness. Is it conceivable that He Who expecteth to lose His life at any moment should seek after worldly vanities? How very strange the imaginings of those who speak as prompted by their own caprices, and who wander distractedly in the wilderness of self and passion! Erelong shall they be called upon to account for their words, and on that day they shall find none to befriend or help them.[151]

And in this same letter, Baha'u'llah writes to the shah of the persecutions to which his followers have been subjected:

It is clear and evident that, whether this Cause be seen as right or wrong by the people, those who are associated with its name have accepted and embraced it as true, and have forsaken their all in their eagerness to partake of the things of God. That they should evince such renunciation in the path of the love of the All-Merciful is in itself a faithful witness and an eloquent testimony to the truth of their convictions. Hath it ever been witnessed that a man of sound judgement should sacrifice his life without cause or reason? And if it be suggested that this people have taken leave of their senses, this too is highly improbable, inasmuch as such behaviour hath not been confined to merely a soul or two – nay, a vast multitude of every class have drunk their fill of the living waters of divine knowledge, and, intoxicated, have hastened with heart and soul to the field of sacrifice in the way of the Beloved.

If these souls, who have renounced all else but God for His sake and offered up their life and substance in His path, are to be accounted as false, then by what proof and testimony can the truth of what others assert be established in thy presence? . . .

For more than twenty years this people have, day and night, been subjected to the fury of the Sovereign's wrath, and have been scattered by the tempestuous gales of his displeasure, each to a different land. How many the children who have been left fatherless, and how many the fathers who have lost their sons! How many the mothers who have dared not, out of fear and dread, to mourn their slaughtered offspring! How numerous those who, at eventide, were possessed of utmost wealth and affluence, and who, when morning came, had fallen into utter abasement and destitution! No land is there whose soil hath not been tinged with their blood, nor reach of heaven unto which their sighs have not ascended. Throughout the years the darts of affliction have unceasingly rained down from the clouds of God's decree, yet despite all these calamities and tribulations, the flame of divine love hath so blazed in their hearts that even should their bodies be torn asunder they would not forsake their love of Him Who is the Best-Beloved of the worlds, but would welcome with heart and soul whatever might befall them in the path of God.[152]

The Tablet of the Branch was also composed in Edirne. One of the images that Baha'u'llah frequently uses, as mentioned before, is that of the Sadratu'l-Muntaha, the tree at the endpoint beyond which there is no passing, a tree which is the guide and goal of the spiritual traveller. It is a metaphor for the prophet or Manifestation of God. Extending this metaphor, Baha'u'llah called his sons the Branches (*aghsán*) and his daughters Leaves (*varaqát*). The Tablet of the Branch from this period presages the high station that was to be given to Baha'u'llah's son 'Abdu'l-Baha (the Most Great Branch) in the Kitab-i Aqdas and Baha'u'llah's Book of the Covenant (see pp. 180, 190).

THE EARLY 'AKKA PERIOD

Baha'u'llah arrived in 'Akka a prisoner. Reflecting on this imprisonment, Baha'u'llah wrote in the Surat al-Bayan:

> The Ancient Beauty [Baha'u'llah] hath consented to be bound with chains that mankind may be released from its bondage, and hath accepted to be made a prisoner within this most mighty Stronghold that the whole world may attain unto true liberty. He hath drained to its dregs the cup of sorrow, that all the peoples of the earth may attain unto abiding joy, and be filled with gladness. This is of the mercy of your Lord, the Compassionate, the Most Merciful. We have accepted to be abased, O believers in the Unity of God, that ye may be exalted, and have suffered manifold afflictions, that ye might prosper and flourish. He Who hath come to build anew the whole world, behold, how they that have joined partners with God have forced Him to dwell within the most desolate of cities![153]

At a time in late 1871, when his external enemies appeared to have achieved their purpose in cutting him off from communication with his followers and harassing him, and even his own followers were about to betray his teachings by their murder of the three Azalis in 'Akka, Baha'u'llah penned a powerful lament in which he describes his sense of being isolated and a victim of intense persecution. This tablet in the original has, as do many of Baha'u'llah's writings, both a rhyme and a rhythm which is difficult to capture in English translation. It is called in English the Fire Tablet:

> Indeed the hearts of the sincere are consumed in the fire of separation:
> Where is the gleaming of the light of Thy Countenance, O Beloved of the worlds?

Those who are near unto Thee have been abandoned in the darkness of desolation:
> Where is the shining of the morn of Thy reunion, O Desire of the worlds?

The bodies of Thy chosen ones lie quivering on distant sands:
> Where is the ocean of Thy presence, O Enchanter of the worlds? . . .

The infidels have arisen in tyranny on every hand:
> Where is the compelling power of Thine ordaining pen, O Conqueror of the worlds? . . .

Thou seest this Wronged One lonely in exile:
> Where are the hosts of the heaven of Thy Command, O Sovereign of the worlds?

I have been forsaken in a foreign land:
> Where are the emblems of Thy faithfulness, O Trust of the worlds? . . .

Thou seest Me forbidden to speak forth:
> Then from where will spring Thy melodies, O Nightingale of the worlds?

Most of the people are enwrapped in fancy and idle imaginings:
> Where are the exponents of Thy certitude, O Assurance of the worlds?

Bahá is drowning in a sea of tribulation:
> Where is the Ark of Thy salvation, O Saviour of the worlds? . . .

O Supreme Pen, We have heard Thy most sweet call in the eternal realm: Give Thou ear unto what the Tongue of Grandeur uttereth, O Wronged One of the worlds?

Were it not for the cold, how would the heat of Thy words prevail, O Expounder of the worlds?

Were it not for calamity, how would the sun of Thy patience shine, O Light of the worlds?

Lament not because of the wicked. Thou wert created to bear and endure, O Patience of the worlds.

How sweet was Thy dawning on the horizon of the Covenant among the stirrers of sedition, and Thy yearning after God, O Love of the worlds.

By Thee the banner of independence was planted on the highest peaks, and the sea of bounty surged, O Rapture of the worlds.

By Thine aloneness the Sun of Oneness shone, and by Thy banishment the land of Unity was adorned. Be patient, O Thou Exile of the worlds ...

When the swords flash, go forward! When the shafts fly, press onward! O Thou Sacrifice of the worlds.

Dost Thou wail, or shall I wail? Rather shall I weep at the fewness of Thy champions, O Thou Who hast caused the wailing of the worlds.

Verily, I have heard Thy call, O All-Glorious Beloved; and now is the face of Baha flaming with the heat of tribulation and with the fire of Thy shining word, and He hath risen up in faithfulness at the place of sacrifice, looking toward Thy pleasure, O Ordainer of the worlds.[154]

In 'Akka, Baha'u'llah continued his proclamatory letters to the kings and leaders of the world. In his second letter to the Emperor Napoleon III of France (the first was sent from Edirne), he addressed that monarch thus:

O King of Paris! Tell the priests to ring the bells no longer. By God, the True One! The Most Mighty Bell hath appeared in the form of Him Who is the Most Great Name, and the fingers of the Will of Thy Lord, the Most Exalted, the Most High, toll it out in the heaven of Immortality in His name, the All-Glorious. Thus have the mighty verses of Thy Lord been again sent down unto thee, that thou mayest arise to remember God, the Creator of earth and heaven, in these days when all the tribes of the earth have mourned, and the foundations of the cities have trembled, and the dust of irreligion hath enwrapped all men, except such as God, the All-Knowing, the All-Wise, was pleased to spare. Say: He Who is the Unconstrained is come, in the clouds of light, that He may quicken the world with the breezes of His name, the Most Merciful, and unify its peoples, and gather all men around this Table which hath been sent down from heaven. Beware that ye deny not the favour of God after it hath been sent down unto you. Better is this for you than that which ye possess; for that which is yours perisheth, whilst that which is with God endureth.[155]

Baha'u'llah condemns Napoleon's justification for going to war with Russia (the Crimean War of 1853–56), and prophesies that he will be punished for his hypocrisy and loose his kingdom – a prophecy that was realised at the battle of Sedan in 1870, when Napoleon was defeated by Prussia and was forced into exile.

> O King! We heard the words thou didst utter in answer to the Czar of Russia, concerning the decision made regarding the war. Thy Lord, verily, knoweth, is informed of all. Thou didst say: 'I lay asleep upon my couch, when the cry of the oppressed, who were drowned in the Black Sea, wakened me.' This is what We heard thee say, and, verily, thy Lord is witness unto what I say. We testify that that which wakened thee was not their cry but the promptings of thine own passions, for We tested thee, and found thee wanting . . .
>
> For what thou hast done, thy kingdom shall be thrown into confusion, and thine empire shall pass from thine hands, as a punishment for that which thou hast wrought. Then wilt thou know how thou hast plainly erred. Commotions shall seize all the people in that land, unless thou arisest to help this Cause, and followest Him Who is the Spirit of God in this, the Straight Path. Hath thy pomp made thee proud? By My Life! It shall not endure; nay, it shall soon pass away, unless thou holdest fast to this firm Cord. We see abasement hastening after thee, whilst thou art of the heedless.[156]

Since France was the main protector of the Roman Catholic Church within the Ottoman Empire, Baha'u'llah also addresses the monks of Christendom in this same tablet:

> Say: O concourse of monks! Seclude not yourselves in your churches and cloisters. Come ye out of them by My leave, and busy, then, yourselves with what will profit you and others. Thus commandeth you He Who is the Lord of the Day of Reckoning. Seclude yourselves in the stronghold of My love. This, truly, is the seclusion that befitteth you, could ye but know it. He that secludeth himself in his house is indeed as one dead. It behoveth man to show forth that which will benefit mankind.

He that bringeth forth no fruit is fit for the fire. Thus admonisheth you your Lord; He, verily, is the Mighty, the Bountiful.[157]

In his letter to Czar Alexander II of Russia, Baha'u'llah accords the Czar a high station as recognition of the help which the Russian Ambassador had given Baha'u'llah in Tehran but warns the Czar not to barter this away.

> O Czar of Russia! Incline thine ear unto the voice of God, the King, the Holy, and turn thou unto Paradise, the Spot wherein abideth He Who, among the Concourse on high, beareth the most excellent titles, and Who, in the kingdom of creation, is called by the name of God, the Effulgent, the All-Glorious . . . Whilst I lay chained and fettered in the prison, one of thy ministers extended Me his aid. Wherefore hath God ordained for thee a station which the knowledge of none can comprehend except His knowledge. Beware lest thou barter away this sublime station.[158]

With Queen Victoria, on the other hand, Baha'u'llah adopts a much milder tone than he does with the other sovereigns. He commends her for two actions of the British government, its efforts to halt the slave trade and the movement towards democracy.

> O Queen in London! Incline thine ear unto the voice of thy Lord, the Lord of all mankind, calling from the Divine Lote-Tree: Verily, no God is there but Me, the Almighty, the All-Wise! Cast away all that is on earth, and attire the head of thy kingdom with the crown of the remembrance of thy Lord, the All-Glorious. He, in truth, hath come unto the world in His most great glory, and all that hath been mentioned in the Gospel hath been fulfilled. The land of Syria hath been honoured by the footsteps of its Lord, the Lord of all men, and north and south are both inebriated with the wine of His presence.
>
> We have been informed that thou hast forbidden the trading in slaves, both men and women. This, verily, is what God hath enjoined in this wondrous Revelation. God hath, truly, destined a

reward for thee, because of this. He, verily, will pay the doer of
good his due recompense . . .

We have also heard that thou hast entrusted the reins of
counsel into the hands of the representatives of the people.
Thou, indeed, hast done well, for thereby the foundations of the
edifice of thine affairs will be strengthened, and the hearts of all
that are beneath thy shadow, whether high or low, will be tran-
quillized. It behoveth them, however, to be trustworthy among
His servants, and to regard themselves as the representatives of
all that dwell on earth. This is what counselleth them, in this
Tablet, He Who is the Ruler, the All-Wise.[159]

In this tablet, Baha'u'llah states that since the rulers of the
world have rejected his plan for the Most Great Peace (peace on
a spiritual basis brought about through the teachings of
Baha'u'llah), they should strive for the Lesser Peace (which is a
political peace to be brought about by political negotiation)
and he lays out the principle of collective security for achieving
that.

Now that ye have refused the Most Great Peace, hold ye fast
unto this, the Lesser Peace, that haply ye may in some degree
better your own condition and that of your dependents.

O rulers of the earth! Be reconciled among yourselves, that ye
may need no more armaments save in a measure to safeguard
your territories and dominions. Beware lest ye disregard the
counsel of the All-Knowing, the Faithful.

Be united, O kings of the earth, for thereby will the tempest of
discord be stilled amongst you, and your peoples find rest, if ye
be of them that comprehend. Should any one among you take
up arms against another, rise ye all against him, for this is
naught but manifest justice.[160]

In his later writings, Baha'u'llah calls on the kings and leaders of
the world to convene an international conference at which a
treaty binding on all nations would be agreed whereby this principle of collective security (see p. 211) would be implemented,
thus allowing all nations to divert expenditure away from
weapons and towards reconstruction and development.

To Pope Pius IX, who was one of the most notable popes in history and established the doctrine of papal infallibility, Baha'u'llah announced his claim to be the one promised in the Gospels, the return of Christ in the glory of the Father.

> O Pope! Rend the veils asunder. He Who is the Lord of Lords is come overshadowed with clouds, and the decree hath been fulfilled by God, the Almighty, the Unrestrained . . . He, verily, hath again come down from Heaven even as He came down from it the first time. Beware that thou dispute not with Him even as the Pharisees disputed with Him without a clear token or proof.
>
> Consider those who opposed the Son, when He came unto them with sovereignty and power. How many the Pharisees who were waiting to behold Him, and were lamenting over their separation from Him! And yet, when the fragrance of His coming was wafted over them, and His beauty was unveiled, they turned aside from Him and disputed with Him. Thus do We impart unto thee that which hath been recorded in the Books and Scriptures. None save a very few, who were destitute of any power amongst men, turned towards His [Jesus'] face. And yet today every man endowed with power and invested with sovereignty prideth himself on His Name! In like manner, consider how numerous, in these days, are the monks who, in My Name, have secluded themselves in their churches, and who, when the appointed time was fulfilled, and We unveiled Our beauty, knew Us not, though they call upon Me at eventide and at dawn. We behold them clinging to My name, yet veiled from My Self. This, verily, is a strange thing.
>
> The Word which the Son concealed is made manifest. It hath been sent down in the form of the human temple in this day. Blessed be the Lord Who is the Father! He, verily, is come unto the nations in His most great majesty. Turn your faces towards Him, O concourse of the righteous!
>
> This is the day whereon the Rock [Peter] crieth out and shouteth, and celebrateth the praise of its Lord, the All-Possessing, the Most High, saying: 'Lo! The Father is come, and that which ye were promised in the Kingdom is fulfilled!' This is the Word which was preserved behind the veils of grandeur, and

which, when the Promise came to pass, shed its radiance from the horizon of the Divine Will with clear tokens.

O Supreme Pontiff! Incline thine ear unto that which the Fashioner of mouldering bones counselleth thee, as voiced by Him Who is His Most Great Name. Sell all the embellished ornaments thou dost possess, and expend them in the path of God, Who causeth the night to return upon the day, and the day to return upon the night. Abandon thy kingdom unto the kings, and emerge from thy habitation, with thy face set towards the Kingdom, and, detached from the world, then speak forth the praises of thy Lord betwixt earth and heaven. Thus hath bidden thee He Who is the Possessor of Names, on the part of thy Lord, the Almighty, the All-Knowing.[161]

In 1873, Baha'u'llah completed his most important book, the Kitab-i Aqdas. In this book, Baha'u'llah lays down the laws of his religion, such as those of prayer, fasting, marriage, divorce and burial. He lays certain obligations upon his followers, such as obedience to government, the education of children, and engaging in a trade or profession, and abrogates a number of the social and religious institutions of the past, such as slavery, begging, carrying arms unless essential, priesthood, the concept of ritual uncleanness or impurity, the confession of sins to another human being and monasticism. He institutes the successorship and bestows upon his successor (whom he later in the Book of the Covenant identifies as 'Abdu'l-Baha) the function of being the authoritative interpreter of Baha'u'llah's writings, thus ensuring that after him disagreements over the correct interpretation of the scripture do not cause schism in the Baha'i community as they have in other religious communities. He also institutes the 'House of Justice' and defines its functions.

Shoghi Effendi, who was appointed leader of the Baha'i Community in succession to 'Abdu'l-Baha, gives this assessment of the importance and historical position of that work:

Unique and stupendous as was this Proclamation [to the kings and leaders of the world], it proved to be but a prelude to a still mightier revelation of the creative power of its Author, and to what may well rank as the most signal act of His ministry – the promulgation of the Kitáb-i-Aqdas. Alluded to in the Kitáb-i-Íqán; the principal repository of that Law which the Prophet Isaiah had anticipated, and which the writer of the Apocalypse had described as the 'new heaven' and the 'new earth,' as 'the Tabernacle of God,' as the 'Holy City,' as the 'Bride,' the 'New Jerusalem coming down from God,' this 'Most Holy Book,' whose provisions must remain inviolate for no less than a thousand years, and whose system will embrace the entire planet, may well be regarded as the brightest emanation of the mind of Bahá'u'lláh, as the Mother Book of His Dispensation, and the Charter of His New World Order.[162]

The first two verses of the Kitab-i Aqdas summarise two of the most important Baha'i teachings: the need to recognize the Manifestation of God and to follow his teachings:

> The first duty prescribed by God for His servants is the recognition of Him Who is the Dayspring of His Revelation and the Fountain of His laws, Who representeth the Godhead in both the Kingdom of His Cause and the world of creation. Whoso achieveth this duty hath attained unto all good; and whoso is deprived thereof hath gone astray, though he be the author of every righteous deed. It behoveth every one who reacheth this most sublime station, this summit of transcendent glory, to observe every ordinance of Him Who is the Desire of the world. These twin duties are inseparable. Neither is acceptable without the other. Thus hath it been decreed by Him Who is the Source of Divine inspiration.
>
> They whom God hath endued with insight will readily recognize that the precepts laid down by God constitute the highest means for the maintenance of order in the world and the security of its peoples. He that turneth away from them is accounted among the abject and foolish. We, verily, have commanded you to refuse the dictates of your evil passions and corrupt desires, and not to transgress the bounds which the Pen of the Most High hath fixed, for these are the breath of life unto all created things. The seas of Divine wisdom and Divine utterance have risen under the breath of the breeze of the All-Merciful. Hasten

to drink your fill, O men of understanding! They that have violated the Covenant of God by breaking His commandments, and have turned back on their heels, these have erred grievously in the sight of God, the All-Possessing, the Most High.[163]

Among the numerous different subjects dealt with in this book is a condemnation of all those who seek spiritual progress and religious leadership with insincere motives and hypocrisy in their hearts:

Amongst the people is he who seateth himself amid the sandals by the door whilst coveting in his heart the seat of honour. Say: What manner of man art thou, O vain and heedless one, who wouldst appear as other than thou art? And among the people is he who layeth claim to inner knowledge, and still deeper knowledge concealed within this knowledge. Say: Thou speakest false! By God! What thou dost possess is naught but husks which We have left to thee as bones are left to dogs. By the righteousness of the one true God! Were anyone to wash the feet of all mankind, and were he to worship God in the forests, valleys, and mountains, upon high hills and lofty peaks, to leave no rock or tree, no clod of earth, but was a witness to his worship – yet, should the fragrance of My good pleasure not be inhaled from him, his works would never be acceptable unto God. Thus hath it been decreed by Him Who is the Lord of all. How many a man hath secluded himself in the climes of India, denied himself the things that God hath decreed as lawful, imposed upon himself austerities and mortifications, and hath not been remembered by God, the Revealer of Verses. Make not your deeds as snares wherewith to entrap the object of your aspiration, and deprive not yourselves of this Ultimate Objective for which have ever yearned all such as have drawn nigh unto God . . .

Amongst the people is he whose learning hath made him proud, and who hath been debarred thereby from recognizing My Name, the Self-Subsisting; who, when he heareth the tread of sandals following behind him, waxeth greater in his own esteem than Nimrod . . .

O concourse of divines! When My verses were sent down, and My clear tokens were revealed, We found you behind the veils.

> This, verily, is a strange thing. Ye glory in My Name, yet ye recognized Me not at the time your Lord, the All-Merciful, appeared amongst you with proof and testimony. We have rent the veils asunder. Beware lest ye shut out the people by yet another veil.[164]

Instead, people are enjoined to detach themselves from the things of this world and strive to acquire spiritual virtues:

> Say: Rejoice not in the things ye possess; tonight they are yours, tomorrow others will possess them. Thus warneth you He Who is the All-Knowing, the All-Informed. Say: Can ye claim that what ye own is lasting or secure? Nay! By Myself, the All-Merciful, ye cannot, if ye be of them who judge fairly. The days of your life flee away as a breath of wind, and all your pomp and glory shall be folded up as were the pomp and glory of those gone before you . . . Happy the days that have been consecrated to the remembrance of God, and blessed the hours which have been spent in praise of Him Who is the All-Wise. By My life! Neither the pomp of the mighty, nor the wealth of the rich, nor even the ascendancy of the ungodly will endure. All will perish, at a word from Him. He, verily, is the All-Powerful, the All-Compelling, the Almighty . . .
>
> Adorn your heads with the garlands of trustworthiness and fidelity, your hearts with the attire of the fear of God, your tongues with absolute truthfulness, your bodies with the vesture of courtesy. These are in truth seemly adornings unto the temple of man, if ye be of them that reflect.[165]

Typical of the words of Baha'u'llah is the following passage in which he links a social principle, prohibition of trading in slaves, with a spiritual principle, the equality of all human beings before God:

> It is forbidden you to trade in slaves, be they men or women. It is not for him who is himself a servant to buy another of God's servants, and this hath been prohibited in His Holy Tablet. Thus, by His mercy, hath the commandment been recorded by the Pen of justice. Let no man exalt himself above another; all are but bondslaves before the Lord, and all exemplify the truth that there is none other God but Him. He, verily, is the All-Wise, Whose wisdom encompasseth all things.[166]

One of the most far-reaching of the changes made in this book is the abolition of the very concept of impurity and uncleanness which is the source of much prejudice and religious fanaticism in the world:

> God hath, likewise, as a bounty from His presence, abolished the concept of 'uncleanness', whereby divers things and peoples have been held to be impure. He, of a certainty, is the Ever-Forgiving, the Most Generous. Verily, all created things were immersed in the sea of purification when, on that first day of Ridván, We shed upon the whole of creation the splendours of Our most excellent Names and Our most exalted Attributes. This, verily, is a token of My loving providence, which hath encompassed all the worlds. Consort ye then with the followers of all religions, and proclaim ye the Cause of your Lord, the Most Compassionate; this is the very crown of deeds, if ye be of them who understand.[167]

The Kitab-i Aqdas also can be said to have completed the proclamation of Baha'u'llah's message to the kings and leaders of the world, which had begun a decade previously in 1863 in Istanbul. Several monarchs are addressed in this book. Emperor Franz Joseph of the Austro-Hungarian Empire is chided for having visiting Jerusalem but having ignored Baha'u'lllah. Wilhelm I of Prussia is reminded of the fate that had by this time befallen Napoleon III and advised to reflect upon it. Ominously Baha'u'llah writes: 'O banks of the Rhine! We have seen you covered with gore, inasmuch as the swords of retribution were drawn against you; and you shall have another turn. And We hear the lamentations of Berlin, though she be today in conspicuous glory.'[168] Baha'u'llah also addressed the Rulers and Presidents of the Americas in this book:

> O concourse of rulers! Give ear unto that which hath been raised from the Dayspring of Grandeur: 'Verily, there is none other God but Me, the Lord of Utterance, the All-Knowing.' Bind ye the broken with the hands of justice, and crush the oppressor who flourisheth with the rod of the commandments of your Lord, the Ordainer, the All-Wise.[169]

Associated with the Kitab-i Aqdas are such subsidiary writings as the answers to a series of questions about the text which Baha'u'llah himself commissioned and the texts of the obligatory prayers that Baha'u'llah has said should be recited daily. There are three of these and Baha'is are free to choose any of them. The following is the short obligatory prayer which should be said once daily between noon and sunset:

> I bear witness, O my God, that Thou hast created me to know Thee and to worship Thee. I testify, at this moment, to my powerlessness and to Thy might, to my poverty and to Thy wealth. There is none other God but Thee, the Help in Peril, the Self-Subsisting.[170]

There are numerous other prayers, communes and meditations that Baha'u'llah has given for use whenever Baha'is feel the need to pray individually or communally. Some are for specific purposes but many are general. The following are a few short prayers:

> O my God! O my God! Unite the hearts of Thy servants, and reveal to them Thy great purpose. May they follow Thy commandments and abide in Thy law. Help them, O God, in their endeavor, and grant them strength to serve Thee. O God! Leave them not to themselves, but guide their steps by the light of Thy knowledge, and cheer their hearts by Thy love. Verily, Thou art their Helper and their Lord.[171]

> Thy name is my healing, O my God, and remembrance of Thee is my remedy. Nearness to Thee is my hope, and love for Thee is my companion. Thy mercy to me is my healing and my succour in both this world and the world to come. Thou, verily, art the All-Bountiful, the All-Knowing, the All-Wise.[172]

> Create in me a pure heart, O my God, and renew a tranquil conscience within me, O my Hope! Through the spirit of power confirm Thou me in Thy Cause, O my Best-Beloved, and by the light of Thy glory reveal unto me Thy path, O Thou the Goal of my desire! Through the power of Thy transcendent might lift me up unto the heaven of Thy holiness, O Source of my being, and by the breezes of Thine eternity gladden me, O Thou Who art

my God! Let Thine everlasting melodies breathe tranquillity on me, O my Companion, and let the riches of Thine ancient countenance deliver me from all except Thee, O my Master, and let the tidings of the revelation of Thine incorruptible Essence bring me joy, O Thou Who art the most manifest of the manifest and the most hidden of the hidden![173]

THE LATER 'AKKA PERIOD

In what Baha'u'llah wrote after the Kitab-i Aqdas, he expands on many of the themes in that book and on the social teachings of his religion. In a series of important tablets, such as the Bisharat (Glad Tidings), Tarazat (Ornaments), Tajalliyat (Effulgences), Ishraqat (Splendours), the Words of Paradise and the Tablet of the World, Baha'u'llah expands on themes such as unity, the importance of education and of religion, the role of religion, the need for moderation, the functioning of the Universal House of Justice, the Lesser Peace and the Most Great Peace (see above), prohibition of certain religious activities (such as monasticism, shunning those of other religions and holy war), and various ethical injunctions. The following is a sampling from these tablets:

The twelfth Glad-Tidings
It is enjoined upon every one of you to engage in some form of occupation, such as crafts, trades and the like. We have graciously exalted your engagement in such work to the rank of worship unto God, the True One . . . Waste not your time in idleness and sloth. Occupy yourselves with that which profiteth yourselves and others.

The fifteenth Glad-Tidings
Although a republican form of government profiteth all the peoples of the world, yet the majesty of kingship is one of the signs of God. We do not wish that the countries of the world should remain deprived thereof. If the sagacious combine the two forms into one, great will be their reward in the presence of God.

The second Taraz

is to consort with the followers of all religions in a spirit of friendliness and fellowship, to proclaim that which the Speaker on Sinai hath set forth and to observe fairness in all matters.

The sixth Taraz

Knowledge is one of the wondrous gifts of God. It is incumbent upon everyone to acquire it. Such arts and material means as are now manifest have been achieved by virtue of His knowledge and wisdom . . .

In this Day the secrets of the earth are laid bare before the eyes of men. The pages of swiftly-appearing newspapers are indeed the mirror of the world. They reflect the deeds and the pursuits of divers peoples and kindreds . . . However, it behoveth the writers thereof to be purged from the promptings of evil passions and desires and to be attired with the raiment of justice and equity. They should enquire into situations as much as possible and ascertain the facts, then set them down in writing.

The third Tajalli

is concerning arts, crafts and sciences. Knowledge is as wings to man's life, and a ladder for his ascent. Its acquisition is incumbent upon everyone. The knowledge of such sciences, however, should be acquired as can profit the peoples of the earth, and not those which begin with words and end with words. Great indeed is the claim of scientists and craftsmen on the peoples of the world.

The word of God which the Supreme Pen hath recorded on the sixth leaf of the Most Exalted Paradise is the following:

The light of men is Justice. Quench it not with the contrary winds of oppression and tyranny. The purpose of justice is the appearance of unity among men . . . Verily I say, whatever is sent down from the heaven of the Will of God is the means for the establishment of order in the world and the instrument for promoting unity and fellowship among its peoples.[174]

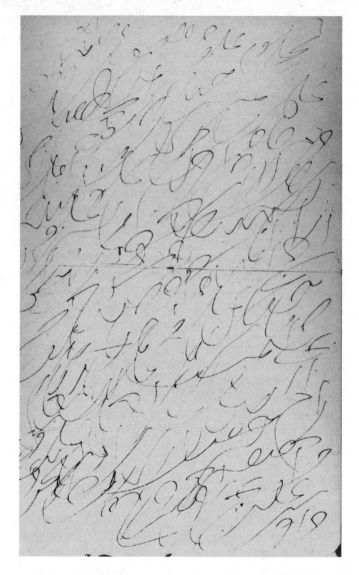

"Revelation Writing". Baha'u'llah would dictate so rapidly that, in order to keep up, his secretary Mirza Aqa Jan developed a special shorthand script that only he could read. The text written here is the Third Tajalli, see p. 187

There were other important tablets such as the Tablet of Wisdom, which deals with philosophical matters; the Most Holy Tablet, addressed to Christians; the Tablet of the Proof, addressed to a senior Iranian cleric who had persecuted the Baha'is and was addressed by Baha'u'llah as 'the Wolf'; and the Words of Wisdom, a series of epigrammatic statements concerned with religious and mystical matters.

During the last of Baha'u'llah's visits to Haifa, in 1891, he went to the cave of Elijah and also, while standing near the Christian monastery there, he recited the Tablet of Carmel, a tablet which was regarded by Shoghi Effendi, Baha'u'llah's second successor, as the charter for the development of the Baha'i World Centre in the Haifa–'Akka area:

> All glory be to this Day, the Day in which the fragrances of mercy have been wafted over all created things, a Day so blest that past ages and centuries can never hope to rival it, a Day in which the countenance of the Ancient of Days hath turned towards His holy seat. Thereupon the voices of all created things, and beyond them those of the Concourse on High, were heard calling aloud: 'Haste thee, O Carmel, for lo, the light of the countenance of God, the Ruler of the Kingdom of Names and Fashioner of the heavens, hath been lifted upon thee.'
>
> Seized with transports of joy, and raising high her voice, she thus exclaimed: 'May my life be a sacrifice to Thee, inasmuch as Thou hast fixed Thy gaze upon me, hast bestowed upon me Thy bounty, and hast directed towards me Thy steps. Separation from Thee, O Thou Source of everlasting life, hath well nigh consumed me, and my remoteness from Thy presence hath burned away my soul. All praise be to Thee for having enabled me to hearken to Thy call, for having honoured me with Thy footsteps, and for having quickened my soul . . .
>
> 'Call out to Zion, O Carmel, and announce the joyful tidings: He that was hidden from mortal eyes is come! His all-conquering sovereignty is manifest; His all-encompassing splendour is revealed. Beware lest thou hesitate or halt. Hasten forth and circumambulate the City of God that hath descended from heaven, the celestial Kaaba round which have circled in adoration the

favoured of God, the pure in heart, and the company of the most
exalted angels . . . Ere long will God sail His Ark upon thee, and
will manifest the people of Bahá who have been mentioned in
the Book of Names.'[175]

It was during 'Abdu'l-Baha's visit to Beirut in 1880 that
Baha'u'llah produced the Tablet of the Land of Ba' (Beirut), a
tablet that clearly portends the successorship and great honours
to be bestowed on 'Abdu'l-Baha. This was then confirmed in
Baha'u'llah's will, the Kitab Ahdi (Book of My Covenant),
which was written at least two years before his passing but only
read out after his passing. This document instituted the doctrine
of the Covenant, which, as will be described later in this book, is
the foundation of the unity of the Baha'i community. In this document, he names 'Abdu'l-Baha (Ghusn-i A'zam, the Most
Mighty Branch) as the one to whom all must turn, the one whom
the Kitab-i Aqdas had stated should be consulted in case of anything in Baha'u'llah's writings that was not understood,
the one about whom the following is stated in the Tablet of the
Branch (see p. 172–3):

> Render thanks unto God, O people, for His appearance; for ver-
> ily He is the most great Favour unto you, the most perfect
> bounty upon you; and through Him every mouldering bone is
> quickened. Whoso turneth towards Him hath turned towards
> God, and whoso turneth away from Him hath turned away
> from My beauty, hath repudiated My Proof, and transgressed
> against Me. He is the Trust of God amongst you, His charge
> within you, His manifestation unto you and His appearance
> among His favoured servants.[176]

The last major work of Baha'u'llah was the Epistle to the Son of
the Wolf. This letter, which is of the proportions of a book, is
addressed to Aqa Najafi, the cleric who, together with his father,
was responsible for most of the persecutions of the Baha'is in the
Isfahan area. This work can be regarded as Baha'u'llah's own
anthology of his writings and a summary of his teachings. Given
that it was addressed to a fanatical Muslim cleric, it is of note

that Baha'u'llah refers in this work to religious fanaticism: 'Religious fanaticism and hatred are a world-devouring fire, whose violence none can quench. The Hand of Divine power can, alone, deliver mankind from this desolating affliction.'[177]

In this work, Baha'u'llah also addresses a number of accusations that had been made against him by the Azalis and by his clerical opponents such as Aqa Najafi. Foremost among the accusations being made by such clerics was that Baha'u'llah had blasphemed by claiming to be God. In this work, Baha'u'llah responds by saying that his statements about Divinity are only intended to depict that, with his own utter self-effacement before God, nothing remains but the Divine names and attributes shining through him. If a Burning Bush can have manifested God in this way in the time of Moses, why not a human being now? He furthermore cites a number of Islamic Traditions that refer to the future appearance of God on earth and asserts that his is the only meaningful explanation of such Traditions.

> O Shaykh! This station is the station in which one dieth to himself and liveth in God. Divinity, whenever I mention it, indicateth My complete and absolute self-effacement. This is the station in which I have no control over mine own weal or woe nor over my life nor over my resurrection.
>
> O Shaykh! How do the divines of this age account for the effulgent glory which the Sadrah [Lote-Tree] of Utterance hath shed upon the Son of 'Imrán [Moses] on the Sinai of Divine knowledge? He [Moses] hearkened unto the Word which the Burning Bush had uttered, and accepted it; and yet most men are bereft of the power of comprehending this, inasmuch as they have busied themselves with their own concerns, and are unaware of the things which belong unto God . . . What explanation can they give concerning that which the Seal of the Prophets [Muhammad] . . . hath said?: 'Ye, verily, shall behold your Lord as ye behold the full moon on its fourteenth night.' . . .
>
> In truth I say, and for the sake of God I declare: This Servant, this Wronged One, is abashed to claim for Himself any existence whatever, how much more those exalted grades of being! Every man of discernment, while walking upon the earth,

feeleth indeed abashed, inasmuch as he is fully aware that the thing which is the source of his prosperity, his wealth, his might, his exaltation, his advancement and power is, as ordained by God, the very earth which is trodden beneath the feet of all men. There can be no doubt that whoever is cognizant of this truth, is cleansed and sanctified from all pride, arrogance, and vain-glory. Whatever hath been said hath come from God. Unto this, He, verily, hath borne, and beareth now, witness, and He, in truth, is the All-Knowing, the All-Informed.[178]

EIGHT

The Claims of Baha'u'llah

Having examined the life of Baha'u'llah and his writings, it is necessary to try to bring together what it was that Baha'u'llah was claiming to be. Baha'u'llah's claim is situated within a picture of the universe which he set out in his writings so in order to understand his claims his view of existence must be understood. Baha'u'llah's claim also needs to be examined historically as it evolved during his lifetime. The following is a necessarily brief and simplified account of this.

THE ULTIMATE REALITY (GOD)

In common with most other religions, Baha'u'llah states that there is a highest reality, which the Western religions call God and the Eastern religions call by different names such as Brahman, Dharma, Shunyata and the Tao. This highest reality is described in different ways in each religion but Baha'u'llah says that this is because human beings whose minds are limited can never comprehend this ultimate reality which is infinite. All descriptions of this ultimate reality are made from a particular viewpoint and are therefore limited by that viewpoint. All descriptions are therefore correct from their viewpoint but are really only partial truths. Baha'u'llah calls this ultimate reality 'God' but states that:

> To every discerning and illuminated heart it is evident that God, the unknowable Essence, the Divine Being, is immensely exalted beyond every human attribute, such as corporeal existence, ascent and descent, egress and regress. Far be it from His glory that human tongue should adequately recount His praise, or that human heart comprehend His fathomless mystery. He is, and hath ever been, veiled in the ancient eternity of His Essence, and will remain in His Reality everlastingly hidden from the sight of men.[179]

Therefore Baha'u'llah states that all those descriptions of God or of the ultimate reality that have been given by religious people down the ages are created in their minds and are therefore a reflection of their minds and not of that reality itself:

> All that the sages and mystics have said or written have never exceeded, nor can they ever hope to exceed, the limitations to which man's finite mind hath been strictly subjected. To whatever heights the mind of the most exalted of men may soar, however great the depths which the detached and understanding heart can penetrate, such mind and heart can never transcend that which is the creature of their own conceptions and the product of their own thoughts. The meditations of the profoundest thinker, the devotions of the holiest of saints, the highest expressions of praise from either human pen or tongue, are but a reflection of that which hath been created within themselves, through the revelation of the Lord, their God. Whoever pondereth this truth in his heart will readily admit that there are certain limits which no human being can possibly transgress. Every attempt which, from the beginning that hath no beginning, hath been made to visualize and know God is limited by the exigencies of His own creation . . . Immeasurably exalted is He above the strivings of human mind to grasp His Essence, or of human tongue to describe His mystery. No tie of direct intercourse can ever bind Him to the things He hath created, nor can the most abstruse and most remote allusions of His creatures do justice to His being.[180]

THE FOUNDERS OF THE WORLD RELIGIONS (THE MANIFESTATIONS OF GOD)

This does not mean to say that there is no connection between this Ultimate Reality and human beings, however. Baha'u'llah states that this Ultimate Reality communicates with humanity through a small number of individuals – those individuals who have been the founders of the major religions of the world. Baha'u'llah describes this relationship thus:

> The door of the knowledge of the Ancient of Days being thus closed in the face of all beings, the Source of infinite grace . . . hath caused those luminous Gems of Holiness to appear out of the realm of the spirit, in the noble form of the human temple, and be made manifest unto all men, that they may impart unto the world the mysteries of the unchangeable Being.[181]

Baha'u'llah states that these individuals, the founders of the world religions, being the channels of communication with the Ultimate Reality, are in effect the representatives of God on earth. They are also the perfect manifestations of all of the Divine names and attributes – names and attributes such as justice, love and patience. They are therefore called the Manifestations of the Names and Attributes of God (Manifestations of God for short) by Baha'u'llah:

> He [God] hath manifested unto men the Day Stars of His divine guidance, the Symbols of His divine unity, and hath ordained the knowledge of these sanctified Beings to be identical with the knowledge of His own Self. Whoso recognizeth them hath recognized God. Whoso hearkeneth to their call, hath hearkened to the Voice of God, and whoso testifieth to the truth of their Revelation, hath testified to the truth of God Himself. Whoso turneth away from them, hath turned away from God, and whoso disbelieveth in them, hath disbelieved in God. Every one of them is the Way of God that connecteth this world with the realms above, and the Standard of His Truth unto every one in the kingdoms of earth and heaven. They are the Manifestations

of God amidst men, the evidences of His Truth, and the signs of His glory.[182]

Because human beings can have no direct access to God and because these Manifestations of God bear the message of God and reflect the names and attributes of God, they are 'as God' in relation to human beings: 'Were any of the all–embracing Manifestations of God to declare: "I am God," He, verily, speaketh the truth, and no doubt attacheth thereto. For it hath been repeatedly demonstrated that through their Revelation, their attributes and names, the Revelation of God, His names and His attributes, are made manifest in the world.'[183]

However Baha'u'llah goes on in this same passage to clarify that this is a statement that is true relative to humanity. In their relationship with God, these Manifestations of God have a position of complete servitude and utter nothingness.

> And were they to say: 'We are the servants of God,' this also is a manifest and indisputable fact. For they have been made manifest in the uttermost state of servitude, a servitude the like of which no man can possibly attain. Thus in moments in which these Essences of being were deeply immersed beneath the oceans of ancient and everlasting holiness, or when they soared to the loftiest summits of divine mysteries, they claimed their utterance to be the Voice of divinity, the Call of God Himself. Were the eye of discernment to be opened, it would recognize that in this very state, they have considered themselves utterly effaced and non–existent in the face of Him Who is the All–Pervading, the Incorruptible. Methinks, they have regarded themselves as utter nothingness, and deemed their mention in that Court an act of blasphemy. For the slightest whispering of self within such a Court is an evidence of self–assertion and independent existence. In the eyes of them that have attained unto that Court, such a suggestion is itself a grievous transgression.[184]

The purpose of these Manifestations of God is to communicate to humanity the guidance that human beings need both for their spiritual and their social life. This function of the Manifestations of God is portrayed in Baha'u'llah's writings in various ways.

For example he gives the analogy of the Manifestation of God as the Divine Physician:

> The Prophets of God should be regarded as physicians whose task is to foster the well-being of the world and its peoples, that, through the spirit of oneness, they may heal the sickness of a divided humanity. To none is given the right to question their words or disparage their conduct, for they are the only ones who can claim to have understood the patient and to have correctly diagnosed its ailments. No man, however acute his perception, can ever hope to reach the heights which the wisdom and understanding of the Divine Physician have attained.[185]

Since these Divine Physicians are the manifestations of the same reality and perform the same function, they can in one sense be regarded as one reality. It is in this sense that there are prophecies in many religions about the return of the founder of that religion (for example, the return of Christ or the return of the Buddha). The coming of each of these Manifestations of God is thus the return of the previous one.

> ... if thou callest them all by one name, and dost ascribe to them the same attributes, thou hast not erred from the truth ... It is clear and evident to thee that all the Prophets are the Temples of the Cause of God, Who have appeared clothed in divers attire. If thou wilt observe with discriminating eyes, thou wilt behold Them all abiding in the same tabernacle, soaring in the same heaven, seated upon the same throne, uttering the same speech, and proclaiming the same Faith. Such is the unity of those Essences of Being, those Luminaries of infinite and immeasurable splendour! Wherefore, should one of these Manifestations of Holiness proclaim saying: 'I am the return of all the Prophets,' He, verily, speaketh the truth. In like manner, in every subsequent Revelation, the return of the former Revelation is a fact, the truth of which is firmly established.[186]

Baha'u'llah sums up the fundamental purpose of the coming of all of the Manifestations of God thus: 'The fundamental purpose animating the Faith of God and His Religion is to safeguard the interests and promote the unity of the human race, and to foster the spirit of love and fellowship amongst men.'[187]

The condition of humanity is however constantly changing and its needs vary from age to age. The means by which these Divine Physicians achieve their fundamental purpose must therefore necessarily change. They must adjust the remedy they give to the needs of humanity in the age in which they come.

> Little wonder, then, if the treatment prescribed by the physician in this day should not be found to be identical with that which he prescribed before. How could it be otherwise when the ills affecting the sufferer necessitate at every stage of his sickness a special remedy? In like manner, every time the Prophets of God have illumined the world with the resplendent radiance of the Day Star of Divine knowledge, they have invariably summoned its peoples to embrace the light of God through such means as best befitted the exigencies of the age in which they appeared. They were thus able to scatter the darkness of ignorance, and to shed upon the world the glory of their own knowledge . . . The whole of mankind is in the grip of manifold ills. Strive, there-fore, to save its life through the wholesome medicine which the almighty hand of the unerring Physician hath prepared.[188]

It is on account of these varying human needs that there are vari-ations in the teachings that the founders of the world religions have given. This is the main source of the differences that arise between religions.

> The other station is the station of distinction, and pertaineth to the world of creation, and to the limitations thereof. In this respect, each Manifestation of God hath a distinct individuality, a definitely prescribed mission, a predestined revelation, and specially designated limitations. Each one of them is known by a different name, is characterized by a special attribute, fulfils a definite mission, and is entrusted with a particular Revelation.
>
> It is because of this difference in their station and mission that the words and utterances flowing from these Well Springs of Divine knowledge appear to diverge and differ. Otherwise, in the eyes of them that are initiated into the mysteries of Divine

wisdom, all their utterances are, in reality, but the expressions of one Truth. As most of the people have failed to appreciate those stations to which We have referred, they, therefore, feel perplexed and dismayed at the varying utterances pronounced by Manifestations that are essentially one and the same.[189]

In summary then, Baha'u'llah's teaching is that as humanity evolves socially and conditions change over time, God sends the teachings that are relevant and necessary to each age through a Manifestation of God who appears in that age. The Manifestations of God mentioned by Baha'u'llah included Moses, Zoroaster, Jesus and Muhammad. Based on his assertion that the founders of all the world's religions were Manifestations of God, Baha'u'llah's appointed successor as leader of the Baha'i Faith, 'Abdu'l-Baha, added Krishna and the Buddha to this list. The teachings of these Manifestations of God have been the main impetus for the evolution of human society into ever more complex forms. This has been so important for humanity that the teaching of each of them has given rise to a new religion, although when seen from the viewpoint of Baha'u'llah teachings, it could equally well be said that the reality of these Manifestations of God is one and that there has in fact only ever been a single, evolving religion of God. Indeed Baha'u'llah states that one meaning of the 'oneness of God' is the concept of this one religion of God brought to humanity by these individuals who are, in their inner reality, one.

THE CLAIM OF BAHA'U'LLAH

Baha'u'llah's claim is thus to be the latest in the long line of these Manifestations of God that have come. As with the previous ones, he claims to have come with a particular message that is needed by humanity at the present time. He states that humanity has now reached the stage when the peoples of the world need to put aside their differences and come together and form a united world; that humanity has now reached the threshold of

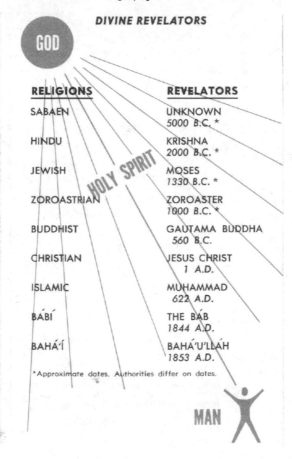

DIVINE REVELATORS

GOD

RELIGIONS | REVELATORS

SABAEN — UNKNOWN 5000 B.C. *

HINDU — KRISHNA 2000 B.C. *

JEWISH — MOSES 1330 B.C. *

ZOROASTRIAN — ZOROASTER 1000 B.C. *

BUDDHIST — GAUTAMA BUDDHA 560 B.C.

CHRISTIAN — JESUS CHRIST 1 A.D.

ISLAMIC — MUHAMMAD 622 A.D.

BÁBÍ — THE BÁB 1844 A.D.

BAHÁ'Í — BAHÁ'U'LLÁH 1853 A.D.

HOLY SPIRIT

*Approximate dates. Authorities differ on dates.

MAN

A typical Baha'i representation of the relationship between God
and humanity with the Manifestations of God as intermediary.
From a pamphlet published by the American Baha'i community
in the 1960s

its collective maturity and therefore new social structures are
needed to reflect this new reality (these teachings are dealt with
in more detail in the next chapter). His coming, Baha'u'llah
claims, represents the fulfilment of the prophecies to be found in
every religion concerning the coming of a future figure who will

introduce a golden age of peace and unity. This future figure is given various names in the different religions (such as the Messiah, the return of Christ, the fifth Buddha, Kalki Avatar) but Baha'u'llah claims that all such designations refer to him: 'Say: O people! The Day, promised unto you in all the Scriptures, is now come. Fear ye God, and withhold not yourselves from recognizing the One Who is the Object of your creation. Hasten ye unto Him. Better is this for you than the world and all that is therein. Would that ye could perceive it!'[190]

Because it is the day promised in all the scriptures of the religions of the world and is the day of the coming together of all humanity, the importance of this age and the significance of this stage in human development is very great and the allusions made to it in the scriptures of the world are striking.

> This is the Day which the Pen of the Most High hath glorified in all the holy Scriptures. There is no verse in them that doth not declare the glory of His holy Name, and no Book that doth not testify unto the loftiness of this most exalted theme. Were We to make mention of all that hath been revealed in these heavenly Books and holy Scriptures concerning this Revelation, this Tablet would assume impossible dimensions.[191]

In his work the Book of Certitude (Kitáb-i Íqán), Baha'u'llah describes how throughout religious history, human beings have always rejected the teachings of God when they have been brought by each new Manifestation of God, despite the fact that the new Manifestation had been prophesied in the scriptures of the previous religion and was expected. People have nevertheless clung to their preconceived ideas of what the new Manifestation of God should do and have rejected him. This is also of course what happened to Baha'u'llah. Although many followed his teachings, the majority of humanity, including its statesmen, religious leaders and intellectuals rejected or ignored him and his teachings. Some even rose up in opposition and did their best to attack him or undermine him. There are also some passages in the writings of Baha'u'llah that reveal his dismay and despair at his rejection by the people and the ferocious attacks that were launched against him:

> Glorified art Thou, O Lord my God! Look Thou upon this wronged one, who hath been sorely afflicted by the oppressors among Thy creatures and the infidels among Thine enemies, though he himself hath refused to breathe a single breath but by Thy leave and at Thy bidding. I lay asleep on my couch, O my God, when lo, the gentle winds of Thy grace and Thy loving–kindness passed over me, and wakened me through the power of Thy sovereignty and Thy gifts, and bade me arise before Thy servants, and speak forth Thy praise, and glorify Thy word. Thereupon most of Thy people reviled me. I swear by Thy glory, O my God! I never thought that they would show forth such deeds, aware as I am that Thou hast Thyself announced this Revelation unto them in the Scrolls of Thy commandment and the Tablets of Thy decree, and hast covenanted with them concerning this youth in every word sent down by Thee unto Thy creatures and Thy people.[192]

THE HISTORICAL DEVELOPMENT OF BAHA'U'LLAH'S CLAIM

During the time of the Bab, Baha'u'llah was regarded as one of his followers. Although he had a high social standing and was therefore an eminent Babi, he occupied no place in the Babi hierarchy that had the Letters of the Living at its head. As recounted in chapter 2, however, he was sufficiently highly regarded to be asked to lead the prayers at the Conference of Badasht at which many eminent Babis were assembled.

According to Baha'u'llah's own words, his mission began with his experience in the Black Pit of Tehran in 1852 (see chapter 2). And yet, he did not immediately announce this. His writings during the Baghdad period were written as a Babi, advancing the claims of the Bab and not putting forward any claim of his own (although, as we have indicated, there are some hints of this here and there, see pp. 164–5). At the end of the Baghdad period, Baha'u'llah announced his mission to a small number of his followers in the Garden of Ridvan. This was, however, just an oral announcement and was not immediately reflected in his writings, except by allusions. The Babi doctrine involved seeing the Bab as the return of the Hidden Imam expected by the Shi'is. There were however a number of other holy figures who were expected also to return with the Hidden Imam. It would appear that Baha'u'llah, partly based on his writings of this period, came to be regarded at this time as the return of one of the most important of these, the Imam Husayn.

Then in Edirne in the Spring of 1866, Baha'u'llah openly made the claim that he was the figure that the Bab had prophesied in many of his writings, He whom God shall make manifest. This figure, according to the writings of the Bab, would inaugurate a new religious dispensation that would be immeasurably greater than that of the Bab.

This claim was then extended by Baha'u'llah during the 'Akka period to the followers of all religions. In his letter to Pope Pius IX, he claims to be the return of Christ that the Christians are expecting. In other letters addressed to Muslims, Jews, and Zoroastrians, he also claimed to be the messianic figure that those religions were expecting. Extending this to all religions and peoples, he states: 'The time foreordained unto the peoples and kindreds of the earth is now come. The promises of God, as recorded in the holy Scriptures, have all been fulfilled.'[193]

During the 'Akka period, Baha'u'llah explained and defined the nature of his claim in numerous works. He expanded on his claim to be the Divine Physician with the remedy for the ills of today's world by writing of social and political solutions for the problems of the world. He was also engaged in defending himself against those who asserted that he had made exaggerated claims (see pp. 191–2).

NINE

The Teachings of Baha'u'llah

The teachings given in the writings of Baha'u'llah were then developed by his son 'Abdu'l-Baha, whom Baha'u'llah authorised to succeed him and be the interpreter and expounder of his teachings. 'Abdu'l-Baha in turn appointed his grandson Shoghi Effendi to perform the same role after him. In a single chapter of a small book, it is impossible to give a full account of this process whereby the seeds to be found in the writings of Baha'u'llah were developed and evolved by his successors; indeed this process cannot even be said to be finished in that the Universal House of Justice, which is now the highest authority in the Baha'i Faith, is continuing the process of eliciting and elucidating the implications of Baha'u'llah's teachings. Therefore in this chapter the account that is given is of the Baha'i teachings in their present form. For a fuller explanation of the Baha'i teachings, the reader should refer to some of the other books described in the 'Sources and References'.

ONENESS OF HUMANITY

If one were to try to summarise the teachings of Baha'u'llah, one could say that they all revolve around the implication of a single word: 'unity'. We have already seen in the previous chapter that Baha'u'llah teaches that God is one – that the Ultimate Reality described in various ways in the different religions of the world is in fact one reality; that the founders of the world religions are, in fact, one in their underlying reality even though each has brought a different message suited to the age in which they have come; and that therefore the different religions of the world should be seen as the progressive unfolding of one Truth. This theme of unity is then carried over to the human level. Baha'u'llah states that human beings should also regard themselves as one. Alone of all creatures, human beings are potentially able to manifest all of the names and attributes of God. They are able to be loving, just, wise, pure and so forth. In this respect therefore they are all equal and indeed should regard themselves as one interdependent reality.

> O Children of Men! Know ye not why We created you all from the same dust? That no one should exalt himself over the other. Ponder at all times in your hearts how ye were created. Since We have created you all from one same substance it is incumbent on you to be even as one soul, to walk with the same feet, eat with the same mouth and dwell in the same land, that from your inmost being, by your deeds and actions, the signs of oneness and the essence of detachment may be made manifest. Such is My counsel to you, O concourse of light! Heed ye this counsel that ye may obtain the fruit of holiness from the tree of wondrous glory.[194]

The oneness and interconnectedness of the human world is already a reality in terms of transport, finance, trade, the sciences and technology, the arts, communications and many other fields. This has yet to penetrate the consciousness of many people however. Human beings have been used to thinking of themselves in terms of narrowly defined identities and loyalties: 'I am British', 'I am Muslim', 'I am Yoruba', 'I am working class'. Baha'u'llah states that we now need to widen our identities and loyalties to the global level, to think in terms of all being citizens of one world.

That one indeed is a man who, today, dedicateth himself to the service of the entire human race. The Great Being saith: Blessed and happy is he that ariseth to promote the best interests of the peoples and kindreds of the earth. In another passage He hath proclaimed: It is not for him to pride himself who loveth his own country, but rather for him who loveth the whole world. The earth is but one country, and mankind its citizens.[195]

As this global consciousness of the oneness of humanity gains ground, it pushes out the prejudices, fanaticism and discrimination that cause so many of the problems of the world today.

A NEW SOCIAL ORDER

This teaching of human oneness that Baha'u'llah gives, is not, however, just left as a pious aspiration; it affects every aspect of Baha'u'llah's social teachings and the structure and administration of the Baha'i community. The key to understand how it moves from aspiration to social realization is in Baha'u'llah's statement that humanity as a whole has reached the threshold of maturity.[196] For at least the last 6000 years, humanity has organised itself into hierarchical formations of power – people at the top of each social unit have commanded and controlled the actions of those below them. These hierarchical structures affect all areas of life: government, business, education, entertainment and religion. Their presence is so pervasive that most people assume that this is the inevitable and unalterable way in which human beings organise themselves. Baha'u'llah says, however, that this is not the case. These hierarchies of power may be likened to the parent–child relationship and were only necessary during humanity's childhood. Now that humanity has reached maturity, the competition, conflict and even violence that is inherent in them are producing detrimental effects in the world, from the oppression of women and minorities to the belligerence and lack of co-operation in international affairs, to environmental degradation due to aggressive competitiveness in business and industry, to violence and hooliganism in sports. Other ways of organising human society are needed. These alternative social structures and processes are not something that can just suddenly and immediately replace the old structures but must be learned and gradually adopted by humanity. Baha'u'llah states that all human beings should regard themselves as being of equal rank;[197] emphasising that power, whether temporal or spiritual, can no longer be held by individuals, Baha'u'llah states: 'From two ranks amongst men power hath been seized: kings and ecclesiastics.'[198]

Baha'u'llah has therefore instilled the principles of what is needed into the structures and processes of the Baha'i community. His successors as leaders of the Baha'i community have been gradually putting these principles into place. Although a great deal could be written about the social organisation that the Baha'i teachings prescribe to replace the hierarchical models of present society, for the present purposes we will focus on two main features, one structural and one procedural. The structural element involves a removal of all elements of personal power. No individuals in the Baha'i community structure have power over others. There is an authority structure in the Baha'i community but the authority does not reside in individuals but in elected councils. These councils are called 'houses of justices' by Baha'u'llah, which emphasises the important role that is envisaged for justice in this social order. They are elected at the local, national and international levels. The local and national councils are, for the present and in order not to cause misunderstandings with governments, called 'spiritual assemblies' while the international elected council is called the Universal House of Justice. None of the individuals on these councils have, however, any individual power or authority by virtue of being elected. The councils have chairpersons but there is no chairperson's casting vote or any special powers for the chairperson or any other member. Members of a national spiritual assembly, for example, are under the authority of the local spiritual assembly of their hometown in relation to local affairs. There are individuals called Counsellors and the members of their Auxiliary Boards who are appointed to their positions but these individuals have only a role in encouragement and support of the Baha'i community and have no power.

The second notable element is a procedural one and this is the process called 'consultation' which occurs at all levels of Baha'i community life. Decisions are arrived at through consultation in the elected councils and on committees that the councils may appoint. Consultation occurs between the community and the local council at Nineteen-Day Feasts, which are held on the first day of each Baha'i month (the Baha'i calendar consists of nineteen months of nineteen days each and four or five intercalary days to put the calendar in line with the solar year). Consultations occur at the annual convention held to elect the national assembly and the five-yearly international convention held to elect the Universal House of Justice. There are a number of features that make Baha'i consultation different from the activity carried out in this name elsewhere. It is considered a spiritual activity, and is therefore carried out in a prayerful atmosphere. It is considered essential that all present be given a chance, and be encouraged to express their views. This is especially important in the case of women and individuals from minority groups and disadvantaged social classes who will often feel intimidated and reluctant to express their views in mixed company. The ideas being discussed in the consultation process should be divorced from the personalities expressing the ideas and therefore individuals should not feel hurt if their idea is criticised or rejected. The ideal is for the idea to evolve through the process of consultation into a better proposition and for there to be a consensus at the end of the process; if no consensus is reached, a vote is taken. In this way, the collective wisdom of the community can be tapped. Thus Baha'u'llah states: 'Take ye counsel together in all matters, inasmuch as consultation is the lamp of guidance which leadeth the way, and is the bestower of understanding.'[199]

The Baha'i consultation process, once learned within the Baha'i community, can also be used in many other situations such as: making family decisions; discovering the meaning of scripture; solving personal problems; involving all elements of society in social decision-making and action; and in evolving social and economic development plans in such a way that all feel that they are involved.

There is no space here to deal with other aspects of the Baha'i community which also help to remove power and competition and conflict from social processes (such as the Baha'i election process which involves no candidates, no electioneering and no formation of parties). In all, however, it is through such structures and processes that individuals who, under the present social structure, are relegated to the bottom of the hierarchy and

A Baha'i Social and Economic Development Project: The Barli Vocational Institute for Rural Women in Indore, India, trains village and tribal women in literacy, hygiene, family health and gives them a vocational skill to enable them to return to their homes with skills that will help them to earn a living and be of service to their community

feel they have no voice and no stake in society (leading to frustration expressed as vandalism, gang culture and violence) can be engaged and involved in shaping community policy and action.

An account of Baha'u'llah's teaching on social order would not, however, be complete without mentioning the great importance that Baha'u'llah gives to the family in the Baha'i teachings. The foundation of unity in society is unity and love in the family. Indeed whatever we wish to produce in society, whether this be equality of men and women or freedom from prejudices and violence, can be more easily spread throughout society if it is first established within the family.

These structures and processes within the Baha'i community are intended to serve as a model for the world of how communities can be organised that move beyond the culture of contest and conflict that our present hierarchical societies promote. The implications of this are spelled out in some of the social teachings of the Baha'i Faith such as the equality of women and men; the need to remove racial and class prejudices; and the need to guarantee all individuals certain human rights. Only by following the path described in his teachings, states Baha'u'llah, can social peace and stability be attained. As long as we persist in our present hierarchically arranged societies, social unrest and instability will continue. We are no longer living in a world where people are willing to live quietly and submissively at the bottom level of power hierarchies, no matter how benign these may be. A radical restructuring of society itself is needed.

GLOBAL TEACHINGS

At the global level, the Baha'i concern for unity is expressed as a belief that human social evolution and technological development has now reached the stage where we are living in a single, interconnected world society. In his message to the kings and leaders of the world, Baha'u'llah offered a vision of the ultimate stage of world unity based on spiritual teachings which he called the Most Great Peace. He wrote, however, that since the kings and leaders rejected his call, humanity should now strive towards the Lesser Peace, a stage of political peace by treaty, which would then gradually evolve into the Most Great Peace. As a first step, Baha'u'llah called for a world conference which all the rulers of the world would attend:

> It is their duty to convene an all–inclusive assembly, which either they themselves or their ministers will attend, and to enforce whatever measures are required to establish unity and concord amongst men. They must put away the weapons of war, and turn to the instruments of universal reconstruction. Should one king rise up against another, all the other kings must arise to deter him. Arms and armaments will, then, be no more needed beyond that which is necessary to insure the internal security of their respective countries. If they attain unto this all–surpassing blessing, the people of each nation will pursue, with tranquillity and contentment, their own occupations . . .[200]

Ultimately, however, to achieve true unity and peace, the world needs a global authority to regulate it. Therefore the Baha'i teachings envisage a world legislature, elected by the peoples of the world, a world executive and a world tribunal that can adjudicate on all international disputes. Only by moving on to this next stage in human social development can global problems such as war, injustice in world trade, environmental degradation, global warming, the regulation of multi-national corporations, and the bullying of weaker nations by stronger ones be tackled. It is futile to try to tackle these problems under the present world order that is based on the political realities of the nineteenth century.

INDIVIDUAL FREEDOM

Among the subjects covered in various places in the writings of Baha'u'llah is that of liberty. Baha'u'llah encourages such moves towards human liberty as democracy and education but warns that if liberty is taken to extremes, it 'causeth man to overstep the bounds of propriety, and to infringe on the dignity of his station. It debaseth him to the level of extreme depravity and wickedness.'[201] Therefore Baha'u'llah emphasises the importance of the principle of moderation: 'Whatsoever passeth beyond the limits of moderation will cease to exert a beneficial influence. Consider for instance such things as liberty, civilization and the like. However much men of understanding may favourably regard them, they will, if carried to excess, exercise a pernicious influence upon men.'[202]

Although some may think that the Baha'i teachings about a global structure outlined above would lead to excessive centralization and bureaucratic or authoritarian control, there is in fact running through Baha'i structures a strong element of subsidiarity – that everything that is best decided and supervised at the local level should be done at that level and only matters that are of national or global concern should be passed up to the higher levels for a decision. Indeed the very existence of a global level of governance gives the individual greater freedom and rights because, within the Baha'i administrative system, decisions made at local or national level can be appealed at the international level if the individual feels unjustly treated or feels that they are wrong on principle.

There is a further factor which gives freedom to the individual and that is the fact that although the institutions of the Baha'i Faith have authority to make decisions and lay out plans, the power to carry out these plans lays with the individual. The institutions do not have the power to compel individuals to take part in their plans. This is of course in line with the concept of the maturity of humanity. It lays the responsibility for one's actions firmly in the individual's lap. Furthermore, since there are no religious leaders, no priesthood or professional learned class in the Baha'i Faith, responsibility for carrying forward the affairs of the religion also lays in the lap of the individual. The Baha'i community is currently engaged in a series of plans aimed at developing this sense of personal responsibility and universal participation in the affairs of the Baha'i community.

Baha'i Social and Economic Development project: Students and teacher at the Ocean of Light School in Nuku'alofa, Tonga. As well as the standard academic curriculum, the children at the school study one virtue each week

The main factor, however, that maintains both the unity of the Baha'i community as well as allowing individual freedom is the doctrine of the Covenant. While in other religions it may be adherence to a theological creed or following a holy law that is the marker of faith, in the Baha'i Faith, it is following the doctrine of the Covenant that occupies this position. On becoming a Baha'i, the individual asserts his or her loyalty to the centre of the Faith. Historically this Centre of the Covenant was Baha'u'llah's son, 'Abdu'l-Baha, who led the Baha'i community from 1892 to 1921; the latter's grandson, Shoghi Effendi, who was the leader from 1922 to 1957; and since 1963, it has been the Universal House of Justice, the elected international Baha'i council. While this doctrine of the Covenant may appear to give the centre of the Faith the last word, in fact this ultimate authority is only exercised in situations where there is a disagreement and the danger of a split in the community. The rest of the time,

Baha'is are operating in an area where they are free to read and interpret the Baha'i scriptures for themselves and to decide the level of their involvement in Baha'i affairs. The relationship between the individual Baha'i and the Centre of the Covenant is thus not seen by most Baha'is as one of power and authority but as one of love and guidance. It is Baha'i belief that the guidance given by Baha'u'llah is continued through the Centre of the Covenant.

Thus when Baha'u'llah writes of a 'new world order', he is not advocating just a rearrangement of the present political and economic order as some others who have used this phrase envisage. The changes that Baha'u'llah proposes are based upon a much more radical and fundamental change in the very structure of human society: 'The world's equilibrium hath been upset through the vibrating influence of this most great, this new World Order. Mankind's ordered life hath been revolutionized through the agency of this unique, this wondrous System – the like of which mortal eyes have never witnessed.'[203]

SPIRITUAL AND MYSTICAL TEACHINGS

The above description of Baha'i social teachings should not lead one to think that the Baha'i Faith is primarily a social movement. On the contrary, the foundation and springboard for all of the Baha'i social teachings is a spiritual one. The political and economic ills of the world, for example, are seen in the Baha'i teachings as primarily a spiritual problem (injustice, corruption, excessive materialism and greed, a misplaced view of what constitutes human happiness, etc.). Therefore it is considered that no application of an economic theory and no amount of political management can solve these problems. It is only a spiritual transformation of the individuals in society that can hope to tackle these problems effectively.

Human beings are considered in the Baha'i teachings to possess a physical aspect, which humanity has in common with animals, and a spiritual aspect, which is the eternal reality of human beings. If all of the attention is concentrated on satisfying the physical needs, this cannot lead to human happiness as the spiritual side is neglected. Indeed, the purpose of human life is described in the writings of Baha'u'llah as being to acquire and perfect divine attributes (such as love, patience, justice, and trustworthiness); it is only if human beings are proceeding along this path that they will be happy. While in most religions this pursuit of the mystical path is the concern of a small number of people who form mystical communities, in the Baha'i community, it becomes the concern of all.

In order to proceed along this path, Baha'u'llah has given a number of spiritual exercises and practices that will help by turning the attention of the individual towards the spiritual. These exercises and practices include daily prayer, reading of the scripture and meditation and an annual period of fasting. The structure and function of the Baha'i community also serve to assist in pursuing the mystic path. Thus, for example, guidance is provided in other mystic communities by the leader, the guru or the shaykh of a Sufi order or the abbot of a monastery. Baha'u'llah has, however, as indicated above, prohibited all forms of individual religious leadership which give power to one human being over another. In its place, guidance for Baha'is on the mystic path comes from their daily spiritual practices. They also gather in groups to study and consult about the meaning of their scriptures. Baha'is believe that the interactions of the consultative process produce insights and wisdom greater than any one individual can achieve. The very process of consultation itself can be an important aid to progress along the mystic path, requiring as it does qualities such as purity of motive, detachment, humility, and patience. The aim of these processes and activities, and indeed of the Baha'i Faith itself, is stated by Baha'u'llah to be that spiritual transformation which has been the aim of the mystics of all religions:

> And yet, is not the object of every Revelation to effect a transformation in the whole character of mankind, a transformation

that shall manifest itself both outwardly and inwardly, that shall affect both its inner life and external conditions? For if the character of mankind be not changed, the futility of God's universal Manifestations would be apparent.[204]

There are many other aspects of Baha'i teachings and Baha'i community life that relate to spirituality and mystical progress but only two more will be mentioned here. The first of these is the role of the tests and difficulties that one comes across in the course of one's life. According to Baha'i teachings, these are often due to attachment to the things of this world, and by overcoming the tests, human beings can become more detached. The Baha'i community, by deliberately aiming to be as diverse as possible and throwing people from every different race, class and culture together, produces many tests and difficulties for the individual Baha'i, but also provides a loving, united framework within which to work through these tests and advance beyond them. The second aspect is the importance of service. The more one engages in service, the more interactions one has with individuals who are unlike oneself, therefore the more tests come one's way. Thus it is also through service that one's spiritual qualities are extended and refined.

In summary then, the teachings brought by Baha'u'llah and the community established by him are designed to produce an interconnected and united society; a society that is no longer organized in the hierarchical manner that may have been suitable in the childhood of humanity but rather one that is suited to the maturity and adulthood of humanity, one that allows all individuals an equal voice and equal respect; that enables all human beings to develop themselves to the limits of their capacities and to grow spiritually. This effort to produce such a society cannot be separated from Baha'u'llah's spiritual and mystical teachings which, through spiritual transformation, render the individual capable and suited to playing a full role in this process. Such a profound change in the individual and society cannot be produced overnight but rather must be gradually and painstakingly built up through a process of education, through overcoming tests and difficulties and by trial and error. This is what the Baha'i community under the guidance of its subsequent leaders, 'Abdu'l-Baha and Shoghi Effendi, and today under the Universal House of Justice, is striving to achieve.[205]

Conclusion

The religion that Baha'u'llah established in his own lifetime was taken forward by his son 'Abdu'l-Baha. Within five years of Baha'u'llah's passing the religion had been established in North America and this spread to the West was consolidated by 'Abdu'l-Baha's own travel to North America and Europe in 1911 to 1913. After the passing of 'Abdu'l-Baha in 1921, his appointed successor, Shoghi Effendi, established the administrative institutions of the Baha'i Faith that had been outlined in the writings of Baha'u'llah and 'Abdu'l-Baha. Having developed this aspect of the religion in the first fifteen years of his ministry, Shoghi Effendi then set these administrative institutions the task of spreading the Baha'i Faith throughout the world in a series of plans that continued up to and beyond his own death in 1957. The Universal House of Justice, which had been called for in the writings of Baha'u'llah, was finally established in 1963 as the crowning institution of the Baha'i administrative order. This institution has continued the planned expansion of the Baha'i Faith. In recent years, however, it has focussed on the development of Baha'i community life and the development of the change in vision and culture needed to bring about Baha'u'llah's teaching of a new way of ordering humanity's social life.

This book has given a necessarily brief survey of the life, the works, the claims and the teachings of Baha'u'llah. We have seen that he emerged as a leading figure in the Babi Faith, a much persecuted religious movement in Iran. As a result of these persecutions, he was exiled in 1853 to Baghdad, then in the Ottoman province of Iraq, from where he succeeded in resuscitating and spreading the Babi religion for ten years. At the end of this time in 1863, as he was about to leave Baghdad, having been summoned by the Sultan to Istanbul, he declared to a few of his followers, that he was the prophetic figure who had been prophesied by the Bab. After he reached Istanbul and was then sent on to Edirne, now in European Turkey, he declared himself openly as the promised one of all religions and sent letters to this effect to the most prominent kings and leaders of his time. In 1868, he was further exiled to the prison-city of 'Akka in Ottoman Syria, where he spent two years confined within the citadel and a further seven under house arrest, before being allowed to take up residence outside the city walls. He passed away in 1892 and his shrine at Bahji near 'Akka is now the central spiritual focus of a

Proclaiming the Baha'i Faith in the Solomon Islands

worldwide religion, the Baha'i Faith, whose adherents are striving to put his teachings into effect.

During his lifetime, Baha'u'llah produced numerous writings in which he gave the teachings, laws and administrative structure of his religion. The foundations of his teachings are a spiritual renewal of the individual. Each individual must strive to become more God-like by acquiring the divine attributes (such as love, justice, trustworthiness, patience, etc.). In doing this, human beings are perfecting their true spiritual nature and preparing themselves for their eternal spiritual journey which continues after death. In order to assist with this task, Baha'u'llah has given his followers prayers and spiritual practices. Guidance on the spiritual path is provided in the writings of Baha'u'llah, in prayer and in the structure of the religion he founded. In particular, the practice of Baha'i consultation is capable of tapping the wisdom of the Baha'i community in exploring the possibilities of the scriptures. According to Baha'u'llah's teaching, the spiritual dynamics of the family are also of great importance in the spiritual progress of the individual.

In his social teachings, Baha'u'llah has provided the theoretical framework for the world unity and peace that he considers the necessary and indeed inevitable next stage of human evolution. This world unity cannot be imposed by the force of powerful nations. It must grow out of a vision of human oneness, out of the development of a global vision for tackling the problems of the world and out of the gradual evolution of world institutions that can produce peace and justice for all the people of the world. Such developments can only succeed if there is universal education, the protection of human rights, the abandonment of religious, racial, and ethnic prejudices and the equality of women and men. Baha'u'llah wrote about these themes out of a conviction that there was no other way to resolve the problems of humanity and he wrote about them passionately as a result of his own experiences. He had after all been subject to unjust imprisonment and torture when he had done no wrong. He had been the victim of a mob whipped up to fanaticism and fury. He had been exiled from his own country and forced to seek asylum and become a refugee in Iraq. He had experienced poverty, extreme cold, hunger and thirst in the course of his journeys of exile. He had been subjected to overcrowded living spaces, unjust and corrupt officials and persecution and harassment by the state. He had watched his children die as a result of these deprivations and had lived through his followers being persecuted, beaten and killed for no reason other than the faith they followed. He had therefore shared in the sufferings of the poor and downtrodden of the world and so when he wrote of the need for a new basis for society, it was not just a theoretical and dispassionate discourse.[205]

Nor did Baha'u'llah just leave his social teachings on a level of theory and proposals. He outlined in the structures and processes of the Baha'i community some of the ways in which a participative and non-hierarchical society can be established. Only by radically changing the hierarchical way in which society has been organized for the past 6000 years or more can the aim of producing a society in which all can participate on a basis of equality and respect be achieved. The structures of the Baha'i community aim to bring such a society into being while its processes, such as consultation and its election methods, are designed to allow even the most reticent and oppressed minorities in society to gain the confidence to emerge and contribute.

Some have considered Baha'u'llah to have been a charlatan and a mischief-maker, some that he was merely an inspired social reformer, while his followers consider him to have been the voice of God giving humanity the necessary guidance for dealing with its current problems. Whatever one's reactions to his claims, it cannot be denied that he produced a great effect on those around him. Many of his followers were prepared to die rather than deny their faith in him during his lifetime and many others have continued to do this up to the present time. His teachings have spread throughout the world and are as avidly studied by his followers on the islands of the Pacific Ocean and in the heart of India as they are in the villages of the Andes and the huts of Africa. These adherents are striving to follow these teachings in their personal lives and also to use them to set up a new type of non-hierarchical participative society. Only the future will disclose the extent of their success.

Bibliography

(Most of the Baha'i scriptural references in this book can be found online at: http://reference.bahai.org)

'Abdu'l-Bahá, *Khatábát-i Hadrat-i 'Abdu'l-Bahá*. 3 vols. Cairo, 1340 A.H./1921–2
——, *Memorials of the Faithful*. Wilmette, IL: Bahá'í Publishing Trust, 1971
——, *Muntakhabát az Makatíb Hadrat 'Abdu'l-Baha*. Vol. 5, Hofheim, Bahá'í-Verlag, 2000
——, *Some Answered Questions*. Wilmette, IL: Bahá'í Publishing Trust, 1981.
——, *A Traveller's Narrative Written to Illustrate the Episode of the Báb* (ed. and trans. Edward G. Browne). 2 vols. Cambridge: Cambridge University Press, 1891
Alkan, Necati, 'Midhat Pasha and 'Abdu'l-Baha in 'Akka: The Historical Background of the Tablet of the Land of Bá'. *Baha'i Studies Review* 13 (2005) 1–13
——, 'Ottoman Reform Movements and the Bahá'í Faith, 1860s–1920s'. in Moshe Sharon (ed.), *Studies in Modern Religions, Religious Movements and the Bábí-Bahá'í Faiths*, Leiden: Brill, 2004, pp. 253–74
Amanat, Abbas, *Resurrection and Renewal*. London: Cornell University Press, 1989
Báb, The, *Selections from the Writings of the Báb* (trans. Habib Taherzadeh et al.). Haifa: Bahá'í World Centre, 1976
Bahá'í Prayers. Wilmette, IL: Bahá'í Publishing Trust, 1991

Bahá'u'lláh, *Ad'iyyih-yi Hadrat Mahbúb*. Original edition: Faraju'lláh al-Kurdí, Egypt, 76 B.E./1920; reprint Germany 1980

——, *Epistle to the Son of the Wolf*. Wilmette, IL: Bahá'í Publishing Trust, 1988

——, *Gems of Divine Mysteries*, Haifa: Bahá'í World Centre, 2002

——, *Gleanings from the Writings of Bahá'u'lláh*. Wilmette, IL: Bahá'í Publishing Trust, 1983

——, *Hidden Words*. Wilmette, IL: Bahá'í Publishing Trust, 1990

——, *Ishráqát va Chand Lawh-i Dígar*. Bombay, n.d.

——, *The Kitáb-i-Aqdas*. Haifa: Bahá'í World Centre, 1992

——, *The Kitáb-i-Íqán, the Book of Certitude* (trans. Shoghi Effendi). 2nd edn. Wilmette, IL: Bahá'í Publishing Trust, 1974

——, *Prayers and Meditations*. Wilmette, IL: Bahá'í Publishing Trust, 1987

——, *The Seven Valleys and the Four Valleys*. Wilmette, IL: Bahá'í Publishing Trust, 1991

——, *Summons of the Lord of Hosts*. Haifa: Bahá'í World Centre, 2002

——, *Tablets of Bahá'u'lláh revealed after the Kitáb-i-Aqdas*. Haifa: Bahá'í World Centre, 1978

Bahíyyih Khánum, the Greatest Holy Leaf: A Compilation from Bahá'í Sacred Texts and Writings of the Guardian of the Faith and Bahíyyih Khánum's Own Letters. Haifa: Bahá'í World Centre, 1982

Balyuzi, Hasan M., *'Abdu'l-Bahá, The Centre of the Covenant of Bahá'u'lláh*. Oxford: George Ronald, 2nd edn. with minor corr. 1987

——, *Bahá'u'lláh, The King of Glory*. Oxford: George Ronald, 1980

——, *Eminent Bahá'ís in the Time of Bahá'u'lláh: with some Historical Background*. Oxford: George Ronald, 1985

Blomfield, Lady [Sara Louise], *The Chosen Highway*. Wilmette, IL: Bahá'í Publishing Trust, 1967

Browne, Edward G., *A Literary History of Persia*. Vol. 4, Cambridge: University Press, 1924, reprinted 1969

Faizi, Muhammad 'Alí, *Hayát-i Hadrat-i Bahá'u'lláh*. Tehran: Mu'assih Millí Matbú'át Amrí, 125 B.E.

Furutan, 'Ali-Akbar, *Stories of Bahá'u'lláh* (trans. Katayoun and Robert Crerar). Oxford: George Ronald, 1986

Gulpáygání, Abu'l-Fadl, *Fará'id*. Cairo 1315 A.H./1897

——, *Letters and Essays, 1886–1913* (trans. J.R. Cole). Los Angeles: Kalimát Press, 1985

[Isfahani], Hájí Mírzá Haydar-'Alí, *Stories from the Delight of Hearts: The Memoirs of Hájí Mírzá Haydar-'Alí* (trans. and abridged by A.Q. Faizi). Los Angeles: Kalimát Press, 1980

Ishráq-Khávarí, 'Abdu'l-Hamíd, *Ayyám Tis'ih*, 3rd ed., Tehran: Mu'assih Millí Matbú'át Amrí, 121 B.E./1964

——, *Má'idih-yi Ásmání*, Tehran: Mu'assih Millí Matbú'át Amrí, 9 vols., 121–29 B.E./1964–1972

Karlberg, Michael, *Beyond the Culture of Contest*, Oxford: George Ronald, 2004

Kolstoe, John E., *Consultation: A Universal Lamp of Guidance.* Oxford: George Ronald, 1985

Malik-Khusraví, Muhammad 'Alí, *Iqlím-i-Núr*. Tehran: Mu'assih Millí Matbú'át Amrí, 118 B.E./1961

Mázandarání, Fádil, *Tárikh-i Zuhúr al-Haqq*, Vols. 4 and 5, copies of unpublished manuscripts in Afnan Library, London

Munírih Khánum: Memoirs and Letters (trans. Sammireh Anwar Smith). Los Angeles: Kalimát Press, 1986

Momen, Moojan, *The Bábí and Bahá'í Religions, 1844–1944: Some Contemporary Western Accounts.* Oxford: George Ronald, 1981

——, *The Bahá'í Faith: A Short Introduction*, Oxford: Oneworld, 1997

Momen, Wendi, *Understanding the Baha'i Faith*, Edinburgh: Dunedin Academic Press, 2005

——, *A Basic Bahá'í Dictionary*. Oxford: George Ronald, 1989

Nabíl [Zarandí, Nabíl-i-A'zam], *The Dawn-Breakers: Nabíl's Narrative of the Early Days of the Bahá'í Revelation.* (ed. and trans. Shoghi Effendi) Wilmette, IL: Bahá'í Publishing Trust, 1970

Phelps, Myron H., *The Master in 'Akká.* Los Angeles: Kalimát Press, 1985

Qazvini, Muhammad Javád, *Tarikh*, copy of manuscript, dated Dec. 1909, in Afnan Library

Qumi, Sayyid Asadu'lláh, *Hizár Dástán.* Copy of unpublished manuscript in Afnan Library, London

Root, Martha, 'White Roses of Persia' – Part 1, *The Bahá'í Magazine*, vol. 23 (1932) pp. 71–4

Ruhe, David S., *Door of Hope.* Oxford: George Ronald, 1983

Salmani, Muhamamd 'Ali, *My Memories of Baha'u'llah* (trans. Marzieh Gail). Los Angeles: Kalimát Press, 1982

Samandari, Tarazullah, *Moments with Bahá'u'lláh* (trans. Mehdi Samandari and Marzieh Gail), Los Angeles: Kalimát Press, 1995

Shoghi Effendi, *God Passes By*. Wilmette, IL: Bahá'í Publishing Trust, rev. edn. 1974

——, *Messages to America*. Wilmette, IL: Bahá'í Publishing Committee, 1947

——, *The Promised Day is Come*. Wilmette, IL: Bahá'í Publishing Trust, rev. edn. 1980

——, *World Order of Baha'u'llah*. Wilmette, IL: Bahá'í Publishing Trust, 1991

Smith, Peter, *A Concise Encyclopedia of the Bahá'í Faith*. 2nd ed., Oxford: Oneworld, 2002

——, *The Bábí and Bahá'í Religions: From Messianic Shi'ism to a World Religion*. Cambridge: Cambridge University Press, 1987

——, *The Bahá'í Religion: A Short Introduction to its History and Teachings*. Oxford: George Ronald, 1988

——, *A Short History of the Bahá'í Faith*. Oxford: Oneworld, 1996

Sours, Michael, *The Station and Claims of Bahá'u'lláh*. Wilmette, IL: Bahá'í Publishing Trust, 1997

Sulaymání, 'Azízu'llah, *Masábíh Hidáyat*, Vol. 1, Tehran: Mu'assih Millí Matbú'át Amrí, 121 B.E./1964

Taherzadeh, Adib, *The Revelation of Bahá'u'lláh*, 4 vols., Oxford: George Ronald, 1974–87

Zarqání, Mahmúd, *Badáyí'u'l-Athár*. 2 vols. Bombay, Vol. 1, 1914 and vol. 2, 1921

Zayn, Núru'd-Dín, *Khátirát Hayát dar Khidmat-i Mahbúb*, 2 vols., copy of typescript in Afnan Library

Sources and References

INTRODUCTION

1. With the exception of the Vatican.
2. There are a number of countries, mainly Islamic states and communist countries, where the Baha'i community is legally prevented from establishing its institutions.

1. EARLY LIFE

Information about Nur, Baha'u'llah's ancestry and Baha'u'llah's father: Malik-Khusravi, *Iqlim-i-Nur*, pp. 2–16, 90–152; see also Balyuzi, *Baha'u'llah*, pp. 9–18. Baha'u'llah's childhood and early life: Balyuzi, *Baha'u'llah*, pp. 19–25. Story of Banu Qurayza: Ishraq-Khavari, *Ma'idih-yi Asmani*, vol. 7, pp. 135–6. Story of Shaykh Muhammad Taqi 'Allamih Nuri: Talk of 'Abdu'l-Baha recorded in Zarqani, *Badayi' al-Athar* vol. 2, pp. 139–40; see also Balyuzi, *Baha'u'llah*, p. 22. Story of the cleric with a large turban and the visit to Qumm: Baha'u'llah, *Ishraqat*, p. 39. Baha'u'llah's marriages and children: Malik-Khusravi, *Iqlim-i-Nur*, pp. 139, 153–9; Mazandarani, *Zuhuru'l-Haqq*, vol. 5, pp. 482–3; Balyuzi, *Baha'u'llah*, pp. 13–18. Quch-Hissar: Nabil, *Dawn-Breakers*, pp. 120–22, Balyuzi, *Eminent Baha'is*, pp. 339–45.

3. When in later years he wrote 'The learning (*al-'ulúm*) current amongst men I studied not; their schools (*al-madáris*) I entered

not', the word *'ulúm* refers to the Islamic sciences that were taught at the religious colleges (*al-madáris*) which were the only form of higher education available in Iran. See Tablet to Nasiru'd-Din Shah in Baha'u'llah, *Summons of the Lord of Hosts*, p. 98

4. Baha'u'llah, *Summons of the Lord of Hosts*, para 12–17, pp. 165–6
5. Blomfield, *Chosen Highway*, pp. 39–40
6. Mazandarani, *Zuhuru'l-Haq*, vol. 5, p. 511
7. Blomfield, *Chosen Highway*, p. 40

2. THE CAUSE OF THE BAB

On the Bab and the Letters of the Living, see Nabil, *Dawn-Breakers*, pp. 47–96; Amanat, *Resurrection and Renewal*, pp. 153–207. On the meeting of Baha'u'llah and Mulla Husyan Bushru'i, see Balyuzi, *Baha'u'llah*, pp. 32–7; Nabil, *Dawn-Breakers*, 97–108. On Baha'u'llah's trip to Nur, see Balyuzi, *Baha'u'llah*, pp. 39–40; Nabil, *Dawn-Breakers*, 109–19; 'Abdu'l-Baha, *Muntakhabat*, vol. 5, pp. 6–8. On Murgh Mahallih: 'Abdu'l-Baha, *Muntakhabat*, vol. 5, p. 15. On Tahirih and the Conference of Badasht: Nabil, *Dawn-Breakers*, pp. 268–300; Balyuzi, *Baha'u'llah*, pp. 41–47; 'Abdu'l-Baha, *Memorials of the Faithful*, pp. 197–203; Shoghi Effendi, *God Passes By*, pp. 31–4. Episode in Bandar Jaz: Ishraq-Khavari, *Ma'idih-yi Asmani*, vol. 5, pp. 170–1; Balyuzi, *Baha'u'llah*, pp. 48–50. Baha'u'llah at Shaykh Tabarsi: Nabil, *Dawn-Breakers*, pp. 347–9; Balyuzi, *Baha'u'llah*, pp. 50–51. Baha'u'llah's imprisonment in Amul: 'Abdu'l-Baha, *Khatabat-i Hadrat-i 'Abdu'l-Baha*, vol. 1, pp. 116–20; 'Abdu'l-Baha, *Muntakhabat*, vol. 5, pp 9–10; Balyuzi, *Baha'u'llah*, pp. 56–60; Nabil, *Dawn-Breakers*, pp. 368–77, 461–2, 583–4. Baha'u'llah's visit to Karbala: Nabil, *Dawn-Breakers*, pp. 586–94; Balyuzi, *Baha'u'llah*, pp. 66–8. The Attempt on the Life of the Shah and the Siyah Chal: Nabil, *Dawn-Breakers*, pp. 595–642; Balyuzi, *Baha'u'llah*, pp. 74–90; Mazandarani, *Zuhuru'l-Haqq*, vol. 5, pp. 59–100, 110–13; Blomfield, *Chosen Highway*, pp. 39–45; Shoghi Effendi, *God Passes By*, pp. 62–105. Takur: Nabil, *Dawn-Breakers*, pp. 638–42; Balyuzi, *Baha'u'llah*, pp. 90–93; Mazandarani, *Zuhuru'l-Haqq*, vol. 5, pp. 100–106. Journey to Baghdad: Balyuzi, *Baha'u'llah*, pp. 99–105; Mazandarani, *Zuhuru'l-Haqq*, vol. 5, pp. 117–23; Shoghi Effendi, *God Passes By*, pp. 108–9.

8. Passages from the Qayyúmu'l-Asmá, the first book of the Bab; excerpts translated in *Selections from the Writings of the Bab*, pp. 41, 41–2, 44, 61, 49

9. Mulla Muhammad earned his living teaching the children of the nobility in Tehran and, since he told Bushru'i that he frequently visited the house of Baha'u'llah, it seems likely that he had been engaged by Baha'u'llah to teach the children in his household, which in addition to his own children included some of his younger brothers and sisters. Nabil recalls taking 'Abdu'l-Baha for classes one day to the Pay-Minar (Mirza Salih) College where Mulla Muhammad resided (see Nabil, *Dawn-Breakers*, p. 441).

10. Nabil, *Dawn-Breakers*, p. 107

11. This form of divination by looking at random verses either of the Qur'an or of the poetry of Hafiz was and still is very popular in Iran.

12. 'Abdu'l-Baha, *Memorials of the Faithful*, p. 201

13. Gulpaygani, *Letters and Essays*, p. 56. The function of leading prayers is trad-itionally given to the most senior and learned of those present.

14. Nabil, *Dawn-Breakers*, p. 461

15. Because Mulla 'Abdu'l-Karim Qazvini was being hunted by the authorities, he took the name Mirza Ahmad and he is frequently referred to by that name in the sources.

16. Translated from Qazvini, *Tarikh*, p. 21

17. Nabil, *Dawn-Breakers*, p. 591

18. [Zarandi], *The Dawn-breakers*, p. 599. Haji Sulayman Khan also managed to meet twice with Baha'u'llah (Mazandarani, *Zuhur al-Haqq*, vol. 4, p. 60).

19. Nabil, *Dawn-Breakers*, pp. 607–8

20. Baha'u'llah, *Epistle to the Son of the Wolf*, pp. 20–1, 77

21. Baha'u'llah as quoted by Nabil Zarandi, in Furutan, *Stories of Baha'u'llah*, p. 108

22. Zarqani, *Badayi' al-Athar*, vol. 2, p. 206; translated in Balyuzi, *'Abdu'l-Baha*, pp. 11–12

23. Letter from Captain Alfred von Gumoens, dated 29 August 1852, published in *Oesterreichischer Soldatenfreund* on 12 October 1852. Translation by E. G. Browne; see Momen, *Babi and Baha'i Religions*, pp. 133–4

24. Baha'u'llah, *Epistle to the Son of the Wolf*, pp. 21–2

25. Baha'u'llah, *Summons of the Lord of Hosts*, p. 5

26. Blomfield, *Chosen Highway*, pp. 46–7

27. Quoted by Shoghi Effendi in *God Passes By*, p. 109

3. BAGHDAD

The first year in Baghdad: Balyuzi, *Baha'u'llah*, pp. 106–14; Mazandarani, *Zuhuru'l-Haqq*, vol. 5, pp. 124–37; Shoghi Effendi, *God Passes By*, pp. 108–120. Period in the mountains of Kurdistan and the town of Sulaymaniyyih: Balyuzi, *Baha'u'llah*, pp. 115–22; Mazandarani, *Zuhuru'l-Haqq*, vol. 5, pp. 137–59; Shoghi Effendi, *God Passes By*, pp. 120–6. On events in Baghdad 1854–58: Mazandarani, *Zuhuru'l-Haqq*, vol. 5, pp. 161–68, 174–197, 244; Balyuzi, *Baha'u'llah*, pp. 122–136; Shoghi Effendi, *God Passes By*, pp. 127–142. On Nabil Qa'ini, see Sulaymani, *Masabih Hidayat*, vol. 1, pp. 425–542, esp. pp. 444–8; Mazandarani, *Zuhuru'l-Haqq*, vol. 5, pp. 203–5; Balyuzi, *Eminent Baha'is*, pp. 112–5. On Fitnih, see Mazandarani, *Zuhuru'l-Haqq*, vol. 5, pp. 183–7n. Opposition to Baha'u'llah, 1858–63: Mazandarani, *Zuhuru'l-Haqq*, vol. 5, 197–203, 206–11, 236–44; Balyuzi, *Baha'u'llah*, pp. 136–150; Shoghi Effendi, *God Passes By*, pp. 142–6. Departure from Baghdad: Mazandarani, *Zuhuru'l-Haqq*, vol. 5, pp. 250–64; 'Abdu'l-Baha, *Muntakhabat*, vol. 5, pp. 36–9; Balyuzi, *Baha'u'llah*, pp. 154–8; Shoghi Effendi, *God Passes By*, pp. 147–50. The Garden of Ridvan: Mazandarani, *Zuhuru'l-Haqq*, vol. 5, pp. 264–70; Balyuzi, *Baha'u'llah*, pp. 168–76; Taherzadeh, vol. 1, pp. 257–82; Blomfield, *Chosen Highway*, pp. 122–3; Shoghi Effendi, *God Passes By*, pp. 151–55. The journey to Istanbul: Mazandarani, *Zuhuru'l-Haqq*, vol. 5, pp. 270–86; Balyuzi, *Baha'u'llah*, pp. 168–96; Shoghi Effendi, *God Passes By*, pp.155–7.

28. Baha'u'llah, *Tablets of Baha'u'llah*, p. 131
29. Shoghi Effendi, *God Passes By*, p. 118
30. Shoghi Effendi, *God Passes By*, p. 119
31. Blomfield, *Chosen Highway*, p. 54
32. Baha'u'llah, *Kitab-i-Iqan*, pp. 250–1
33. Shoghi Effendi, *God Passes By*, p. 122
34. Baha'u'llah, *Kitab-i-Iqan*, p. 251
35. Shoghi Effendi, *God Passes By*, p. 125
36. Blomfied, *Chosen Highway*, p. 47
37. Salmani, *My Memories of Baha'u'llah*, pp. 16–17 (translation slightly adapted)
38. Words of Nabil Zarandi in Shoghi Effendi, *God Passes By*, p. 137
39. Quoted in Shoghi Effendi, *God Passes By*, p. 137
40. Shoghi Effendi, *God Passes By*, p. 133
41. See translation of part of this poem in Browne, *Literary History*, vol. 4, pp. 173–7

42. From the notes of Lutfu'llah Hakim, translated in Balyuzi, *Baha'u'llah*, pp. 143–4
43. Mazandarani, *Zuhuru'l-Haqq*, vol. 4, p. 243
44. Abdu'l-Baha, *Some Answered Questions*, pp. 28–30; see also Baha'u'llah, *Gleanings*, no. 67, pp. 131–2 for Baha'u'llah's own shorter account of this.
45. Baha'u'llah, *Summons of the Lord of Hosts*, paras, 1.206–7, pp. 106–7
46. Shoghi Effendi, *God Passes By*, p. 150
47. Nabil Zarandi quoted in Shoghi Effendi, *God Passes By*, p. 153
48. Salmani, *My Memories of Baha'u'llah*, p. 22
49. Quoted in Phelps, *The Master in 'Akka*, pp. 38–9
50. Talk of 'Abdu'l-Baha delivered at Bahji on 29 April 1916, in Ishraq-Khavari, *Ayyam Tis'ih*, pp. 329–30
51. Baha'u'llah, *Gleanings*, no. 14, pp. 27–9
52. See note 112
53. Baha'u'llah, *Epistle to the Son of the Wolf*, p. 167
54. 'Abdu'l-Baha in *Star of the West*, vol. 13, no. 10 (January 1923), p. 278

4. ISTANBUL AND EDIRNE

The period in Istanbul: Mazandarani, *Zuhuru'l-Haqq*, vol. 4, pp. 286–302; Balyuzi, *Baha'u'llah*, pp. 197–216; Shoghi Effendi, *God Passes By*, pp. 157–62. Edirne: the open proclamation of Baha'u'llah's claim and the split with Azal: Mazandarani, *Zuhuru'l-Haqq*, vol. 4, pp. 303–24, vol. 5, pp. 2–10, 21–46; Balyuzi, *Baha'u'llah*, pp. 217–45; Shoghi Effendi, *God Passes By*, pp. 161–76. Banishment from Edirne: Balyuzi, *Baha'u'llah*, pp. 246–68; Mazandarani, *Zuhuru'l-Haqq*, vol. 5, pp. 46–84; Shoghi Effendi, *God Passes By*, pp. 176–82.

55. Baha'u'llah, *Gleanings*, no. 65, p. 122
56. Furutan, *Stories of Baha'u'llah*, p. 36
57. Baha'u'llah, *Summons of the Lord of Hosts*, para 5.30–2, 5.59, 5.81–2; pp. 197–8, 209–10, 218–9
58. Words of Baha'u'llah, translated by Shoghi Effendi in *God Passes By*, pp. 160–1
59. Quoted in Phelps, *The Master in 'Akka*, pp. 47–8
60. Baha'u'llah, *Summons of the Lord of Hosts*, para 5.75, pp. 216–17
61. Salmani, *My Memories of Baha'u'llah*, pp. 50–2

62. See summaries of the papers of this Commission of Investigation in Momen, *Babi and Baha'i Religions*, pp. 198–200
63. Quoted in Phelps, *The Master in 'Akka*, p. 67
64. Dispatches of Blunt to the British Ambassador in Istanbul Elliot, No. 54, 6 Aug. 1868 and No. 59, 15 Aug. 1868: FO 195 901; see Momen, *Babi and Baha'i Religions*, pp. 189, 193
65. Surih-yi Ra'is, 211–13, in Baha'u'llah, *Summons of the Lord of Hosts*, pp. 145–6
66. Baha'u'llah, *Summons of the Lord of Hosts*, para. 3.3, p. 162
67. Aqa Husayn Ashchi in Furutan, *Stories of Baha'u'llah*, p. 41
68. Quoted in Phelps, *The Master in 'Akka*, p. 69
69. Quoted in Lawh-i Ra'is, Baha'u'llah, *Summons of the Lord of Hosts*, para. 3.25, p. 170
70. Baha'u'llah, *Summons of the Lord of Hosts*, paras. 2.2, 2.4, pp. 141–2
71. Baha'u'llah, *Epistle to the Son of the Wolf*, p. 69

5. THE EARLY 'AKKA PERIOD

Imprisonment in the Citadel: Balyuzi, *Baha'u'llah*, pp. 269–92; Mazandarani, *Zuhuru'l-Haqq*, vol. 5 pp. 84–93, 97–111; Shoghi Effendi, *God Passes By*, pp. 183–9. Badi' and the letters to the kings and leaders: Balyuzi, *Baha'u'llah*, pp. 293–310; Mazandarani, *Zuhuru'l-Haqq*, vol. 5, pp. 111–23. The death of Mirza Mahdi: Balyuzi, *Baha'u'llah*, pp. 311–4; Mazandarani, *Zuhuru'l-Haqq*, vol. 5, pp. 126–7; Shoghi Effendi, *God Passes By*, pp. 188–9. Residence in the House of 'Udi Khammar: Balyuzi, *Baha'u'llah*, pp. 315–38, 351–3; Mazandarani, *Zuhuru'l-Haqq*, vol. 5, pp. 128–34, 157–207; Shoghi Effendi, *God Passes By*, pp.189–92. The Marriage of 'Abdu'l-Baha: Balyuzi, *Baha'u'llah*, pp. 339–48; Blomfield, *Chosen Highway*, pp. 84–90; *Munirih Khanum*, pp. 42–51. Last Years in 'Akka: Mazandarani, *Zuhuru'l-Haqq*, vol. 5, pp. 213–27, 236–8; Balyuzi, *Baha'u'llah*, pp. 353–61 (in this source the story of Shaykh 'Ali Miri persuading Baha'u'llah to leave 'Akka is in relation to Mazra'ih rather than the Garden of Ridvan).

72. Report of Eldridge, British Consul in Beirut to Layard, Ambassador at Istanbul, No. 14, 4 Feb. 1878: FO 195 1201; see Momen, *Babi and Baha'i History*, pp. 203–4
73. Baha'u'llah, *Summons of the Lord of Hosts*, paras 3.4, 3.27, pp. 162, 171
74. Blomfield, *Chosen Highway*, p. 66

75. Quoted in Phelps, *The Master in 'Akka*, pp. 80–1

76. A Persian translation of the text of the decree is given in the memoirs of Nuru'd-Din Zayn; *Khátirát Hayát dar Khidmat-i Mahbúb*, vol. 1, pp. 73–7

77. Quoted in Phelps, *The Master in 'Akka*, pp. 82–4

78. Faraydun Rahimi, *The Biography of Áqá 'Abdu'r-Rahím-i-Bushrú'í*, translated in Furutan, *Stories of Baha'u'llah*, pp. 44–5

79. Translated by E.G. Browne in 'Abdu'l-Baha, *Traveller's Narrative*, vol. 2, pp. 391–2

80. This account was written down by Muhammad Vali Khan Tunukabuni who heard it from the executioner himself; Balyuzi, *Baha'u'llah*, pp. 305–7

81. Blomfield, *Chosen Highway*, p. 64

82. Quoted in Phelps, *The Master in 'Akka*, pp. 87–8

83. Shoghi Effendi, *Messages to America*, p. 34

84. Shoghi Effendi, *God Passes By*, p. 188

85. Quoted in Phelps, *The Master in 'Akka*, pp. 90–1

86. Baha'u'llah, *Prayers and Meditations*, pp. 200–1

87. Quoted in Momen, *Babi and Baha'i Religions*, pp. 211–2

88. Abdu'l-Baha, *Memorials of the Faithful*, p. 16

89. Mazandarani, *Zuhuru'l-Haqq*, vol. 5, pp. 161–2

90. Quoted in Phelps, *The Master in 'Akka*, p. 98

91. Quoted in Phelps, *The Master in 'Akka*, 100n.

92. Baha'u'llah, *Gleanings*, no. 115, p. 243

93. Quoted in Momen, *Babi and Baha'i Religions*, p. 213

94. Quoted in Phelps, *The Master in 'Akka*, pp. 101–3

95. Quoted in Phelps, *The Master in 'Akka*, pp. 120–1

96. Translated from Zayn, *Khátirát*, vol. 1, pp. 89–90

97. From recollections of Mirza 'Ali-Akbar Kashani, translated in Furutan, *Stories of Baha'u'llah*, p. 56

98. Translated from Zayn, *Khatirat*, vol. 1, pp. 138–9

99. Taherzadeh, *Revelation of Baha'u'llah*, vol. 2, pp. 372–3

100. Balyuzi, *Baha'u'llah*, p. 151

6. THE LATER 'AKKA PERIOD

Mazandarani, *Zuhuru'l-Haqq*, vol. 5, pp. 238–9, 248–9, 259–61, 358–65; Balyuzi, *Baha'u'llah*, pp. 362–419; Shoghi Effendi, *God Passes By*, pp. 192–6. On Midhat Pasha: see Alkan, 'Midhat Pasha and 'Abdu'l-Baha'. Contacts with statesmen and reformers: Alkan, 'Ottoman Reform Movements'. Events in Iran: Shoghi Effendi, *God Passes By*, pp. 197–203. The Passing of Baha'u'llah: Mazandarani,

Zuhuru'l-Haqq, vol. 5, pp. 433–75; Balyuzi, *Baha'u'llah*, pp. 420–8; Shoghi Effendi, *God Passes By*, pp. 221–3.

101. Tuba Khanum in Blomfield, *Chosen Highway*, p. 97
102. Unpublished diaries of Dr J.E. Esslemont, entry for 26 January 1920, Port Said
103. Quoted in Ruhe, *Door of Hope*, p. 99
104. Alkan, 'Midhat Pasha and 'Abdu'l-Baha in 'Akka'
105. Husayni is a form of kebab made in Isfahan in which the meat is cut into small pieces and barbequed on thin wooden stakes. Barg is a more commonly made form of kebab using larger thin chunks of meat and usually barbequed on metal stakes.
106. Translated from Zayn, *Khátirát*, vol. 1, pp. 146–8
107. Qumi, *Hizár Dástán*, pp. 160–1
108. Browne in 'Abdul-Baha, *Traveller's Narrative*, vol. 2, pp. xxix–xl
109. Samandari, *Moments with Baha'u'llah*, pp. 51–5
110. Translated from an article in the journal *Al-Hidáya*, no. 9, Dhu'l-Qa'da 1314, quoted in Gulpáygání, *Fará'id*, pp. 512. Gulpáygání quotes the views and poetry of several eminent Arab scholars and poets concerning Bahá'u'lláh.
111. Emin Arslan, 'Une Visite au Chef du Babisme,' *Revue Bleu: Revue Politique et Literature*, 4th series, vol. 4, Paris, 1896, p. 316. Translated from the French in Momen, *The Bábí and Bahá'í Faiths*, p. 225
112. This headdress was worn throughout the Middle East and is known as a fez in Morocco. The fact that it is stated that he wore it firmly on his head is because Sufis often wore it loosely placed and skewed.
113. This was notable because the usual oriental custom was to sit or recline on the floor.
114. Mazandarani, *Zuhuru'l-Haqq*, vol. 5, pp. 472–4
115. Recounted by his grandson Jalal Nakhjavani and translated in Furutan, *Stories of Baha'u'llah*, pp. 69–70
116. Account recorded by Elizabeth McKenty, *Bahá'í News*, no. 517 (April 1974), p. 10
117. Samandari, *Moments with Bahá'u'lláh*, pp. 60–1, 62–5
118. Mirza Habibu'llah Afnan, quoted in Balyuzi, *Baha'u'llah*, p. 413
119. 'Azizu'llah Varqa, translated in Martha Root, 'White Roses of Persia' – Part 1, p. 73–4
120. Translated from Zayn, *Khátirát*, vol. 1, p. 145
121. Unpublished diaries of Dr J.E. Esslemont, entry for 26 January 1920, Port Said

122. Translated from Zayn, *Khátirát*, vol. 1, pp. 170–1
123. [Isfahani], *Stories from the Delights of Hearts*, pp. 105–6
124. Qumi, *Hizár Dástán*, pp. 139–40
125. Tuba Khanum in Blomfield, *Chosen Highway*, p. 94
126. Tuba Khanum in Blomfield, *Chosen Highway*, p. 98
127. See, for example, [Isfahani], *Stories from the Delights of Hearts*, p. 106; Samandari, *Moments with Bahá'u'lláh*, pp. 9–11; Mirza Habibu'llah Afnan, translated in Balyuzi, *Baha'u'llah*, p. 415, 417
128. Samandari, *Moments with Bahá'u'lláh*, pp. 19–20
129. Mirza Habibu'llah Afnan, translated in Balyuzi, *Baha'u'llah*, p. 417
130. *Bahiyyih Khanum*, p. 3
131. Extracted from Shoghi Effendi, *Messages to America*, p. 35
132. Baha'u'llah, *Epistle to the Son of the Wolf*, pp. 35–6, 72, 122, 123, 74
133. Baha'u'llah, *Kitab-i-Aqdas*, v. 54
134. Taherzadeh, *Revelation of Baha'u'llah*, vol. 4, p. 415
135. Samandari, *Moments with Bahá'u'lláh*, pp. 35–7
136. Free translation by Ahang Rabbani and Anthony A. Lee; text in Mazandarani, *Zuhuru'l-Haqq*, vol. 5, pp. 444n.–445n.

7. THE WRITINGS OF BAHA'U'LLAH

On the writings of Baha'u'llah, see Taherzadeh, *Revelation of Baha'u'llah*, 4 vols.: volume 1 deals with the Baghdad period; volume 2 with Istanbul and Edirne; volume 3 deals with 'Akka 1868–77; and volume 4 with 'Akka 1877–92. Story of the Kitab-i Iqan: Taherzadeh, *Revelation of Baha'u'llah*, vol. 1, pp. 153–9; Balyuzi, *Baha'u'llah*, pp. 163–5; Mazandarani, *Zuhuru'l-Haqq*, vol. 5, pp. 211–23.

137. Baha'u'llah, *Epistle to the Son of the Wolf*, p. 115
138. Personal communication from Baha'i World Centre, 3 Feb. 2004
139. Baha'u'llah, *The Seven Valleys*, pp. 13–15; the three traditional Islamic arch-angels mentioned in this passage are Izra'il the angel of death, Gabriel the angel who brings guidance and revelation to the prophets, and Israfil the angel who announces the Day of Resurrection.
140. Translation in Balyuzi, *Baha'u'llah*, p. 149
141. Baha'u'llah, *Hidden Words*, Arabic, nos. 1, 2, 3; Persian no. 1
142. Matt. 24:29; Mark 13:24; in the King James Authorised Version of the Bible the word 'tribulation' is used in place of 'oppression'. This

makes no difference to the argument that follows and the word 'tribulation' can be inserted in place of 'oppression' in the following passage without making any difference to the sense.

143. Baha'u'llah, *Kitab-i-Iqan*, pp. 29–32
144. Sayyid Yusif from the village of Sihdih, near Isfahan.
145. Baha'u'llah, *Gems of Divine Mysteries*, para. 104, p. 71
146. *Baha'i Prayers*, pp. 220–3
147. Baha'u'llah, *Tablets*, pp. 75–6
148. Baha'u'llah, *Gleanings*, no. 52, pp. 105–7
149. Baha'u'llah, *Gleanings*, no. 152, p. 322
150. Baha'u'llah, *Summons of the Lord of Hosts*, paras. 5.2, 5.3, 5.8–11, 5.15, pp. 185–6, 188–9, 191; quoting John 14:28 and 16:13
151. Baha'u'llah, *Summons of the Lord of Hosts*, paras. 1.192, 1.196, pp. 98, 100
152. Baha'u'llah, *Summons of the Lord of Hosts*, paras. 1.218–20, pp. 112–14
153. Baha'u'llah, *Gleanings*, no. 45, pp. 99–100
154. *Baha'i Prayers*, pp. 213–19
155. Baha'u'llah, *Summons*, para 1:131, pp. 67–8
156. Baha'u'llah, *Summons*, paras. 1:137–8, pp. 71–2
157. Baha'u'llah, *Summons*, para. 1:136, p. 70
158. Baha'u'llah, *Summons*, para. 1:158, p. 83
159. Baha'u'llah, *Summons*, paras 1.171–3, pp. 88–90
160. Baha'u'llah, *Summons*, paras 1:179–82, pp. 93–4
161. Baha'u'llah, *Summons*, 1.102, 108, 112, 113, 118, pp. 54, 58, 59, 57–8, 61
162. Shoghi Effendi, *God Passes By*, p. 213
163. *Kitab-i-Aqdas*, vv. 1–2
164. *Kitab-i-Aqdas*, v. 36, 41, 165
165. *Kitab-i-Aqdas*, v. 39, 40, 120
166. *Kitab-i-Aqdas*, v. 72
167. *Kitab-i-Aqdas*, v. 75
168. *Kitab-i-Aqdas*, v. 90
169. *Kitab-i-Aqdas*, v. 88
170. Baha'u'llah, *Prayers and Meditations*, p. 313
171. *Baha'i Prayers*, p. 203
172. Baha'u'llah, *Prayers and Meditations*, pp. 262–3
173. Baha'u'llah, *Prayers and Meditations*, p. 248
174. Baha'u'llah, *Tablets of Baha'u'llah*, pp. 26, 28, 35–36, 39–40, 51–2, 66–7
175. Baha'u'llah, *Tablets of Baha'u'llah*, pp. 3–4

176. Translated in Shoghi Effendi, *World Order of Baha'u'llah*, p. 135
177. Baha'u'llah, *Epistle to the Son of the Wolf*, p. 13
178. Baha'u'llah, *Epistle to the Son of the Wolf*, pp. 41–2, 44

8. THE CLAIMS OF BAHA'U'LLAH

Shoghi Effendi, *God Passes By*, pp. 93–100; Shoghi Effendi, *World Order of Baha'u'llah*, pp. 100–19; Sours, *The Station and Claims of Baha'u'llah*.

179. Baha'u'llah, *Gleanings*, no. 19, pp. 46–7
180. Baha'u'llah, *Gleanings*, no. 148, pp. 317–8
181. Baha'u'llah, *Gleanings*, no. 19, pp. 46–7
182. Baha'u'llah, *Gleanings*, no. 21, p. 50
183. Baha'u'llah, *Kitab-i-Iqan*, p. 178
184. Baha'u'llah, *Kitab-i-Iqan*, pp. 179–80
185. Baha'u'llah, *Gleanings*, no. 34, p. 80
186. Baha'u'llah, *Gleanings*, no. 22, pp. 51–2
187. Baha'u'llah, *Gleanings*, no. 110, p. 215
188. Baha'u'llah, *Gleanings*, no. 34, pp. 80–1
189. Baha'u'llah, *Gleanings*, no. 22, pp. 52–3
190. Baha'u'llah, *Gleanings*, no. 144, p. 314
191. Baha'u'llah, *Gleanings*, no. 10, pp. 13–14
192. Baha'u'llah, *Prayers and Meditations*, pp. 306–7
193. Baha'u'llah, *Gleanings*, no. 10, pp. 12–13

9. THE TEACHINGS OF BAHA'U'LLAH

There are many introductory books on the Baha'i Faith which outline the teachings of Baha'u'llah. See for example: Moojan Momen, *Baha'i Faith: A Short Introduction*; Wendi Momen, *Understanding the Baha'i Faith*; Smith, *The Baha'i Religion*. Good general reference works on the Baha'i teachings and the Baha'i community include Momen, *Basic Baha'i Dictionary*; Smith, *Concise Encyclopedia of the Baha'i Faith*. On the hierarchical nature of society and the Baha'i community, see Karlberg, *Beyond the Culture of Contest*. On Consultation, see Kolstoe, *Consultation*.

194. Baha'u'llah, *Hidden Words*, Arabic no 68
195. Baha'u'llah, *Gleanings*, no. 117, p. 249
196. Baha'u'llah, *Gleanings*, no. 33, p. 77

197. This statement is made in the Tablet of Unity which is published in Baha'u'llah, *Ad'iyyih-yi Hadrat-i Mahbub*, p. 396, but has not yet been translated
198. Quoted in Shoghi Effendi, *Promised Day is Come*, p. 70
199. Tablet of Maqsud, in Baha'u'llah, *Tablets* , p. 168
200. Baha'u'llah, *Epistle to the Son of the Wolf*, pp. 30–1
201. *Kitab-i-Aqdas*, v. 123
202. Tablet of Maqsud, in Baha'u'llah, *Tablets*, p. 169
203. Baha'u'llah, *Gleanings*, no. 57, p. 136
204. Baha'u'llah, *Kitab-i-Iqan*, p. 240

CONCLUSION

For a survey of Baha'i history, see Smith, *Short History of the Baha'i Faith*. A more detailed academic account is Smith, *The Babi and Baha'i Religions*. For more general information about the Baha'i Faith and the Baha'i community, go to: http://www.bahai.org.

205. The author is grateful to Dr Wendi Momen for first suggesting the idea of this passage. He would also like to thank Dr Necati Alkan for assistance with Turkish spellings and Dr Marleen Chase and Antony Lee for scanning two of the pictures used in this book.

Index

In this index there is full transliteration according to the Bahá'í system of all names and Arabic and Persian words (with the exception that underlining of pairs of letters as used in the Bahá'í system is not used). This is a word-for-word index, ignoring articles, prepositions (including al-), and titles such as Aqa, Mirza, Mulla and Sayyid. Page numbers for illustrations are given in bold.

240 *Index*